Early praise for *Metaphors of Internet*

"The Internet has disappeared. This exceptional book brings it back into focus—through richly illustrated histories, artworks, and reflections. It is both a historical document and an exploration of possible futures. On top of that, Annette and Katrin have given us a profoundly inspirational glimpse of what truly creative scholarship looks like."

Mark Deuze,
Professor of Journalism and Media Culture,
University of Amsterdam, author of *Media Life*

"*Metaphors of the Internet* is an extraordinary book, which zooms from the early days of cyberspace to the present moment to ask how we might conceptualise what the internet is, feels and means. Curated by the fabulous duo of Annette Markham and Katrin Tiidenberg this book presents a new vision and mode of encountering the internet in everyday lives and biographies. It presents an at once collective and carefully crafted, but also deeply personalised and reflexive, series of metaphors and stories through which the internet and life can be conceptualised as part of the same world. It invites us to acknowledge and contemplate anew how our own and others' lives are entangled in the creativity and politics of everyday environments, that are never not digital. *Metaphors of the Internet* is essential, fascinating and accessible reading for anyone from any academic or practice-based discipline who is interested in understanding the internet."

Sarah Pink,
Professor of Design and Emerging Technologies,
Monash University,
author of *Situating Everyday Life: Practices and Places* and
Doing Sensory Ethnography

"What language will internet research speak in the years to come? Read this innovative collection and find out what you will be thinking about, researching, and dreaming about, when you talk technology. A fun and forward thinking patchwork of ideas weaved together by scholars known for being ahead of their time."

Zizi Papacharissi
Professor and Head of Communication,
Professor of Political Science,
University of Illinois at Chicago

Metaphors of Internet

Steve Jones
General Editor

Vol. 122

The Digital Formations series is part of the Peter Lang Media and Communication list. Every volume is peer reviewed and meets the highest quality standards for content and production.

PETER LANG
New York • Bern • Berlin
Brussels • Vienna • Oxford • Warsaw

Metaphors of Internet

Ways of Being in the Age of Ubiquity

Edited by
Annette N. Markham and
Katrin Tiidenberg

PETER LANG
New York • Bern • Berlin
Brussels • Vienna • Oxford • Warsaw

Library of Congress Cataloging-in-Publication Data

Names: Markham, Annette N., editor. | Tiidenberg, Katrin, editor.
Title: Metaphors of internet: ways of being in the age of ubiquity /
edited by Annette N. Markham and Katrin Tiidenberg.
Description: New York: Peter Lang, 2020.
Series: Digital formations, vol. 122 | ISSN 1526-3169
Includes bibliographical references and index.
Identifiers: LCCN 2019059859 | ISBN 978-1-4331-7449-0 (hardback: alk. paper)
ISBN 978-1-4331-7450-6 (paperback: alk. paper) | ISBN 978-1-4331-7451-3 (ebook pdf)
ISBN 978-1-4331-7452-0 (epub) | ISBN 978-1-4331-7453-7 (mobi)
Subjects: LCSH: Internet—Social aspects. | Internet—Terminology.
Classification: LCC HM851 .M466 2020 (print) | LCC HM851 (ebook) |
DDC 302.23/1—dc23
LC record available at https://lccn.loc.gov/2019059859
LC ebook record available at https://lccn.loc.gov/2019059860
DOI 10.3726/b16196

Bibliographic information published by **Die Deutsche Nationalbibliothek.**
Die Deutsche Nationalbibliothek lists this publication in the "Deutsche
Nationalbibliografie"; detailed bibliographic data are available
on the Internet at http://dnb.d-nb.de/.

The paper in this book meets the guidelines for permanence and durability
of the Committee on Production Guidelines for Book Longevity
of the Council of Library Resources.

29 Broadway, 18th floor, New York, NY 10006
www.peterlang.com

Printed in the United States of America

Table of contents

Figures and Table

FIGURES

TABLE

Acknowledgments

This book is a collaborative effort of all the contributors, who spent more than two years working together in Google docs to draft, critique, and revise their pieces. This is not an easy process and their persistence, patience, and willingness to be part of this experiment is remarkable. For this, we thank our fellow curators and co-authors: Andee Baker, Anette Grønning, Anna Shchetvina, Carmel L. Vaisman, Cathy Fowley, Craig Hamilton, Cristina Nuñez, Crystal Abidin, Daisy Pignetti, Jeff Thompson, Jessa Lingel, Katie Warfield, Kevin Driscoll, Maria Schreiber, Nadia Hakim-Fernández, Patricia Prieto-Blanco, Polina Kolozaridi, Priya C. Kumar, Ryan Milner, Sarah Raine, Sarah Schorr, Son Vivienne, Terri Senft, Tijana Hirsch, Tobias Raun, Whitney Phillips, xtine burrough, Winnie Soon.

Annette: Speaking from my own perspective on the project, I admit I enjoyed the creative process much more than the management required to bring this volume to fruition. I liked tinkering with the order of chapters, the titles of various sections, the wording of authors' sentences. I cherished the gift of editing the other authors' texts to build what we hope reads as a strong cohesion across the chapters. In this meandering and playful curating process, I cannot begin to express my deep appreciation for Katrin's continuous work to keep the project moving toward completion. Without her alternately fierce and gentle pressure, I would still be tweaking and fussing with the details of each of the contribution. Katrin skillfully managed the personalities, the logistics, and me. She is a brilliant scholar and a true pleasure to work with. I consider myself one of the lucky few who get to work with her.

Katrin: Annette is the bravest scholar I have ever worked with—a pioneer, an innovator, an inspiration. She has the inimitable capacity to propose just-shy-of-outrageous ideas as a legitimate plan and the charisma to mobilize people around those ideas. Working with her is a transformative experience, an adventure and a privilege. Without Annette, I would not have dared to ask our collaborators for the trust needed for, nor taken on the monumental task of closely editing and remixing nearly 30 chapters after they had already gone through a rigorous and creative process of co-creation. Yet this is what we did, and this is what our amazing collaborators allowed us to do. I am so grateful to have been a part of this book and to have had the chance to learn so much from co-editing it with Annette.

We also thank the editorial team at Peter Lang, the Digital Formations series editor Steve Jones, The Cultural Transformations Research Programme at Aarhus University for their wonderful writing retreats, and the community of AoIR, the Association of Internet Researchers, who made space for this work in various conferences along the way.

SECTION 1

Introducing the Metaphors of the Internet

CHAPTER ONE

Ways of Being in the Digital Age

ANNETTE N. MARKHAM

Between 1995 and 1997, I conducted an ethnographic study of people who considered themselves "heavy users" of the internet. Representing only a small slice of lived experience in the early digital age, my participants taught me to move, emote, and build my identities in their own worlds. It was a time when terms like Virtual Reality and Cyberspace were used without irony. The creative use of text produced images, maps, and emotions. In this space, I:

> wanted to know why people spent so much time online. I wondered what cyberspace meant to them, how it affected or changed their lives. I wanted to know how they were making sense of their experiences as they shifted between being in the physical world and being in these textual worlds created by the exchange of messages, where they could re-create their bodies, or leave them behind. (1998, p. 17)

The book that emerged from this ethnography, *Life Online: Researching Real Experiences in Virtual Space*, is a document of its era. The early Internet. This was a time in history when some people would spend 2 hours online and call that "heavy use" while others would spend 18. The visual web didn't exist on any large scale yet. The people I observed and interviewed for the book used it for many different reasons, with different degrees of attachment and commitment. Most considered it a playful space, a way to constitute the self … "to try on different forms and identities, engage in meaningful activities with other people, and evolve as members of various communities" (Markham, 1998, pp. 157–158).

In popular discourse, however, the rhetoric was often anxious. A creepy photo of a child threatened by cyberporn haunted the cover of the July 3, 1995 *Time* magazine. This was one of many panic-inducing headlines in these early years depicting the wild, alluring, and dangerous internet frontier. In 1996, "internet addiction disorder" entered the medical lexicon. My participants, like many people in the public sphere at the time, avidly talked about this addictive feature of the internet, but in stark contrast to the moral panics in the news, their discourse described a strong sensibility about the fact that their bodies were the center of their existence and there were limits of the internet, whether it was a tool, place, or a way of being.

As Kevin Driscoll notes in his chapter (this volume), many of us remain nostalgic about those days of the early internet. In the 1990s, there was a certain giddiness in the Western world about the potentiality of the internet. From my perspective in the thick of it, our[1] beliefs in the transformative potential of the internet were driven by the imaginaries built through common stories floating through fiction, film, news, and the internet itself.

METAPHORS OF THE INTERNET OF THE 1990S

In the nineties, we paid attention to the internet as a place precisely because we could be there but our bodies were both absent from the scene and still viscerally feeling so very much. After all, vast communities and intimate relationships were accomplished through the exchange of white or green ASCII text on dark desktop screen backgrounds (see Figure 1.1). If you were lucky, your interface might have different colors (Figure 1.2).

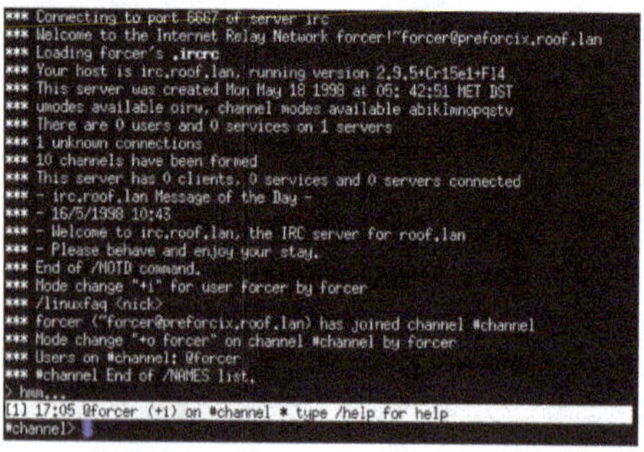

Figure 1.1: IRC chat client, basic interface in 1998. Source: Google image search, unknown provenance

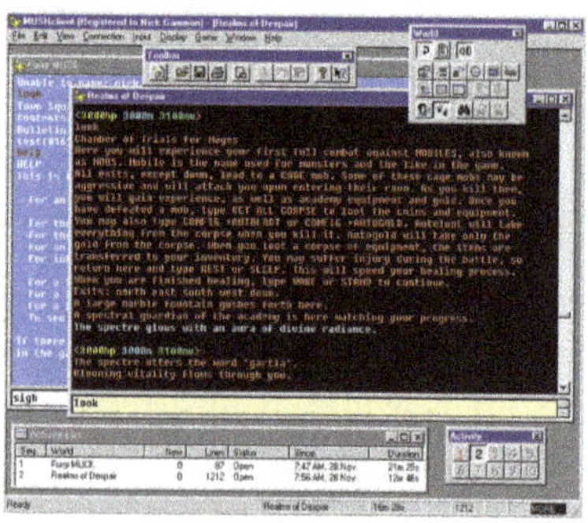

Figure 1.2: MUSH client for interacting in multiple multi user dimensions at once, circa 1998, actual date unknown. Source: Image CC BY 3.0 AU. Attributed to Nick Gammon

1 By 'our' or 'we', I mean to generalize across academics, pop culture authors, filmmakers, developers, and enthusiastic users situated in the midst of the internet revolution of the early 1990s. And primarily in the English-speaking West.

While people would use artistic renderings of text to create maps (Figure 1.3) or convey facial expressions:-) or gestures ¯_(ツ)_/¯, in general, the visual plainness of the interfaces belied the intensity of what was happening.

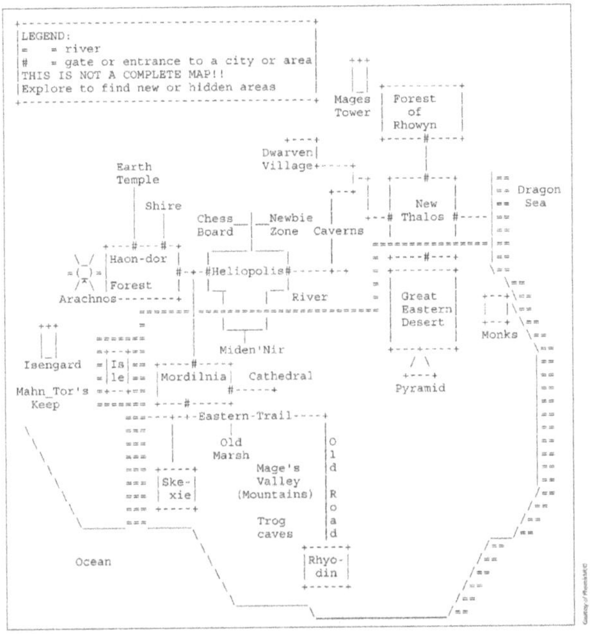

Figure 1.3: ASCII text map of PhoenixMUD, photographer unknown. Source: Image CC BY 3.0, Martin Dodge.

It's no wonder that "cyberspace" was such a popular term, as it depicted an Other place, a developed place, where information and people lived, separate from physical—or what some at the time called IRL (In Real Life) or meat—space. This dis-placement gave the opportunity for re-configuring both body and reviving a meaning-centered form of relationality.

Cyberspace collapsed distance, so we could be at a meeting halfway around the world and still be in our pajamas in our home country. We could be inside the most prestigious libraries in the world, browsing through their archives, without actually being there, but with a verisimilitude of being there. Because it was an information space, we were told, it didn't have any physical limits. Its seeming location in nowhere and everywhere facilitated the visual metaphor of an out of body experience. This idea was built and facilitated through various sci-fi books at the time: William Gibson, who coined the term "cyberspace" in 1984, described it as "a consensual hallucination" one could jack into; Iain Banks called it a "cryptosphere" or a "data corpus," where people's minds could be uploaded and accessed after they died (1994); Neal Stephenson called it the "metaverse" (1992). We could use our body fat to power immersive experiences (Pat Cadigan), take a drug to wake us up from our lives in "The Matrix," or otherwise enter and move through data-filled spaces, often occupying avatar bodies of ourselves, other people, or nonhuman entities.

In other words, there were strong visual metaphors of virtual reality, avatars, and disembodiment that dominated conversations about what the Internet was, what happened there, how one could get there, where to find entries and exits, and once there, where one could go. As the web grew into a more commercial enterprise with websites, actual and imagined designs grew even more fantastical for a while. Some of these imaginaries, collected later in the Atlas of Cyberspace (Dodge & Kitchin, 2000), depicted web browsers where our avatars would be transported through portals from one location to another (Figure 1.4) or illustrated real information in three-dimensioned cityspaces, like antarti.ca's creative mapping in 2000 of the world's websites (then two million) onto a map of the continent Antarctica (Figure 1.5), or MIT Media Lab's architectural rendering of an individual's computer (Figure 1 6).

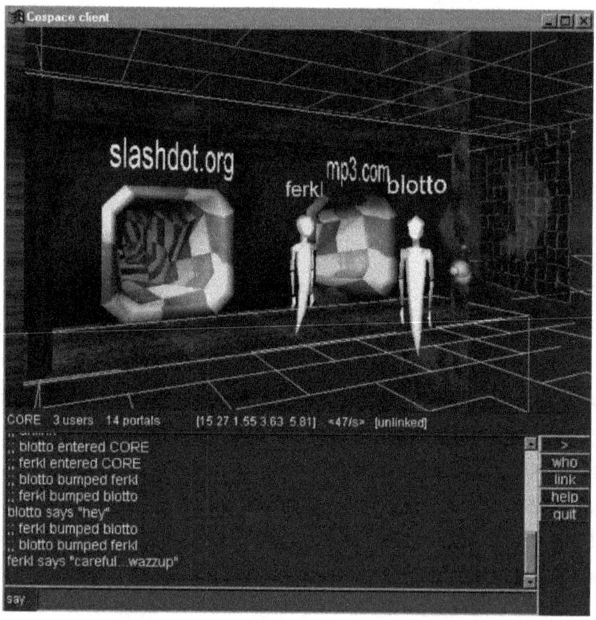

Figure 1.4: Cospace, a browser prototype emphasizing users as avatars and transportation to websites through portals. Source: Screenshot by Martin Dodge for his Atlas of Cyberspace project, permission granted under fair use considerations.

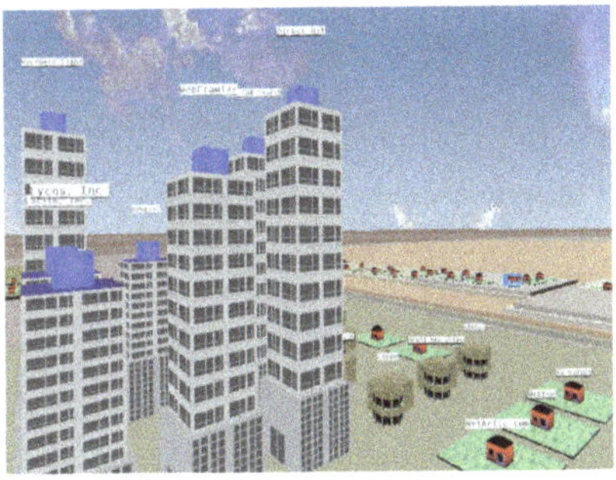

Figure 1.5: Geographic depiction of size of search engines in 2000, as visualized by antarti.ca in 2000. Source: Screenshot by Martin Dodge & Rob Kitchin for the Atlas of Cyberspace. Permission by Dodge granted under fair use considerations.

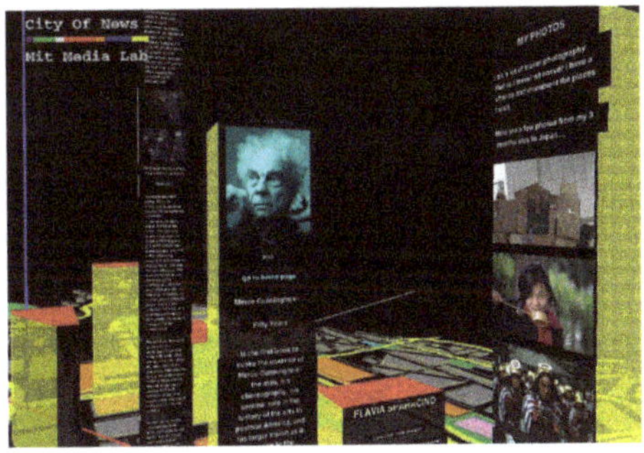

Figure 1.6: CityOfNews interface by Flavia Sparacino, MIT Media Lab, 1996–2000. Source: Screenshot by Martin Dodge & Rob Kitchin for the Atlas of Cyberspace. Permission by Dodge granted under fair use considerations.

Of course, these weren't the only imaginaries. At roughly the same time John Perry Barlow was writing his cyberspace manifesto to proclaim the idea that the internet is a wild frontier, ripe for exploration, a place where we (the privileged) could attain a genuine participatory democracy, others, later represented by then vice president Al Gore, were promoting the concept of the internet as an information superhighway. Both metaphoric imaginaries fueled speculation and development to build particular types of capacities, based on the idea that the internet was a conduit between places as well as the network of places.

The internet was many things at once, as most technologies are. The capacities of the internet enable or facilitate certain actions, movements, and structures. In the late 1990s, because the internet afforded anonymity, we could test out certain ways of being and try certain actions to witness the results. "What if" or "Why not?" became motifs for trying out new experiences of "being with." The experimentation was often humorous. I offer this example from my own experience teaching an online course in 1999 (excerpt from Markham, 2004, p. 371):

> We had met online for six weeks, never meeting face to face, as the participants were both local and distant. We had met in various online environments to assess the impact of each technology on our participation in class as well as the development of individual identity and overall sense of community. One night my students and I met in Internet Relay Chat (IRC), a synchronous anonymous chatting environment. At the request of the students leading class discussion, we adopted colors as our names. I thought I would be satisfied with 'Forest Green', but I got bored, and switched it. As I changed my 'nick', this message appeared on everyone's screens:

*** Forest green is now known as

"GhostlyGreen"

For me, GhostlyGreen was satisfactory for a while (it was very close to Halloween). But I was feeling playful—finally, I could experience a classroom environment in which I was not immediately identified and characterized as Dr Markham. For all they knew, I was just another student.

*** GhostlyGreen is now known as

"babypuke"

Much better. I acted out my 'color identity'—made rude comments, interrupted other participants, and such. Still, I thought, it wasn't really 'me'. I continued my spectrum of development:

*** babypuke is now known as

"RottenJackOrange"

This still did not quite feel right, and I was in an obnoxious student-disrupting-the-class mood, so I shifted my nickname again:

*** RottenJackOrange is now known as

"oatmeal"

I oozed and squelched while the rest of the class attempted to carry on a scholarly conversation. Occasionally they would get into the playful mood with me and "walk around oatmeal," or enact "gets their shoes stuck" in my porridge-ness. One student threatened to "throw oatmeal on you" to another student.

We all had a good laugh about that, which disrupted the class even more. Finally and wisely, the students running class discussion decided it was time to reveal the actual identities behind the colors. As I watched various students reveal themselves, I saw IndigoBlu turn to AnnetteMarkham:

*** IndigoBlu is now known as

"AnnetteMarkham"

Wait! I had never chosen IndigoBlu as my color identity. I thought to myself, "someone's playing a good game." So I went along with it and after all the other students had presumably revealed their actual names, I unmasked as the only unnamed student remaining:

*** oatmeal is now known as

"DennisL"

For the remainder of the class, almost two hours, the rest of the students believed he was the professor and responded to him as if he were me. I played the role of student. They believed I was a student. Afterwards, when Dennis revealed what he had done, none of the other students believed him. But until that point, they had believed he was the professor. Which is a remarkable thing.

The experiences of being computer-mediated were transformative in more meaningful, poignant ways. One of my then-female friends spent a lot of time in virtual worlds as a male because for her, it felt safer. On many occasions she would also say it felt like she could be more authentic as her avatar, to interact and develop relationships as a male. This gave her the experience and confidence to eventually transition in real life into a gender that was a better fit.

Life in semi-anonymous text-based spaces could also be horrific and devastating for communities, as Julian Dibbell's chronicle of *A Rape in Cyberspace* so vividly demonstrated. These brief examples and so many more reminded us that the internet was also a way of being with consequence. The experiences people had in anonymous spaces were every bit as real as they would be anywhere else, if what we mean by 'real' is that they are meaningful, consequential, and actual. Lived. Even as the internet has disappeared, our actual social realities are constructed not just through how we use the internet but also how we rely on it, and what we expect, which in large part emerges from the imaginaries we're using to frame the situation in the first place.

How swiftly different metaphorical frames come and go. Looking back, I believe we were experiencing something that accompanies any historical technological advancement; shocked out of our typical frames for understanding human interaction, we were compelled to confront existential questions of what it means to *be*, and *be with*. Goffman's work in Frame Analysis (1974) usefully articulates how anomalous events in a situation can create frame breaks, whereby the invisible structuring processes of our lives are disrupted. At these moments, the boundaries we use to encapsulate and delimit these situations are revealed. The internet did this in many ways.

The metaphors we use to frame our experiences of the internet (then and now) matter; in that they can construct both the enabling and limiting features of our technologies. These frames spread through everyday terminologies and visual imageries. What we called surfing, we now call sharing. What was once cyberspace and The Net are now platforms. What we once called online or networked is now IOT and smart. All of these are metaphors, but we might be less likely to notice them as such, because this is how dominant metaphors work - as infrastructures of.

Beyond language, the technologies or materialities themselves function metaphorically, as Carmel Vaisman discusses later in this book. What shifts in our thinking when we move from a mode of clicking or pushing buttons, to swiping across screens with our fingertips, and then to positioning screens in front of our faces, aligning our physicality with an invisible grid that confirms a matching digital and physical identity or conversely, enables us to morph our image into something different? Perhaps as many of the works in this book will emphasize, the internet is simultaneously a tool and a way of being. It is materiality and digitality combined, but more, an extension or prosthesis of one or more of our senses, as McLuhan would say of any medium. We are creatures that adapt to our tools, but also vice versa—and in the words of my colleagues writing the future history of machine vision (Rettberg et al., 2019),

> a clear argument is to be made that technologies have predetermined human thought ever since the first stone axe shaped a human hand, or symbolic articulations shaped the human face.

We live now in the age of ubiquity, where the internet is by many experienced as a way of being, a point driven home by the central role of digital media in life, work, exercise, virus tracing, obtaining essentials during the 2020 pandemic lockdown.

If we depict this ubiquity visually, we often see digital information superimposed over materiality, which conveys a sense of invisible, always-on presence of the internet in our everyday lives (Figure 1.7). Far from being separate from us, it encompasses us, like the water encompassing the fish on Mark Deuze's book cover for *Media Life* (Figure 1.8).

Figure 1.7: Corning advertisement envisioning a future with embedded smart technologies. Source: Screenshot of YouTube video by author

Figure 1.8: Mark Deuze's book cover, depicting digital media as water to a fish. Source: Photo of book jacket by Annette Markham

The phrase used by Sarah Pink, Debora Lanzeni, and Elisenda Ardevol in their 2016 book *Digital Materialities* is that the digital and material are "entwined." For many years, the STS community has carried forward Donna Haraway's image of the cat's cradle to emphasize this "entanglement" of human, nonhuman, more than human. For me, the Arab Spring events and Japanese earthquake in 2011 highlighted how most of the world had become "digitally-saturated," and I still use this adjective phrase as a way to try to articulate how the internet is interwoven in our everyday lives.

METAPHORS OF THE INTERNET

For me, this book you read now and perhaps even hold in your hands (not likely) will also be a document of its time. It is written at a time when the internet has disappeared. Who knows when this happened? Maybe it was the moment when Facebook became so prominent as a form of networked sociality globally that many users would claim they didn't use the internet, only Facebook (Samarajiva, 2012). Maybe it was the moment when Samsung advertised its Galaxy SII in 2011, proclaiming that everything we need to be the master of our universe lives in their revolutionary new phone. Maybe it was much earlier, when Google presented us with the epitome of the transparent portal to (all) information: a vanilla screen with nothing but the google logo and a search box.

What new metaphors are suitable in these times? Wherever and whenever the internet as a frame of reference disappeared, the resulting Gestalt (or feeling, or way of being) is just life. The internet is just there, like electricity fifty years after it became common. For those who are very privileged, it's like oxygen. Even if a person doesn't have ready or easy access to the internet, it is not absent from their worldview, it's merely not accessible enough to fulfill their present needs. Within this way of being, metaphors such as tool and place still have relevance. And other metaphors emerge. The collaborators in this book find they are much more situated, nuanced, and understated, since the frame itself is no longer the topic of interest. Rather, what is available or possible takes center stage. This book, then, is about how we experience life because of the unique confluence of digital communication, a globally networked internet, within the continuous development of social media platforms, machine learning, automation, recommendation systems, and other technologically mediating forces (or agents or actants) in our daily lives that we live in different local conditions. For many of the collaborators of this project, the internet is not something to focus on, but it is something we all see through, live through. Whatever else these experiences are, they are tacit enactments of the internet in a time when it has become a taken for granted as a global way of being.

CHAPTER TWO

A Wormhole, a Home, an Unavoidable Place. Introduction to "Metaphors of the Internet"

KATRIN TIIDENBERG

Late in December of 2016, Annette Markham and I invited scholars, artists and activists to work with us on a project that would generate a set of stories about how the internet is experienced by people as we near 2020. This was driven by three shared impulses. The first was personal—I had joined Annette at Aarhus University for a postdoc and we wanted to produce something big and meaningful together to celebrate our collaboration. The second impulse is probably best called ethnographic. We felt the need to push back against, or rather complicate with lived experience, the growing bundle of academic narratives of the internet becoming domesticated (Haddon, 2006), ubiquitous (Bechmann & Lomborg, 2014), even disappearing into a post-internet condition (Olson, 2011). The internet seems only a caveat in these more complicated imaginaries of inextricable entanglements of computation, networked communication technology, environment, capitalism and human experience. It's not that we disagree with these claims. It is more that within the specific contexts of pervasiveness, the internet continues to be experienced, utilized, built, hacked, resisted, felt, imagined and articulated in a myriad of ways by different people, in different settings, for different purposes. And these small stories of the everyday internet matter. The grand stories of the social, ethical, political and economic dimensions of today's internet are comprised of, accepted or resisted based on people's small stories.

Finally, our third impulse can perhaps be called celebratory or even expansionist. Or both. We workshopped a couple of chapters of Annette's 1998 book *Life Online: Researching Real Experience in Virtual Space* with masters level students.

We discussed embodiment, desire, writing and imagination—everything we had previously talked about in the context of social media platforms, visual interaction apps and smart devices that the students use—in the context of the text-based interactions of IRCs, MUDs and MOOs of the 1990s. On one hand, students' reactions to the text showed us the continuing force of everyday narratives and ethnographic craft that *Life Online* so brilliantly foregrounds. On the other hand, their reactions brought into vivid relief the surprising changes and perhaps even more surprising, the consistencies in how people make sense of the internet over all this time. In 1998, Annette gathered the more dominant internet metaphors into three categories—metaphors of the internet as a tool, metaphors of the internet as a place, and metaphors of the internet as a way of being. Twenty years later, these still organize people's articulations of the internet well enough. But they coexist with a new rhetoric for making sense of one's networked experience (cf. Tiidenberg et al., 2017 for an analysis of auto-ethnographies by young people making sense of their own experiences of social media). Occasionally, this coexistence of old and new metaphors is contradictory. A clear transition from old to new cannot be argued and would be an oversimplification. So our third reason for working on this book was to collect stories of "life online" twenty years later. These stories celebrate the endurance of the metaphors of the internet as a tool, a place, and a way of being even when it is ubiquitous, and expand the metaphoric approach by showing the evolution and mutation of how the internet is being made sense of. Most importantly, these metaphors—old and new—that we claim shape and constrain how the internet is experienced and articulated today, are entirely empirical. Our collective claims of their relevance emerge from people's lives.

METAPHORS

Twenty years ago, the Internet was imagined as standing apart from humans; a frontier to explore, a virtual world to experiment with embodiment, and an ultra-high-speed information superhighway. Now, we hardly use the term internet. We don't even "go online." Instead, we chat, tweet, snap, friend, share, and post. We worry about the way algorithms polarize us. News and information, both accurate and fake, streams to us through various feeds. We might worry about how recommendation systems, machine learning, algorithms, largely conflated as "Artificial Intelligence," are more and more involved in filtering information, thus resulting in us living in what is often metaphorically called echo chambers or filter bubbles (cf. Bruns 2019 for a critique of the terms).

Has the internet been absorbed completely into the background of our life-world ? Or do we still think of the internet as a place or a tool? How do we experience the internet in an era when, for all intents and purposes, it disappears?

Starting with the (deceptively) simple premise that the way we talk about certain things shapes the way we think about them, Lakoff and Johnson (1980) remain foundational in helping us understand how metaphors function conceptually to not only reflect but construct our experience of reality. If we say "Annette is a lion" or "the internet is a frontier," the comparison of terms builds or promotes a particular meaning. The term being defined (Annette, internet) is connected to the supposedly more known term (lion, frontier). Pride, fierceness, or a bushy golden mane become lion-esque reference points to help us explain what Annette is like. If we and the reader have in mind the same sort of lion, this can help us find common ground or common understanding about Annette. These characteristics may not be obvious every time we think of Annette, but according to metaphor theory, if the comparison sticks, it will work under the surface not only to reflect, but to influence how we think about her. This transference of meaning is also a translation; important insights about one object are transferred or transposed to the other. This process highlights certain aspects of the described phenomena, but simultaneously obscures others.

What is highlighted and obscured in the metaphors we use for the internet? What if we never use the frontier metaphor directly, but just say, "It's the law of the wild in the Internet?" Are different interest groups partial to particular metaphors?

The rhetoric used and strategically circulated by internet intermediaries and other corporate providers serves its own ideological, political and economic purposes. Nicholas John (2017) has written about the term "sharing" as central to how social media is articulated. In everyday discourse, sharing has multiple, mostly positive connotations (fair distribution, emotionally open communication). These connotations are appropriated by for-profit companies like Facebook and more recently Uber or Airbnb. Calling the practices they want people and organizations to engage in on their platforms—the same practices that generate the value for their business models—sharing, allows the platform owners to make their products and services seem like a natural continuation of the utopian, communal, gift-economy based project of the early internet. Tarleton Gillespie (2017) has argued that the term "platform," which social media companies incorporated into their internal and marketing discourse circa 2010, allowed YouTube and Facebook to ignore the word's computational connotations, and instead draw on older meanings from architecture and politics (platform as a structure from which to speak or act). As Gillespie explains, "calling themselves platforms promised users an open playing field for free and unencumbered participation, promised advertisers a wide space in which to link their products to popular content, and promised regulators that they were a fair and impartial conduit for user activity" (np). Brett Frischmann (2018) similarly critiqued the obfuscated connotations of metaphors like "cloud" and "smart." He says that "cloud" attempts to blackbox the fact that it is merely "someone else's computer." Calling it that would obviously raise more eyebrows and invite anxieties about data security, privacy and surveillance, which is not useful for service providers. "Smart," for Frischmann (2018), conflates different forms of intelligence—smart as wise and learned, versus smart as based on computational analysis of personal (and/or sensor) data. This conflation makes it difficult for us to notice that sometimes we do not actually need a piece of technology to operate with our personal data, and that we would, in fact, much prefer for it to be "dumb," leaving us the agency and responsibility to use it wisely.

Many popular metaphors about the internet have thrived and dwindled over the past three decades. We used to talk about cyberspace and the electronic frontier, then the surfable web, then networked publics, platforms, clouds and the internet of things. Some have fallen out of use, but as Josh Dzieza (2014) aptly points out, even those that might now sound slightly ridiculous, continue to shape discussions of particular spaces on, or functions of the internet. He uses "town square" and "superhighway" as examples. The first used to describe the internet as a whole, but is today often applied to Twitter, in particular when the speaker wants to highlight that Twitter is a public sphere of sorts. The second has transformed into a language of fast and slow lanes within the debates surrounding net neutrality (Dzieza, 2014). This aligns with what other metaphor theorists have argued: that the most powerful metaphors are actually those that are no longer obvious as comparisons, but because they are embedded in our deep structures of meaning, they provide a root system upon which newer metaphors build.

There have been various ways of clustering the metaphors of the internet. Alongside Annette's 1998 framework of the internet as a set of tools, some kind of place, or a way of being, Josh Meyrowitz (1998) encapsulated communication media as vessels/conduits, language, and environment. Marianne van den Boomen (2014) writes about material, processing, transmission, and storage metaphors of new media. Denis Jamet's 2010 analysis of French and English words for verbs around internet use laid out a framework of movement or motion (going on, getting off, and surfing the internet). The most recent Wikipedia entry on internet metaphors divides them into social metaphors (i.e. ones that emphasize community and togetherness), functional metaphors (indicative of how the internet should be used), and visual metaphors (how the internet is visualized, mostly through a partial network of connected nodes) (Wikipedia, 2019). The effort to identify and critically analyze the metaphors we use to encapsulate the experience and use of digital media is important because, as Annette noted in 2003, the more concrete the preferred metaphors for the internet are, the more they construct walls of meaning around us: "reifying a box that we will be asking ourselves to think outside of in the future" (Markham, 2003, p. 1). We see these boxes everywhere: metaphors like virus, backdoor, and cloud have encouraged particular imaginaries about what parts of the internet look like or how they work. "Piracy," a common metaphor for file sharing outside sanctioned networks invokes images of deliberate nonconformity and a culture of violence and thievery, which hardly encapsulates the everyday activity of file sharing between friends. What do we imagine, when we are told that data is the "new oil?" Such discourse matters. Each term we use invites different moral assessment and regulation. The use of particular frames has significant impact and implications, far beyond simply using a metaphor to explain how the internet works in a general conversation (cf. Katzenbach & Larsson, 2017; Wyatt, 2004).

A WORMHOLE, A HOME, AN UNAVOIDABLE PLACE?

This book contributes to ongoing conversations about metaphors by focusing on how and whether Annette's original framework of "tool, place and way of being" still captures the essence of how people make sense of the internet in their everyday lives and work. Through short vignettes, longer essays, artworks, interviews and academic studies, the collaborators share granular details of lived experiences in the US, UK, Australia, Canada, Spain, Israel, Russia, Singapore, Hong Kong, Denmark and Austria. The pieces describe all manner of activities, including blogging, forum posting, image sharing, history telling, music and live video streaming, meme remixing, searching, status updating, mapping, filesharing, video chatting and cloud syncing. Some authors tell their own stories, while others share their informants' stories of mourning, migration, childbirth, trauma, transition, family, vulnerability and activism on, in and with the internet. These are stories about life, but they are also stories about the internet. About how the internet is part of life, how it makes life better, easier, or is described as an intrusion. For our collaborators and their informants the internet is inescapable and boring, necessary and magical, grand and mundane.

"Metaphors of internet" is packed with lived experience and varied modes of finding and expressing meaning about an internet that is viscerally relevant. The pieces, despite being written for an academic book, evoke both the mundanity and shocking transformative potential of the internet in the age of ubiquity. Through images, vignettes, poetry, and dialogues, the chapters bring life to theories so often used to analyze the internet. This vitality was nurtured through a long and arduous process of collectively composing and curating the book. Making a monumental effort towards our vision to build a book collaboratively, our authors wrote their chapters in a shared space online. From the very first drafts, they opened themselves up for comment and critique from the other authors. Because our goal was to create readable, evocative, and creative pieces that were also analytically rigorous, we relentlessly banged that drum every time we interacted with the drafts or engaged in conversation with our collaborators. We were somewhat amazed that they accepted this unconventional, radically open style of writing and engaging in peer review and further, embraced the level of intensity it involved. We are equally grateful for being allowed the great freedom to hands-on edit and remix the texts as they entered the final draft stages. Because of this dual process of multiple rounds of collective reviewing and dialogue on the one hand, and the close editing by Annette and I on the other, the book accomplishes two often incompatible aims: It offers a kaleidoscopic diversity of everyday experiences and articulations of the internet, and maintains a coherence and consistently high quality. This is a book, not a collection of disjointed chapters.

We've organized the book into six sections, titling them to emphasize how much the internet has become a way of being, the third metaphor in Annette's original conceptual continuum. The introductory section lays out some core ideas. In addition to introducing the overall framework of the book and the authors (the piece you're reading now), we include two chapters that highlight historical shifts in how we communicate about the internet, from astounding, marvelous and revolutionary to mundane, routine, and unremarkable. We opened the book with a short piece by Annette Markham, discussing some of the ways internet metaphors have changed over the years, both linguistically and in our everyday visual representations of the internet and our relationship with or in it. That piece helps situate the present book within a larger conversation that began in the mid-1990s about what the internet *is*, an ongoing definitional debate that frames how people will make sense of and interact with this core element (some would say backbone) of digital life. Annette raises a future-oriented question about which metaphors we want to use to reflect, and more importantly shape, our future experiences with digital technologies. Kevin Driscoll's chapter analyzes how the small and privileged group of long-term internet users—those who've had steady access since 1997—make sense of and articulate how the internet has transformed. In his historical treatment, Kevin discusses how nostalgia and narratives of decline have the rhetorical power to "shape debates about Internet policy, technology and culture" (this volume, p. 28). His piece raises the question of how today's mundane and ubiquitous internet could "inspire new senses of wonder, feelings of possibility, and sparkling visions of better tomorrows?" (this volume, p. 34).

Section 2, *Ways of Doing*, presents stories about the everyday performances and practices in and with the help of the internet. Despite the general argument that the internet has disappeared, at least as an obvious frame for experience and interaction, it—and its capacities and affordances—remain central to almost every aspect of contemporary living. The authors in this section highlight some of these capacities of the internet as a tool for getting things done. The two pieces by Nadia Hakim-Fernández and Jeff Thompson illustrate vividly how the capacities of networking enable geographic dispersion, and at the same time, create a reliance on the material means of production—there are machines with cables that require power and network connections. Nadia analyzes how becoming a mobile worker shifts how the internet is lived by mobile freelancers. Her stories surface the invisible luxury of both being connected (to a workplace) and disconnecting (from work), as mobile freelancers face challenges of making one's own workplace at the intersections of wifi-connected cafes, computer configurations, devices that wear out or break, and networks of other gig workers. Jeff's images of the physical workspaces of various Mechanical Turk workers around the world highlights the routine materiality of platform work. The images are even more striking when we compare the materiality of a microworker's desktop to the shiny, hipster-coffee-shop vibe presented in advertisements or stock images of the gig economy. In the following two pieces, Tijana Hirsch and Whitney Phillips depict two very different ideas about what it means to create and connect information on social media networks. On the one hand, the availability of information and tips from new friends stabilize and ease Tijana's participant's efforts to migrate to a different country and try to be a good parent through challenging transitions. For her the internet, or specifically Facebook, is a tool for making migration and parenthood work. On the other hand, Whitney's essay lays bare the chaotic ways that information ricochets through the internet as it is created, remixed, and taken up by stakeholders with radically different ambitions. We conclude this section with my own conceptual work on the micro processes of interactivity involved in looking and showing (through visual image sharing), to clarify how the capacities and affordances of the internet shape our performances of our selves. When we look beyond the fact of visual images, we can explore how the interactive performativity with and in the internet adds up to much more than the sum of its parts. In all, this section offers a nuanced exploration of why the intersection of the activities of the people and the capacities of the internet matter.

Section 3, *Ways of Relating*, focuses attention on being with others, and the relations that emerge as we interact with others through digital technologies, whether we call this "online" or not. Crystal Abidin's analysis introduces us to the ways that people who spend a lot of time cultivating relationships through social media make sense of certain areas of the internet as home. As Crystal compares influencers' activities in their old blogs to cleaning house or rearranging furniture, she vividly reminds us that for many, the internet provides a strong sense of place. In a similar vein, Andrea Baker provides a glimpse of how very early on, Rolling Stones fans created hybrid places for experiencing concerts, being with each other, and their own fandom. For the most part, the snippets of everyday life presented by the authors in this section depict a strong sense of belonging, camaraderie, and shared interest in being together and using the internet to enact and sustain significant parts of personal and familial relationships. Cathy Fowley's piece offers a poignant pastiche of voices, hinting at meaningful conversations among women in a place that no longer exists: *the Pink Place*. Anette Grønning describes the seemingly mundane but powerfully connective ways the internet is woven into the ecology of the Danish families she studies. She builds on the concept of personal ecologies, where feedback is an important component of creating or identifying boundaries, albeit very interconnected ones. Priya Kumar's piece addresses a different aspect of an ecological model for thinking about the digital contexts within which we build and maintain relationships. Building or maintaining relationships in the age of ubiquitous internet means grappling with complicated and often competing demands. While a parent might want to post many images of their children to keep family and friends apprised of their activities, this comes with a pressure of constantly sharing, shifting attention away from the self to focus on the profile of one's child, even before birth. For her participants, various entities have different ideas about where the boundaries of self, personal life, or family life should be drawn. In this piece, readers can conclude the section wondering to what extent our personal ecologies are controllable, or at least, controlled by us, versus other stakeholders.

Section 4, *Ways of Becoming*, addresses the constantly changing, transitioning and transforming aspects of being ourselves and in the world. Although not all the authors in this section use the concept of becoming directly, each addresses aspects of transformation, or how the internet is entangled in the processes, practices and performances of selfhood in flux. We start this section with Son Vivienne's chapter on trans-being. Relying on personal experience and research with gender-diverse storytellers, Son writes of the effects that using the internet and researching other people's internet use has had on them. Son's chapter follows their iterative and creative self-reinvention through social media and other forms of digital self-representation, and in the process, asks if "trans-being" can be posited as a new framework that constitutes both the 'post-gender' and "post-digital" facets of digital living. This piece demonstrates the visceral and deeply felt disconnections and reconnections of filtering, enacting, and articulating the self, for the self and for and with others. The discussion of what experimentation might mean to the potentiality of being continues in the following piece, where Craig Hamilton and Sarah Raine describe how tools, places, and ways of being intermingle in the experience of music streaming. They extend Markham's framework by introducing the "potential of being" involved in using and "hacking" music streaming services. As people manage the current and future impressions they give and give off of themselves as music listeners, they create experiences for their future selves. In the next piece, Maria Schreiber and Patricia Prieto-Blanco offer a deceptively straightforward case study of their own experiences of collaboration in various virtual co-working spaces. Their story offers intriguing conceptual thinking by showing how through everyday co-presence, they are actually co-becoming a new hybrid being—Maria+Patricia+internet. The process of becoming through and with socially-mediated photography of the self is poignantly discussed by artist Cristina Nuñez. In an interview with Kat and Annette, Cristina shares her path through physical, material, and digital experiences, raising important questions about the possibilities and challenges of becoming with technology. Finally, Katie Warfield uses the conceptual lenses of *transgeography* and feminist phenomenology to look at how young people regard their use of social media for self-presentation. She offers a series of what she calls "slippery" metaphors that help reorient our analytical gaze from people or individuals doing things, to the processes of becoming through, with, and in digital and material entanglements across and through geographies that are less about place and more about deeply contextual processes and meanings.

Section 5, *Ways of Being With*, is titled in homage to the notion that being is always relational and dialogic. R.D. Laing would explain that our identity cannot be abstracted from our identity-for-others, our identity-for ourselves, the identities we attribute to others, the identities we think they attribute to us, what we think they think we think, and so on (Markham, 1998, p. 215, citing Laing, 1969, p. 86). Distinct from the focus of section 3 on ways of relating with other people, this section focuses on how we make sense of ourselves, others, and the world through/by being with machines, the digital, and information, as facilitated by the internet. You could also say the pieces we've collected here explore how technologies mediate self, other, and relationality. We open with Tobias Raun's study of how Facebook is experienced as a wormhole between life and death. Based on his conversations with Camilla, a woman whose mother and sister recently passed away, the chapter follows how a deceased person's Facebook page is a portal, enabling a sense of closeness and presence that the gravesite does not. This emotional and eerie chapter is followed by a series of photos by xtine burrough entitled *Vigil for Some Bodies*. Each All Hallow's Eve since 2015, xtine has paid Mechanical Turk workers 25 cents, not to conduct digital piece work as is typical, but to light a candle in remembrance of loved ones. The topic of presence, being with, and the digital/physicality of commemoration is entangled and juxtaposed in xtine's images in ways that raise important questions about the centrality of the internet for everyday sensemaking. Sarah Schorr and Winnie Soon take up related questions, focusing on temporality, being with, and the reappearance of the unerasable in their artworks, *Saving Screens* and *Unerasable Images*, respectively. Building from and reframing the violent metaphorical associations involved in screenshooting, they discuss how the act of cut/copy/paste of the screenshot transitions from a tool of the internet era to a generative sensemaking practice where meanings and memories linger. Daisy Pignetti continues this contemplation of the internet's capacities to revive and re-present information in the next chapter. Daisy relates the story of how her New Orleans childhood home, devastated in 2005 by Hurricane Katrina and subsequently razed to the ground, reappeared in 2010 on Google Maps' Street View. This strange familiarity is one of being—not out of time, but in different layers of time, a consequence of the interconnections between physical referents, mapping technologies, social media activity, and episodes of nostalgia. Annette Markham offers a final brief essay for this section. She offers the metaphor of echolocation as a way of making sense of digital sociality. Comparing the various pings of our social media use to the practices of bats, whales, and dolphins to navigate through space, Annette suggests that through an always-on, always-available internet, people locate their social selves when they are responded to, relational processes that are only visible when the lack of response casts the self into existential doubt.

Our sixth and final section, *Whose Internet? Whose Metaphors?* collects pieces that address the rules, power hierarchies and boundaries in who gets to perceive the internet as theirs, who gets to make the dominant metaphors and what that may mean for imaginaries of the future internet. Carmel Vaisman's chapter tells the history of a blogging platform where teenage girls lived, resisted, appropriated and finally submitted to platform owner's and community manager's tropes of what Israel's blogging platform *Israblog* is—and more importantly, is not—for. Based on her analysis of the battles of meaning, Carmel suggests that as systems become more complex and bureaucratic, people naturalize certain technical constraints, accepting them as given. Jessa Lingel's chapter offers a thought experiment to explore how some of the practices of anarchist groups online demonstrate a stronger democratic or collaborative mode than the automated, ill-functioning content moderation processes adopted by many social media giants. Inspired by anarchist communities she knows via her research and activist work, she offers a generative set of practices for managing online communities. In the following chapter, Polina Kolozaridi, Anna Shchetvina, and I offer a rare insight into Soviet and Post-Soviet understandings of the functionality, meaning and uses of the internet. By analyzing the metaphors used by Russia's internet-pioneers, and contextualizing those within historical Soviet conceptualizations of the interconnections of technology and humans, we propose that different cultures create marked distinctions in what meaning is conveyed within the same root metaphor. Nuancing the metaphors of tool, place and way of being with historical Russian/Soviet connotations emphasizes not how technology is used by individuals, but rather how it participates in relations with collectives. This opens up new avenues to think about the future of the internet. We wrap up this section and the book as a whole with Ryan Milner's chapter. In a sensitive, critical and self-aware analysis of his own early internet use, Ryan opens up the implications, blind spots and exclusions imbricated with the tone, practices and self-perceptions of the young, white, American men, who arrogantly called themselves "The Internet" in the early 2000s. Ryan analyzes that Internet through the metaphor of a "Remix Machine" that runs on a particular form of repurposing, creativity and irony. These practices of remix have become more accessible todiverse groups of internet users, but as Ryan says, the ghosts linger in the machine. As Ryan writes in his chapter, "If 'just a joke' ever requires, even 'ironically,' trotting out the same dehumanizing stereotypes and characterizations that have been sampled time and again to write songs of oppression, then maybe the joke's not funny," (p. 253). He concludes with a call to use our tools to create a place premised on more diverse, more empowering voices.

Together, these chapters weave new and old metaphors into our understanding of what the internet means in an era when it has all but disappeared as an obvious frame for experience. This is what we mean by the subtitle of our book, *Ways of Being in the Age of Ubiquity*. The term "ubiquitous computing" is attributed to Mark Weiser (1991), who believed the best sort of computers were those that receded into the background and simply functioned without our noticing. Without getting into whether or not we agree with this valuation, we take the concept of ubiquity in the way our colleagues in the Association of Internet Researchers (AoIR) did when titling our 2004 annual conference "Ubiquity?" This conference challenged as well as explored the visibility and prevalence of the Internet as everywhere, all at once. The call for papers raised questions such as:

> is the internet everywhere? How and where does the internet appear and act in technical, social, political, or cultural contexts? What does it mean to have access and who does and doesn't have it? How does the presence of the internet affect individuals, communities, families, governments, societies and nation-states? What are the implications of 'internet everywhere'? (excerpt from AoIR mailing list call for papers)

We believe *Metaphors of Internet: Ways of Being in the Age of Ubiquity* illustrates how these sorts of questions often get answered in ways that highlight one particular metaphorical frame over others. The pieces in this book can also help us understand that debates over meaning are not only longstanding, they are rarely recognized as debates in the first place. This is precisely because metaphors move from active or "live" where they startle us into making new sense of something, to dead, where they are still active but function at the deep structure of discourse to simply frame understanding and guide definitions. And of course, things change. New devices, platforms, and capacities come along. Conversations continue. Trends shift, and along with these, the meaning of the internet shifts as well. And while these frames may disappear over time and familiarity, the power of the imaginary remains an influence in how we act, with others, with our technologies.

CHAPTER THREE

Losing Your Internet: Narratives of Decline among Long-Time Users

KEVIN DRISCOLL

Annette Markham's *Life Online* (1998) documents an historical conjuncture in which the visibility of the Internet in popular culture outpaced hands-on access for most Americans. At the time that Markham was completing her fieldwork, approximately one-third of Americans reported using the Internet, most of whom were white, wealthy, highly educated, and male (Rainie, 2017). Yet, for half a decade, news and entertainment media had been saturated with stories of the Internet as a technical marvel, economic opportunity, social revolution, and moral threat (Schulte, 2013; Streeter, 2017). Every few months, the cover of *Time* magazine added a new dimension to the Internet story, from the "info highway" in 1993, to the "cyberporn" panic in 1995, dot-com "golden geeks" in 1996, and the "death of privacy" in 1997. Beyond these sensational headlines, friends and coworkers gossiped about relationships and romances forming online. Early users of the Internet were similarly enthusiastic and many shared a sense that computer-mediated communication might transform the social world. Even Markham described her initial observations of the internet and its growing user population as "astounding" and "extraordinary" (1998, pp. 16–17). At the turn of the century, the Internet seemed charged with unknown possibility.

Twenty years later, the structure of feeling that characterized early encounters with the Internet has changed. For millions of people, computer-mediated communication is now an unremarkable aspect of everyday life. In comparison to the fantastical multi-user environments that Markham described in 1998, typical uses of the internet in 2017 seem quite dull: reading the news, solving a crossword puzzle, shopping for household goods, or arranging meetings with coworkers. Furthermore, in popular media, the Internet seems to oscillate unpredictably from the mundane to the menacing. The same platform used to file income taxes is said to facilitate waves of terrorism, harassment, fraud, and propaganda. Returning to the *Time* archive, we find alarming cover stories about the "secret web where drugs, porn and murder hide online" in 2013 and a failed e-government initiative described as a "nightmare" in 2014. What is striking about these recent headlines, however, is how infrequently the Internet itself is an object of scrutiny. Unlike stories from the 1990s, the presence of the Internet in our homes is now taken-for-granted and the panic lies in its misuse or abuse.

Long-time users, the small group who have enjoyed continuous internet access since 1997, are in a unique position to reflect on the transformation of the Internet from ballyhoo to banality. While any American adult alive in the early 1990s would have been exposed to ideas and arguments about the Internet, only long-time users can compare these narratives with first-hand experience. Long-time users bore witness to several translations in the cultural position of the Internet: from voluntary to compulsory, peripheral to central, marvelous to mundane. For the long-time user, the interleaving of computer-mediated communication and human society is neither taken-for-granted nor natural. And while these transitions unfolded over the course of many years, long-time users are only occasionally prompted to reflect on the changes they have experienced. It is in these moments of self-reflection that we find clues regarding the changing meaning of metaphors over the past two decades.

This chapter focuses on discourses of nostalgia, loss, and decline among long-time users for whom the Internet of the 1990s became, in Markham's analysis, "a way of being" (2003). Almost invariably, long-time users remember the early Internet as a kind of golden age, an electronic Eden in which anyone with a modem was free to play and experiment in relative safety. As one characteristic comment on an historical blog post reads, "[This] brings back some fond memories. [Back then,] the worst thing that would happen was that call waiting would knock me offline!" Undoubtedly, this nostalgia reflects an authentic longing for the excitement one felt standing on the threshold of cyberspace but it also obscures the substantial social barriers and material costs that prevented most people from sharing in that experience. To understand what is at stake in this tension between the nostalgia of long-time users and the on-going expansion and domestication of Internet access, this chapter examines both the contemporary accounts of Internet use captured by Markham in *Life Online* and the retrospective stories told by high-profile figures in the recent past. This comparison reveals the rhetorical power of narratives of decline to shape debates about Internet policy, technology, and culture. As we consider what it means to live online for another two decades, we must critically consider the stories that we tell about Internets of the past.

LOST WAYS OF BEING ON THE INTERNET

The Internet of today is cheaper, faster and more widely accessible than at any point in the past. But these developments have been achieved through a process of continuous change. The Internet is made and re-made as various components are adopted and abandoned, incorporated and disconnected. As the Internet evolves, long-time users mourn the loss of particular programs, practices, services, or interfaces. Favorite sites shut down, loose network connections fade away, daily habits are disrupted. As the technical systems that make up the Internet change, they unsettle the Internet as a way of being.

The consequences of technological change for long-time Internet users are clearest in the transition from desktop terminals to mobile devices. In the mid-1990s, a majority of online social activity unfolded in text-only environments. Even as faster modems, graphical operating systems, and the Web grew more common, the Net of the 1990s was composed of seemingly endless streams of text; row upon row of letters, numbers, and punctuation. In the decades since, text-only applications such as IRC were displaced by interactive video displays that interleave images and text, respond to taps, gestures, swipes, and voices rather than instructions typed out on a keyboard. Although these new interfaces contributed to the growing accessibility of the internet, the transition was not without costs for users accustomed to navigating by text. For several participants in Markham's *Life Online* fieldwork, the text-only interfaces of the 1990s afforded ways of being not available elsewhere in their lives. In the words of one interlocutor, text-only environments like MUDs and MOOs gave rise to "a much more complex life of relationships … centered around being a part of a meaningful community" (p. 176). For some long-time users, the Internet was a way of being because the Internet was made of text.

Text-oriented interfaces also shaped the embodied experiences of users in the 1990s. Markham's interlocutors reported sitting at desks, day and night, in computer labs, offices, and bedrooms. Their hands played across a keyboard or moved a mouse, and their gazes focused on a screen fixed in place. Likewise, the textual environments they inhabited—MOOs, chatrooms, listservs, and newsgroups—maintained a material distinction between being online and offline. To enter one of these spaces required being in a particular place, sitting in front of a machine, and entering the proper sequence of commands to open a network connection. Although the predominance of text seemed to offer an "escape" from the body for some users, Markham found that the bodies of her interviewees stubbornly resisted abandonment, a phenomenon that Megan Boler later described as a "new digital Cartesianism" (2007). Embodiment persists, reflected Markham, even when bodies were rendered, enacted, and performed through text alone (1998, p. 209).

For those users who inhabited the Internet as a way of being in 1997, the Internet was, implicitly, a society of written texts. Though text-only interfaces and text-oriented applications may not have obliterated the flesh, they nevertheless privileged written communication over all other forms of social interaction. As mobile broadband and constant connectivity blurred the boundary between online and offline in the late 2000s, however, written communication lost its status as the principal form of computer-mediated communication. For some of the people profiled in *Life Online*, this transition must have been profoundly unsettling. Consider Sherie, Markham's obtuse interlocutor who insisted that life online is "very textual. very discursive and rhetorical. also poetic" (1998, p. 207). Could a user like Sherie, so committed to text, experience the always-on, broadband internet of 2017 as a way of being?

The growing, changing internet of the 2000s gave rise to new forms of creative expression and provided space for a much broader range of voices, but it also foreclosed the dreams of some long-time users whose way of being depended on the primacy of text. For these users, a text-only environment seemed to offer a form communication free from the prejudices they experienced in embodied environments. Text-mode interaction granted these users a special kind of control, evidenced in their recurring references to the "delete" key, a synecdoche for the entire apparatus of the text-only internet. The most optimistic among them imagined that the spread of internet access—that is, text-mode internet access—would bring about a radical egalitarian society, a "civilization of the Mind" in the words of EFF co-founder John Perry Barlow (1996). But it turned out that the diffusion of access was not enough. As the internet became another medium for entertainment and office work, the paradigm shifting dream of the late 1990s began to sound naïve and out of touch. What could be so revolutionary about baby pictures, cute dogs, celebrity news, and TV dramas? For the cyber-romantic of the 1990s, the lived reality of ubiquitous internet access may be a bit of a letdown.

NOSTALGIA FOR INTERNETS OF THE PAST

Nostalgia shapes the memories of long-time users who have lost the Internet as a way of being. To paraphrase a characteristic recollection about the experience of exploring the online world of the 1990s: "Those were such great days, or should I say long nights." But there is more at stake in the nostalgia of long-time users than fond memories. The stories that long-time users share about the diffusion and domestication of the Internet reflect underlying beliefs about how the Internet ought to be. In the hands of people with power and influence, narratives that glorify the Internet of the past will have material consequences for people who rely on the Internet of the present for personal expression and community support. Excessively sentimental attachment to the early Internet overlooks the most important change in the past two decades: the mutual visibility and increased access for people of different racial and gender identities, socio-economic classes, ages and abilities, geographic locations, and linguistic groups. Paradoxically, of course, the utopic structure of feeling of the 1990s motivated the work that opened the Internet to others.

Recently, two Silicon Valley entrepreneurs, each a long-time user, marshalled stories about the Internet's past to advocate for a particular vision of its future. While each articulated a narrative of decline, they differed in their diagnoses of the problem. One offered a hopeful account of paths-not-taken while the other blamed Internet newcomers and social media speculators for shortsightedness and a lack of ambition. Comparing the uses of history in these two rhetorical moments underscores the importance of memory in the experience of the Internet as a way of being.

In late 2012, long-time blogger Anil Dash published "The Web We Lost," lamenting a decline in "core values" that were once "fundamental to the web world" (2012a). Dash elaborated these values through a chronological series of examples of the design of social technologies and the collective behavior of industrial organizations. The blog post was widely read—Dash lists it among his personal favorite and most popular posts (2012b)—and, shortly after, Dash gave a talk on the topic at the Berkman Center for Internet and Society at Harvard University (2013). In the spoken version, titled "How We Lost the Web," Dash marshalled a narrative of decline to critique the enclosure of the Web by mutually incompatible social media systems, a process that Anne Helmond later characterized as "platformization" (2015).

In Dash's narrative, the "early social web" ran from 1999 to 2005, the period immediately following the conclusion of Markham's fieldwork. First, he acknowledged the scarce documentation of the period—"younger folks may not even know how the web used to be"—and, second, he established his credibility as a first-hand observer, "I got to witness it." In Dash's recollection, blogging was the preeminent activity of the period, a lingering effect of the privileged status of written communication during the 1990s. For Dash's crew of early bloggers, the internet was a way of being: "[blogging] distinguished you and who you were." This shared identity gave rise to a shared culture and a shared set of values involving openness, privacy, control, and creativity. In Dash's narrative of decline, the platform that dominates today's Internet offers no similar shared identity to its users: "Nobody's a 'Facebooker.'"

For Dash, the purpose of sharing this narrative of decline was to inspire an alternative vision of the future in his readers. His personal recollections of an earlier Internet suggest that the platformization of the internet was not pre-ordained, nor universally welcome. He describes the transition from self-hosted blogs to centralized platforms as happening "really, really quickly with almost no public discourse about the implications" (2013). In setting up the present conditions as aberrant, he offers a potential remedy for the future: "The reality is public policy can be a really, really effective part of addressing the problems in the technology industry" (2013). In effect, Dash pitched a "battle" between the past and the present, characterizing the decline as temporary and appealing to readers to join his pursuit toward a different future.

In contrast to Dash's focus on values, a manifesto titled "What happened to the future?" circulated by the venture capital firm Founders Fund in 2011, told a story of the Internet's past characterized by failures of technological achievement (Gibney, 2011). (The manifesto was written by Founders Fund partner Bruce Gibney but authorship is often misattributed to his fellow partner Peter Thiel.) At the time of the essay's publication, journalists covering the tech industry were especially likely to quote a sentence that did not actually appear in the body of Gibney's essay: "We wanted flying cars, instead we got 140 characters" (2011). Coming from a firm closely associated with Facebook, industry insiders interpreted this quip as an attack on competitors and it led to a staged debate between Thiel and Twitter investor, Marc Andreesen (Horowitz, 2013). To the general public, however, the sentence neatly captured a feeling of bitter disappointment.

Reactionary narratives of decline mistakenly blame the loss of the Internet as a way of being on the growth in the size and diversity of the online population. In the 2013 debate with Andreesen, Thiel elaborated his dismissal of Twitter's "140 characters" by targeting the players of casual games and users of social media:

> You have as much computing power in your iPhone as was available at the time of the Apollo missions. But what [is it] being used for [?] It's being used to throw angry birds at pigs[;] it's being used to send pictures of your cat to people halfway around the world; it's being used to check in as the virtual mayor of a virtual nowhere while you're riding a subway from the nineteenth century. (Horowitz, 2013)

These examples reflect Thiel's evaluation of certain Internet applications as low value and undeserving of "computing power." By this logic, the decline of the Internet was caused by an overindulgence in technologies of pleasure, entertainment, community, and kinship.

The resentment evident in narratives such as Thiel's have real consequences for people who have come to rely on the internet. Men like Gibney and Thiel invest financially as well as emotionally in the future of the internet. Their personal feelings, preferences and priorities shape the terms by which they deem new technologies worthy of support and enable them to flourish. For this milieu, the internet of the 1990s provided more than a way of being. Thanks to the irrational exuberance of the dot-com bubble, a mastery of arcane computer technology translated into political power and economic capital. As beneficiaries of that brief moment, industry elites are uniquely positioned among long-time users to act on their narratives of decline.

Weaponized by capital and privilege, narratives of decline can empower dangerously regressive visions of the future. The embittered dotcommer—no longer part of a technical vanguard, bored by an early retirement, alienated by an internet population that better represents the full range of humanity—wants to recapture the openness and optimism they felt when the early internet was their way of being. When this nostalgia gives way to frustration and anger, long-time users may be drawn to arguments like Thiel's, convinced that the decline of the Internet is the fault of new users, new practices, new interfaces, and new techniques. Ironically, in grieving over the sense of novelty they felt on the Internet of the past, they risk missing out on what is exciting and new about the Internet of the present.

WAYS OF BEING ON INTERNETS OF THE FUTURE

At the conclusion of her fieldwork, Markham noticed that her own experience of life online had begun to settle down into the realm of familiar. After three years exploring the Net, she was surprised to touch the boundaries of a system that had once seemed so limitless. "I am amazed that I don't find more weird stuff and more exotic transmutations of the body and mind online" (p. 222). In this moment, Markham anticipated the challenge facing us today: to imagine a future for an unremarkable internet. In a final interview, interlocutor Terri Senft offered a concise portrait of a mundane way of being online: "Sometimes blown away. Sometimes bored. Sometimes angry. Often, I have to pee" (p. 223).

Every vision of the internet's future contains a vision of its decline. Since the publication of *Life Online*, the Internet has become the infrastructure of everyday life, suffused into the most quotidian social exchanges and financial transactions. More people in more places have more of their lives mediated by Internet communications. The predominance of young, white, English-speaking men from Europe and the U.S. with money and education has steadily waned. Yet, over the same period, as the Internet shed its exclusivity, it also lost some of its novelty. The mere act of getting online and interacting with other people through a screen no longer inspires the same popular fascination or moral concern that it once did. Long-time users who experienced the frisson of technological mastery or the industrialized hype of the Internet of 1997 may feel some melancholy at the Internet's transformation. But to carelessly remember that older Internet as a virtual Eden is to indict the millions of users who were structurally excluded from participation. The society of the Mind was a dream of computer-mediated colorblindness; an indifference to difference.

Facing down powerful narratives of decline, long-time users committed to justice must recover alternative memories of the internet's past. One small step in this direction is to narrate the past two decades in terms of a dramatic expansion in the size and diversity of the internet-using population. For many of these 21st century users, the Internet itself is a taken for granted feature of their media environment. Indeed, this mundane Internet may not inspire the same outrageous dreams as the Net of the 1990s but its infrastructural futures are not necessarily any less radical. We have language for the internet at its most mundane—an overgrown garden, or a ship in need of repair. But those who struggle for justice must also capture the internet at its most transcendent. How can the Internet of today—ubiquitous and mundane—inspire new senses of wonder, feelings of possibility, and sparkling visions of better tomorrows?

SECTION 2

Ways of Doing

CHAPTER FOUR

Workplace-Making among Mobile Freelancers

NADIA HAKIM-FERNÁNDEZ

April 19, 2017
11:45 am. Talking to my mobile phone's camera.
I have news. The cable that connects my computer to the power source is breaking, and the cables are sprouting out of the plastic sleeve,

See?

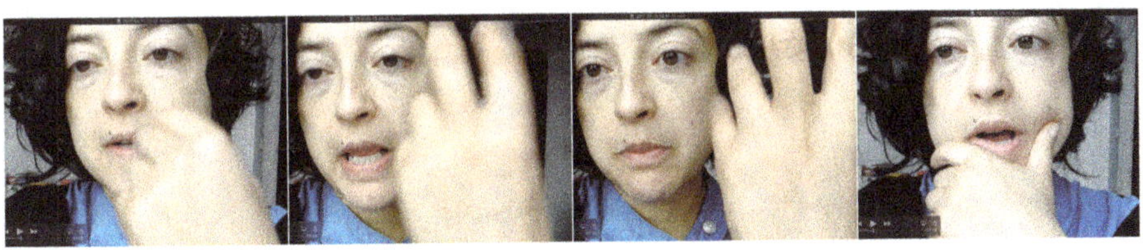

Figure 4.1: Screencaptures of author. Source: Photo by Nadia Hakim-Fernández

I had to put special tape around it, and if I move a lot, it will break apart. Another reminder that I have to buy another computer. But it's 1200 € and I am not sure if I'll be able to spend that kind of money now … I have some savings, but I have bills to pay. This is why I'll have to stay here [at home] for a while, and, you know … speak to myself as I am doing now instead of being in a real workplace with co-workers.

This is part of my auto-ethnography[1] *of what it feels like to be a precarious, mobile, freelancer life. Right now, I'm actually—Sorry, I was interrupted by my mobile phone prompting me to download a new operating system.*

21 April 2017 12:43

I have been working from home since Monday, so for 4 and a half days in a row, (…) I spoke before about the fact that my laptop cable was breaking apart, and this is how it looks today, I mean, it's still connecting by some miracle (Figures 4.1, 4.2 and 4.3):

Figure 4.2: Broken cables. Source: Photo by Nadia Hakim-Fernández

Figure 4.3: The fragility of the internet in the mobile workplace. Source: Photo by Nadia Hakim-Fernández

1 I started this autoethnography (inspired by Ellis & Bochner, 2000; Pensoneau-Conway & Toyosaki, 2011) on December 2015. It is still ongoing. I wrote, filmed and voice recorded fieldwork journals, and recorded interviews both face to face and remotely with eight mobile freelancers working in different fields (university teaching and research, design, digital code developers, and culture related-professions). Constantí, Laura and Thilo are programmers. They are in a better position to find paid labor compared to Muriel, Alvaro, Elena and myself. Muriel is a cultural mediator, she finds "the field of culture much more precarious (…) in Spain [compared to the UK where she used to live]." Alvaro and myself are academic researchers with no access to a well-paid or stable jobs in desirable conditions in the Spanish university system. Loli, a PhD who transitioned from an academic career to an academic freelancer, is able to find projects to

... so I am just using this connector for its last hours. I feel lucky that my partner realized they had a spare computer at work. It belonged to a postdoc who left Madrid (...) so it was just lying there in a box. I can take it for some weeks, not to Colombia, but for a while here in Madrid.

Last night I began downloading the programs I need to be able to work with this computer. I tried to use the in-built migration program, but it didn't work, so I am doing it manually. I have my Dropbox now and it's downloading a ton of files, I have installed my Firefox with all my bookmarks, my Evernote, which doesn't work, because it needs an upgrade. I need to reinstall the program I am using to write. Making the workplace is not a straightforward thing—every time there's something new, some different complication. This time, it involves making these borrowed objects mine through a series of technical transformations. Depending on the objects I borrow, this can take many hours—days, even.

These three desktops are workplaces for me at the moment (Figures 4.4, 4.5, and 4.6):

Figure 4.4: Source: Photo by Nadia Hakim-Fernández

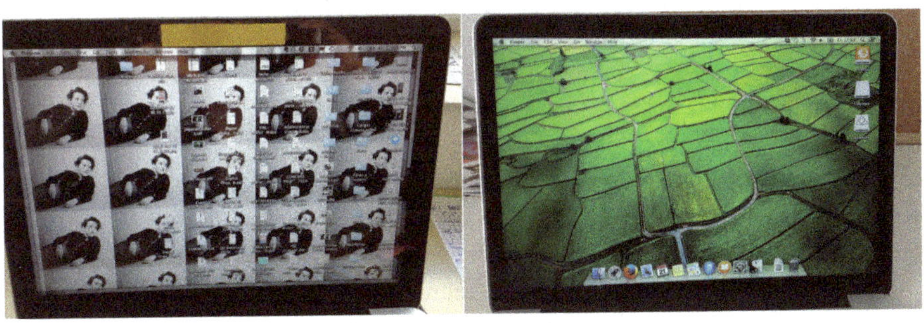

Figure 4.5: Source: Photo by Nadia Hakim-Fernández

work on, but describes the situation as unpredictable and underpaid. Elena is transitioning from being a consultant for public institutions in one country to a writer in another one, and she acknowledges her family's financial support and her own savings as allowing her to continue this personal and professional project.

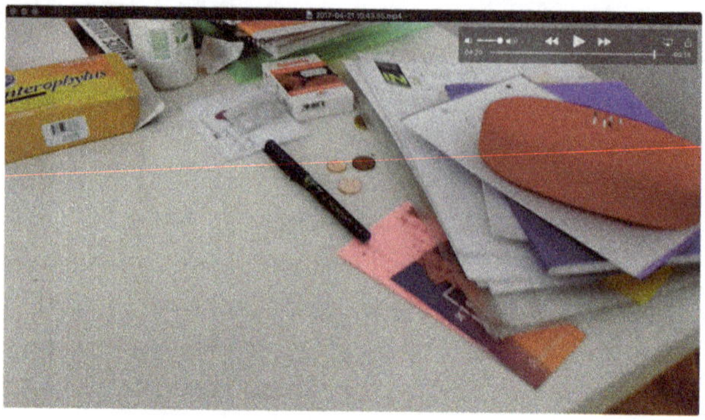

Figure 4.6: Source: Photo by Nadia Hakim-Fernández

INTERNET AND MOBILITY

Technology is designed with explicit purposes and then lived and interpreted by its users in many different ways. What follows is part of a larger project on mobile freelancers (Hakim-Fernández, 2017)—people who do creative and/or intellectual, mostly project-based work, change workplaces and employers frequently, and are constantly on the move, physically and psychically. Mobility is at the heart of this study, and it includes both bodily movement and the flows of information that make the internet what it is. Mobile freelancers don't just "use" the internet and don't just "move" as a lifestyle; they experience and interpret the internet in specific ways while being mobile. I make sense of their experience through Tim Cresswell's (2006, 2014) take on mobility, defined as "movement + meaning + power" (2014, p. 108). This entails both flows and frictions, the latter referring to how power structures and the location of people within it hinder free mobility, not stopping flows completely—as there is no such thing as lack of movement—but redirecting it through specific paths. How we experience and articulate the internet—as a tool, as a place, as a way of being—depends on our capacity to move freely, and the meanings that mobility take, both in positive or negative terms.

While travelling for work and working while in movement are not exclusive to mobile freelancing, doing this without a regular office location or a traditional employment contract is. Mobile freelancers like me are responsible for securing our own jobs—often project-based, often several at a time to make ends meet. The work itself, the place of work, and the schedule of work is for most of us unpredictable. This differentiates mobile freelancers from previous iterations of independent workers (i.e. small shopkeepers in Spain), for whom activities were clearer, there was an established place for commerce, and "high" and "low" seasons were more predictable. Mobility, instability, and a constant 'workplace-making' make mobile freelancers a specific life condition, and this life condition frames how the internet is lived and understood. As Alvaro, one of my informants, a postdoc and adjunct professor at a public University of Barcelona comments: "[i]t is an imposed situation. It's like a permanent instability, in which stability is instability … a stability that never arrives. I feel I focus my energies on searching a stability that will never come."

WHAT IS THE INTERNET FOR MOBILE FREELANCERS?

For the freelancers I studied, the internet is the foundation of their jobs, and the mobile phone the core embodiment of the internet. In the following I explore this through their experiences of materiality, workplace-making and (dis)connection.

Materiality

The "essential survival kit" for mobile freelancers consists of a laptop, a mobile phone, an internet connection, and the complements needed—a notepad and pen, adaptors, keys, money, identification documents, a bottle of water and sometimes something to eat. This set is enough to "do everything," as Constantí notes. However, the most important in this set is still the internet. Markham (2003), building on McLuhan's ideas about media, emphasized the internet as a prosthesis. It provides "vital tools with which we alter the fundamental processes of getting things done." (p. 3). "No internet means I can't do any work. Like when my laptop broke I had to install some backups (…) [from] the internet (…) so really the internet is the most important thing to have." Loli, a freelancer sociologist and consultant based in Barcelona said: "the internet is like electricity to me."

As a material reality, the internet is associated with a screen, and in this case, the mobile screen of a smartphone or a laptop computer. As Laura puts it, her laptop computer screen is important because: "It is a window to the world." Interestingly, Nuria, a freelance web-designer also uses this analogy: "To me, the internet is a window to everything, to work, to my friends who live in other cities, (…) to knowledge." The devices, particularly the screens, are described as the contact points between two worlds. The freelancers use words like "cyberspace" or "virtual world" ("ciberspacio" and "vitual" in Spanish), which could be read to mean they perceive the internet as a place, but it is not the place that is most salient to them, or where they are situated themselves. Instead, they seem to use these terms to describe their sense of distance from a reality that would be invisible if it wasn't for the computer or mobile screen. So the more meaningful metaphor for them may be the idea that the internet is a prosthesis, a conduit.

For many freelancers, there's a tension between the obvious materiality of the device and the invisibility of what we do, or what happens "inside" the computer or the mobile. As Jason Farman (2012) notes when discussing the ideas of visibility and invisibility in locative mobile technologies, most communication technology is designed to be experienced as invisible, and this explains in part why we think of our mobile phones or laptop computers, together with the internet, as immaterial.

Most of the labor performed by knowledge workers, mobile freelancers no exception, is invisible. Muriel's parents, who have experienced work as being visible and touchable, cannot "see" the results of their daughter's work, which gives them a perception of her not having a "real job." She says: "It's not as if I was watching YouTube videos all day! I have to work a lot to be able to get a paid job." Without stacks of papers on desks, and without an office where it's clearer—in a traditional sense—that work happens, it's difficult to visualize for others the materiality of our work.

But the materiality of the internet manifest in a variety of *frictions* (Cresswell, 2006, 2014) in our daily lives. Sometimes the invisible becomes quite materially apparent. Alvaro had to take a trip to a Central-American country, where he was to teach a class. His laptop broke just a week before, so he had to bring an old laptop, which would only turn on when connected to a power source. Alvaro had to worry about not being able to turn it on during security checks at the stop-over airport in the USA. He also couldn't use the precious flight time to prepare his classes. When technology stops working, frictions appear, and the internet becomes material. Friction do not stop the flows of information, work activities and bodies, but makes the material constraints apparent. When this happens, the worker is cut off from significant parts of their workplace(s).

Mobile freelance work and mobile media also have a bodily dimension: the freelancer has to carry the weight of the basic kit on their bodies. As Álvaro puts it, "you never know where you will end up working, you have to take it all with you just in case," an experience Loli describes as a "snail with its shell" and Laura as being "one of those carriage horses in the park." I'm often exhausted by the weight of my workplace. I often find myself staying home just to rest my back. Carrying this equipment is a requirement to get work done, and as I will describe in the next section, to have a workplace we can call our own. The distinction between knowledge/intellectual/creative work and physical work is blurred, when working as a mobile freelancer, and the generally accepted idea about the privileged life conditions entailed by this work type is questioned.

Workplace making

Digital work is often defined as immaterial (Hardt & Negri, 2000, p. 30) and placeless; done anytime, anyplace, without putting a "personal mark on the environment" (Felstead et al., 2005, p. 22). The platforms that organize work are designed to amplify this seeming placelessness (Lehdonvirta, 2016). However, for the mobile freelancers I studied the platforms and software used for, as well as the processes of text processing, design, internet browsing and instant messaging create a sense of a bounded and shared place. For instance, GoogleDocs is a tool frequently used for remote collaborations, and becomes a place where multiple people can be co-present (see chapters by Schreiber and Prieto-Blanco and Raun, this volume). Place and placemaking are relevant for digital labor (Flecker and Schönauer, 2016; Liegl, 2014; Pigg, 2014).

The opening auto-ethnographic vignette showed how different personalizations of our mobile and laptop computers transform standard machines into an intimate place to be alone or with others, to work by oneself or in collaboration. Personalization is accomplished through creative means but also through the affordances of the objects and the platforms and systems within them. Affordance here is understood as "the capacity of an object to help people do something by virtue of its 'interface' features—how it invites and facilitates some particular action" (Molotch, 2011, p. 103). I'm most likely to create personalization through changing preferred settings, adding bookmarks, specifying notifications, using color tags, changing the desktop background. Other mobile freelancers do more or less the same.

Transforming our devices helps make them into stable work places, so that when we log on, we are at work. But it also serves a secondary purpose, helping us transform different types of spaces (semi-public—such as coffee shops—or domestic) into our workplaces for intermittent periods of time, while we move. This, together with the "stuff" stored in people's machines, is similar to the "living space making" Daniel Miller (2011) describes people doing with their households. Work and living place making is influenced by habitus, biography and the material culture available. When Muriel was looking for work, she created a marker system for every museum and gallery in town within her preferred internet browser. Alvaro said: "I prefer working on my laptop because I control the programmes. Working on another PC is very uncomfortable. The one I have available at the Uni is a powerful PC, it's really fast, but my files aren't there and I refuse to have a copy of my Dropbox there [due to privacy issues]." Personalization is key in workplace making, as it creates a sense of privacy and intimacy, which is particularly important for precarious mobile workers.

My laptop computer and mobile phone are my workplaces and so is the coffee shop I am at in Brussels (Figure 4.7).

Finding a place that can temporarily be made one's own is part of the daily work routine for mobile freelancers. It can be extremely time consuming and mentally exhausting. We move with our technologies to find an adaptable place with a wifi, electric sockets and other conditions such as acceptable ambient noise. It is

Figure 4.7: Brussels, 26 December 2016. Source: Photo courtesy of Nadia Hakim-Fernández

of course also important that our activity is welcome. Elena describes her routine of workplace making: "I have two main activities and I do them at different spots of the city. One of them requires writing a lot and being alone, and when I try staying at home, it never works, I cannot concentrate. I'll just settle down and then the doorbell rings and I have to open the door to the gas guy, etc., and there's a thousand other interruptions. I have tried going to libraries, but I need to feel free to answer the phone, move around (…) and the opening hours don't match my schedule. I go to a coffee shop or to my gym that has a big social area, a restaurant, and is very quiet, the coffee is cheaper and I can exercise after work. I normally get up at 8, get my 3-year-old kid ready for school, and I then choose between going to the coffee shop, where we are now, the gym, or returning home. I love home because I can take a nap if I am too tired."

Mobility combined with workplace making is one of the strategies we have to separate what would be otherwise a collapsed work and personal life. Leaving home is important, but maintaining this separation can feel like a struggle. When I was interviewing Constantí at a coffee shop near his home, a phone alert indicated that it was time for him to clean the kitchen. This alert is a reminder for him to stop working and invest some time in his household. He didn't want to interrupt the interview and preferred to stay a while longer, claiming to be "already late in all my [his] tasks anyway." Freelancing requires a sustained effort to be able to create workplaces distinct from personal places. In other words, creating a separation between work and not work through movement, or with the help of technological constraints is fragile; it requires a rejection of some of the affordances designed into our technologies and a lot of self-discipline.

(Dis)connection

> *I disconnect my phone [from the internet] to sleep, and it is an achievement to be able to keep it disconnected until 10:30 am, because you get the feeling that it is getting very late. So the challenge is to wake up and not check the email or whatsapp, but to wake up, exercise a bit, straighten things at home, load the washing machine, and then say OK, now I connect. It's not a big deal to wait until 11 am, and then it's like, OK, 'let the craziness begin'. And you get 40 thousand whatsapps, and mails.*

As Alvaro, all of the interviewed mobile freelancers experience the internet and its related digital technologies inevitable and absorbing, even against their will. This feeling of constant connection to the technologies, to the information and the requirements that come with it, becomes too much. "Disconnection" is a word used by many of my respondents. These mobile freelancers yearn to "escape," to "block" the stream of information and separate work from other aspects of life.

> *A:* *It's that feeling that whether you connect or not, the world changes completely, it's really crazy.*
>
> *N:* *Changes in what sense?*
>
> *A:* *There is a feeling of being intruded on. There are always things there demanding your attention. And I feel a bit persecuted.*

For many mobile freelancers, disconnection, and connection for that matter, present complicated tensions. We recognize it is a matter of boundaries, but these are negotiated with multiple stakeholders—other people, technological devices, and ourselves. Even when we might handle the first two, and that's an ongoing challenge, we might not recognize the third, where we battle to balance our own expectations. On the one hand, we expect that being a freelancer has advantages related to having independence from a boss and sense of "freedom" to create a personal life/work project. On the other hand, we experience keen disadvantages, such as feeling the pressure to work all the time to find material security and feeling as if we must be available all the time. As a result, disconnection carries a double edge.

Disconnection, or more precisely the seemingly constant desire for time and space for oneself, provides compelling evidence for the fact that even if the internet is ubiquitous, it is, for these mobile freelancers, not a seamless way of being. They have a strong object/subject understanding of the internet. It is a tool that moves information, the conduit for that information flow.

This core of feeling that the internet is a tool is evident also in how the freelancers talked about connection and being with others. Of course, the internet provides the freelancer with the necessary, and sometimes only available connection to others. For two hours every week I meet with a colleague sociologist I have only met three times while teaching in Bogotá (see Figure 4.8). We share many interests, and connect just to keep each other company while writing, and to tell each other about our accomplishments or what has been going on during the week.

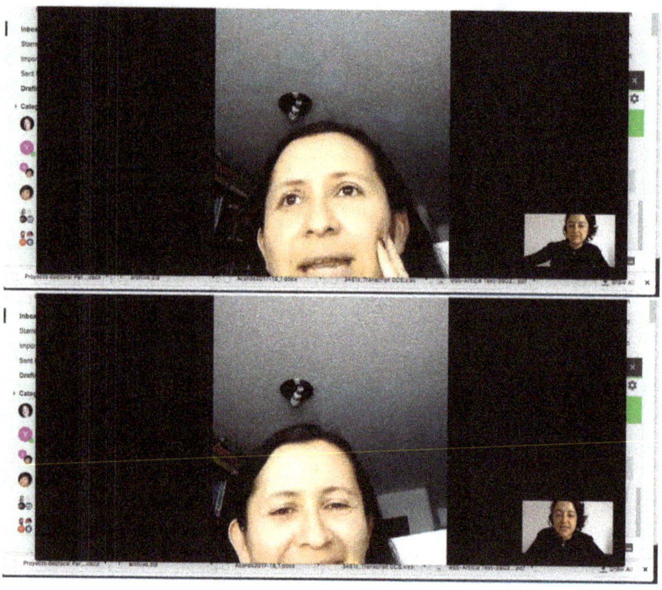

Figure 4.8: Photo of my setting and sessions with Yenny. Source: Image by Nadia Hakim-Fernández

But these internet-mediated platforms for connection don't feel like a replacement for face-to-face encounters, for either of us. In fact, for all of the freelancers I studied, the internet mediated connection alone is inadequate for feeling a sense of being with others. Elena says it is still key to her work to meet others in person, and this is also the case for all the mobile freelancers including myself. Some say they love meeting others in person as part of their jobs. For me, meeting with others in person feels rewarding and productive. It helps me to 'get out of my head' and develop ideas in an informal way.

The connection provided by the internet allows us to be in the life of others who are far away and exchange certain types of information, but for the freelancers I studied it does not translate into a feeling of complete co-presence, or satisfy the need to be in physical contact with others. Quite the opposite, being connected through technologies carries a constant feeling of incompleteness and unfulfillment. The feelings of isolation among remote workers has been widely studied; this literature stresses the importance of "networking opportunities" and the use of, for instance, co-working spaces (Avdikos & Kalogeresis, 2016; Gandini, 2016, pp. 27–44, 97–106; Garrett et al., 2017; Spinuzzi, 2012). Many of us share the feeling that we have to be in places physically with others to do our jobs, and we agree that while these connected technologies are useful, they are—no matter how sophisticated—insufficient. It takes losing just some bits of information during a conversation that is supposed to be synchronous, to also lose the sense of connection and mutual presence. This relates to Markham's critique of the common conflation of information transmission and communication, as if the instrumental means and content of information exchange is the same as meaningful interaction.

CONCLUSION

The metaphors of tool, place, and way of being prove to be useful to analyze mobile freelancer's understandings of the internet. Objectified understandings of the internet and frictions shape the meaning of the Internet and show its limitations. Even though we all have limited resources in time, money and energy, the way mobile freelancers deal with the materiality of digital technologies connected to the internet is specific to life conditions as these resources are usually uncertain, self-provided, and related to constant movement. Even though many of the participants in this research speak about the internet as being virtual and different from physical reality, we endure its materiality every day. Frictions in the flows represented by mobile work and the flow of information manifest when the technologies we use cease to work, and our socio-economic conditions—often precarious—open up for certain possibilities and closes others.

We are involved in a constant placemaking in our devices and through our devices. Place continues to be important and the internet helps create the feeling of a transitory shared work place. This sense of co-presence is nevertheless fragile, and not enough to generate the sense of having a strong bond or to avoid the feeling of isolation. The ability to be in contact and exchange information with others in real time makes certain things possible, but is not enough, because it is understood as an incomplete connection to others. This incompleteness is explained in part by the work conditions of mobile freelancers, where relationships and network opportunities aren't a given and have to be sought for continuously.

As I have shown, project-based and ICT-mediated mobile work does not necessarily represent freedom and a privileged lifestyle. It is certainly a tool for work, but not an emancipatory one. If one is tempted to apply a naïve Marxist analysis regarding the possession of the means of production in the context of capitalism, I have shown that it does not entail freedom from constraints attached in this case to the labor market. The Internet is also a place for the exchange of information, but not a place for being with others and learning informally. The internet as a forced way of being is highlighted when we reflect on how difficult it is to be present or disconnect from our working selves. The internet does not support a free-style identity, which could be supposed from the possibility to personalize and supposedly adapt these technologies to our needs.

CHAPTER FIVE

Turker Computers

JEFF THOMPSON

Turker Computers is a project that sets out to make visible the personal, varied relationship between a person and their computer. A simple request was made on Amazon's crowd-labor site Mechanical Turk over a period of approximately a year: take a photograph of your computer, and include a name (or handle/alias) and where you live (as vague as you like). The responses came from locations across the globe, a selection of which is shown in this art reel. The images from this project turn the webcam around, not showing the people who populate the internet, or make the internet work, but the machines we collaborate with to access it and the spaces in which we use them.

The images of the technology economy we see most often are of hip offices, open floorplans, and ping-pong tables. But many of the online services that we think of as being digital are in fact a modulation of automation and human intervention (cf. Sarah T. Roberts' new book *Behind the Screen* (2019) for a critical take on the invisible work of content moderation). Our experience with our computer, seemingly intimate and one-directional, is very often mirrored on the other end by a tech laborer and their machine. While having humans perform physical computation isn't new,[1] seeing the physical space in which this work happens makes the issue of class very clear. Turkers (the name given by this community for someone

1 For a wonderful account of human computation, see David Alan Grier's (2005) *When Computers Were Human*. This practice overlapped considerably with the era of the digital computer. At its peak, the Mathematical Tables Project, funded by the WPA, employed more than 400 human computers at its site in New York City from the late 1930s through 1948.

who does work on Mechanical Turk) make for an average of $1.20 to $5.00 USD per hour (Folbre, 2013)[2] and do not spend their days in fancy Bay Area offices, taking advantage of unlimited vacation time or free meals. In these images we see where Turkers work: coffee tables, desks in a home office, on top of beds, in the kitchen or basement.[3]

In much of my work as an artist, I am interested in reversing our technological gaze: instead of using a tool or looking through a screen, I am interested in seeing technology as aesthetic, cultural, political objects. The physical relationship we form with our computers is something that is constantly re-written as we upgrade our machines and operating systems, and the history of this relationship is constantly being lost and written over as well. We have many images of server rooms, early mainframes, and depictions of computers in film and television, but we have few images of the everyday ways that we engage our computers—desks strewn with coffee mugs and soda cans, laptops propped up on random objects, spaces to work negotiated within one's home. This project is about capturing a tiny, specific piece of that.

2 https://economix.blogs.nytimes.com/2013/03/18/the-unregulated-work-of-mechanical-turk— My workers were paid $1 USD for their images, and since Amazon provides fairly detailed stats, I can tell this works out to about $8.75/hour—not great but above the minimum wage for the United States. For more on how I tried to balance fairness and a limited artist's budget for this project, see http://www.jeffreythompson.org/blog/2014/11/14/turker-computer-process-notes

3 See the blog post above for further work that shows a shift in Mechanical Turk worker demographics during the run of the project from non-Western to mostly American, due in large part of Amazon changing their policies. This change is evident in the project too, shifting towards Western homes and higher-end computers.

Figure 5.1: Sam.

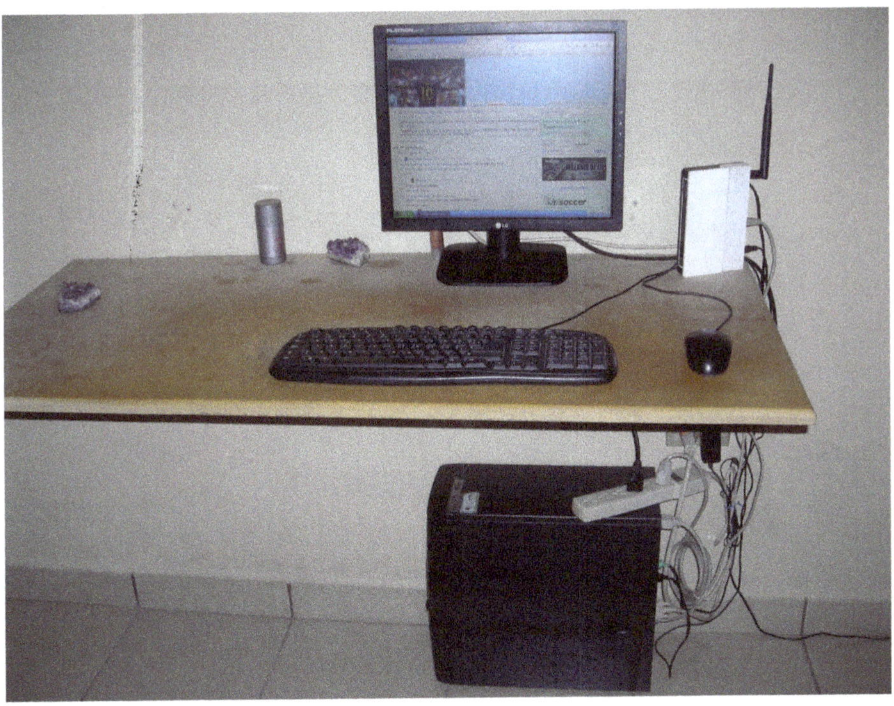

Figure 5.2: Bellevue, USA.

Figure 5.3: Cheddar, USA.

Figure 5.4: Jessica, USA.

Figure 5.5: Tenna, USA.

Figure 5.6: Medford, New York.

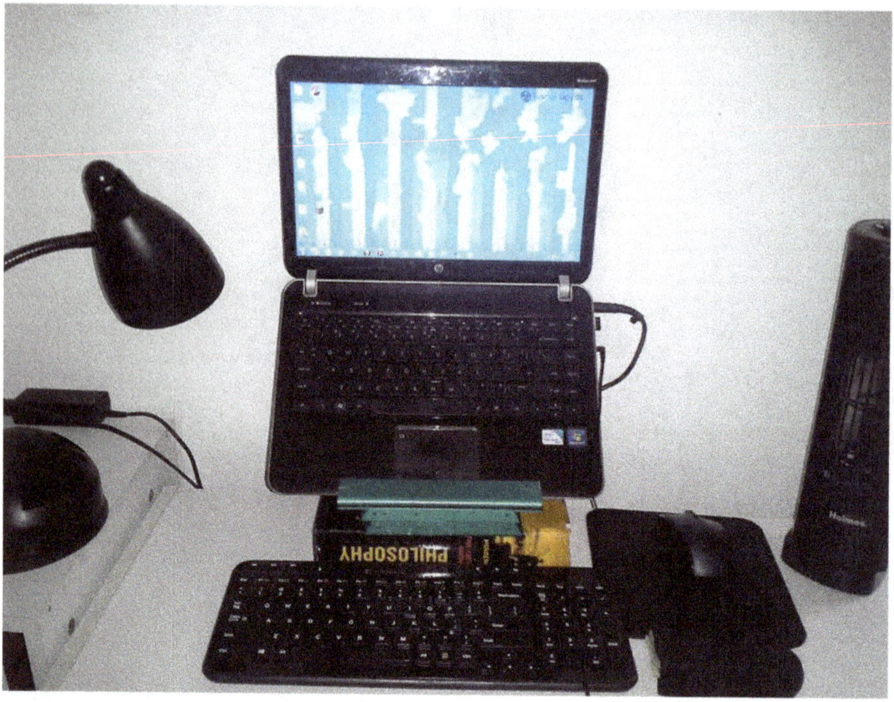

Figure 5.7: Bobbatron, Hawaii.

Figure 5.8: Parkland, Florida.

Figure 5.9: Dylan, Kuala Lumpur.

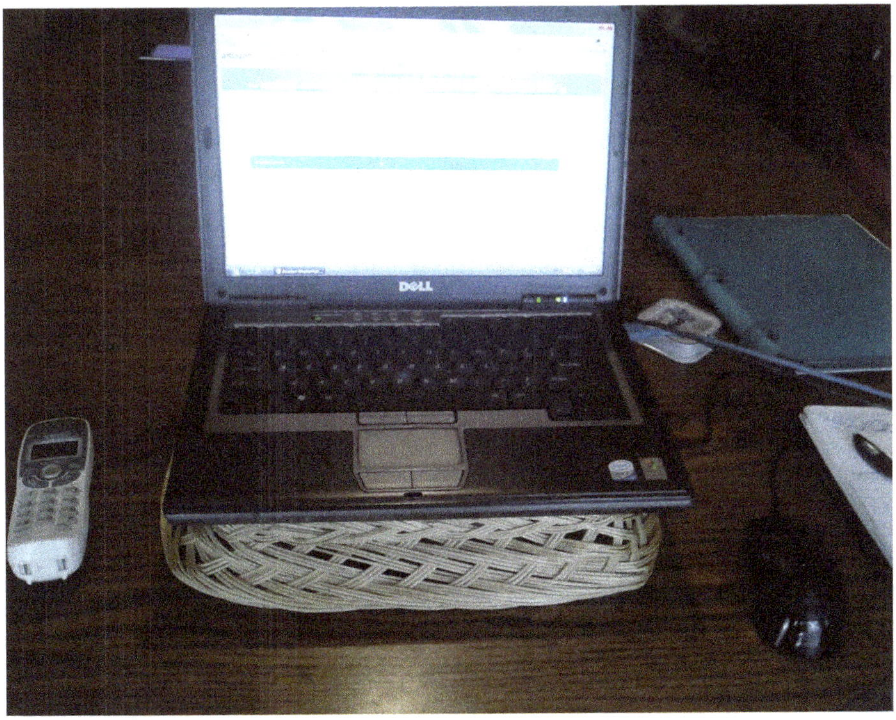

Figure 5.10: Nana, Nettleton.

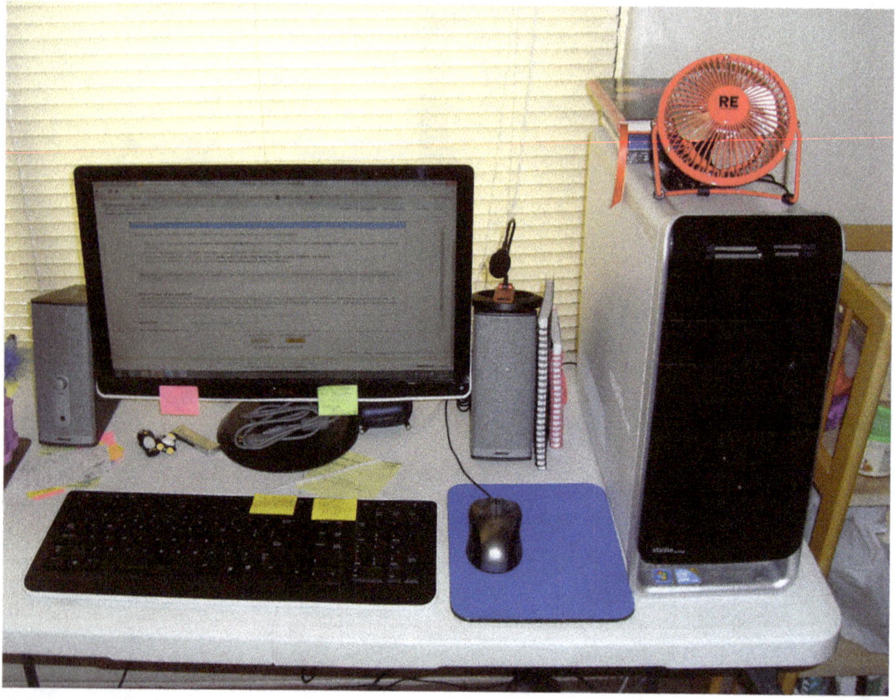

Figure 5.11: White Sands, New Mexico.

Figure 5.12: The Mouse, Portland, Oregon.

CHAPTER SIX

Migration of Self

TIJANA HIRSCH

"My kids say 'shit' occasionally but pronounced 'sheet' so at least I know it is not coming from me as the only English speaking parent in our house. Unfortunately I can't blame gan[1] *for the 'for fucks sake' usage from our little ones—whoops."*

Dania is a transnational settler,[2] a working, now multilingual, professional woman, and a mother to four daughters. She and her Swedish-English-Israeli husband relocated to Israel in 2007, when Dania was in advanced stages of her first pregnancy. I met her at a 'mommy and me' gathering for English speakers initially organized by one of the fellow moms whom I met through a Yahoo Groups posting. Since, Dania and I have met many times, with our growing families and alone, and have over the years had many conversations, online and off, on the topic of migration: the translocation, the settlement, and the language(s). In this piece, I focus on how Dania embraced her networked life "in media" (Deuze, 2011)—in particular in Facebook—after arriving to Israel. I briefly pan, scan, and zoom in

1 Gan—transliterated Hebrew word for daycare/preschool/Pre-K/ Kindergarten.

2 Transnational Settler denotes transnational living patterns in which permanency in the current transnational living situation is a factor but not a given, i.e. a return to the country of origin and/or additional host countries is possible. Transnational settlers maintain significant relationships in countries of origin and/or prior countries of residence, while forging new relationships and viewing their current host country/living situation as potentially permanent (cf. Hirsch and Lee, 2018).

on (Stephens, 1998) her trajectories as an immigrant and a mother, and how those shaped her life in the internet.

Dania already had a Facebook account when she moved to Israel, and considered herself an active internet user. Facebook reached 100 million users in 2008, when Dania's first child was born, and 500 million active users in 2010, when her twins and the Israeli Facebook Baby-Community she helped to co-create were born. As the babies and Facebook grew, so did the number of communities that Dania as an immigrant mother needed, created or joined. Some of the mothers, who had initially been involved in the Baby community with Dania, created a Kid community, then the City Specific Kid community, then many more after that. For Dania, Facebook became a tool for co-creating a digitally mediated and networked communal life. Each community served as a (co)created, (re)used, shared place that different users frequented depending on their stable and/or fleeting interests, needs, desires and hopes. Dania's description of that period of her life paints a picture of fluid movement between various Facebook communities while by those very moves creating those communities and their boundaries. She used the space(s) as needed—for respite and information—as part of her being both an immigrant and a mother. *"My Israeli aunt came over and was shocked that our six year old after three months in school could not read fluently … given that Hebrew is her third language I decided to ignore."*

Like so many others, she used her Facebook communities as an informational tool to ask for and get recommendations for services, places, and businesses within the new, initially strange place that Israel was for her. Similarly, Dania and her peers entered their Facebook communities as places to overcome isolation and loneliness that often comes with early stages of both motherhood and relocation. There they could share their challenges with pregnancies, birth, nursing, and childcare; seek advice or just vent. As Dania made her way to the stores or businesses recommended to her in the Facebook communities, her understanding of the geography of her own life became more and more entwined with the information, the sharing, and the communities themselves. Her mothering was shaped by the advice and experiences of similar others, those new to the country and sharing the difficult task of raising their children in a linguistically, culturally, and geographically new environment. These Facebook communities permeated and represented their lived experiences to an extent where Dania no longer made sense of them as tools or places, but rather, together, her way of being. Nowhere is it clearer than within the City-Specific Facebook Baby Community, where the internet as a tool and place most obviously collide. Listening to how Dania describes the City Specific Facebook Baby Community, it becomes obvious that it was a community online, as opposed to an online community. Of course, members utilized the community as a tool for scheduling and updating others regarding meet-ups, events, and gatherings in physical, material places. However, in the process, these scheduling conversations turned a tool into a place for a much-needed chat or where one could vent and be heard. *"Let's do the park tomorrow. It looks like the weather will hold for another day and I am sure there will be plenty of rainy days to come where we need to stay indoors"* could invite a response as simple as: *"we'll be there x"* to: *"looks like we won't make it today .... struck down with a bug have fun x" to "A couple of our kids are still coughing and wheezing badly after getting through another virus or flu ... any experiences on what help them ..."* As suggested by Markham (2003) these tools for reaching others transformed into a place (and places) to be, hang out, and have a chat. The transition is fluid and natural, not one way. So one could return back to the understanding that this was a conduit or even a prosthesis.

Through seemingly simple observations, Dania and others entered deep explorations of what it meant to be raising their *"'Israeli' kids"* while navigating motherhood as a transnational settler (Hirsch & Lee, 2018) in Israel. *"What is it with our 'Israeli' kids"* Dania once posted: "*... none of them, including ours, eat potatoes ... which are a huge staple of British kids' diets. ...weird. ...just an observation!*" Talk such as this made the communities into places of belonging, wherein similar observations would make sense, be understood, perhaps even eagerly welcomed, as they allowed the members to briefly pause and focus on their experiences of mothering in a new place, maybe sprinkle it with some comic relief. So, when one of Dania's peers, who was new to Israel and its preschool system, turned to her trusted community with how "mortified" she was by the language her child was picking up in preschool, Dania responded with the curse word related confession that started this piece. She shared, cared, and provided some comic relief to a mother who was, in that moment, struggling with the newness of it all.

CHAPTER SEVEN

Pinball Machines, Cardboard Cutouts, and Private Parties: Three Metaphors for Conceptualizing Memetic Spread

WHITNEY PHILLIPS

Once upon a time, a cartoon frog turned into a Nazi.

Understanding this trajectory requires stepping back and considering how memes spread, and what happens to them as they do. Tipping its hat to the usefulness of metaphors when describing the digital, this essay presents three metaphors that aim to add tactile, ricocheting contours to discussions of memes: pinball machines, cardboard standees, and private parties (obviously). These metaphors work against the tendency to describe memes linearly, and/or as singular objects. As these metaphors emphasize, memes are neither linear nor singular. They have been neither linear nor singular for as long as memes have existed.[1] Our discussions about memes will be more accurate, and tell us more about the people who share and remix and laugh at them, if we lean into memes' frenetic, quantum mechanics-like quality.

First though, some background on Pepe, which requires one to gaze longingly to the land before Trump, all the way back to 2006. In that year, cartoonist Matt Furie created Pepe, an anthropomorphic frog character, for his comic series *Boy's Club*. The frog's name is a riff on the relief one experiences when one is able to "go

1 A time frame that long predates the internet, as memes can take any mediated form within any cultural tradition; here I refer to memes in the colloquial "funny picture on the internet" sense, which entered the popular lexicon in the early-2000s

Pepe," that is to say, "pee pee," as Furie explained in an interview with *The Daily Dot* (Khan, 2015). Said piss frog took its first fateful turn in 2008. Some anonymous scholar on one of 4chan's many message boards captioned a frame from Furie's comic with the phrase "feels good man," echoing Furie's original intent. This image spurred the creation of a number of Pepe iterations (notably "feels bad man"), as the meme caught fire not just with the denizens of the original board, and not just with 4chan as a whole, but well beyond 4chan's borders, including Tumblr, Instagram, and the Twitter feeds of pop celebrities like Katy Perry, who used Pepe to complain about Australian jetlag (Kiberd, 2015).

As the meme continued to spread, the original image and its urinary sentiment continued to be remixed into countless new scenarios and emotional states. The more people shared and further tinkered with the Pepe meme, the more it diverged from Furie's original vision, ultimately sustaining a "Rare Pepe Economy," in which participants scoured the internet to find—and if not to find, then to create for themselves—the most unexpected, strangest, and most precious Pepes imaginable (Hathaway, 2017).

And then white nationalists operating under the euphemistic banner of the "alt-right" decided to join the party, taking active shitposting measures to associate Pepe with white supremacist imagery. That's not editorializing; "shitposting" is the term adopted by Trump supporters on 4chan, 8chan, and other white supremacist cesspools who enthusiastically trade in bigotry and targeted perseveration couched in a bad-faith trolling wink. These efforts were wildly successful with Pepe, and organizations like the Anti-Defamation League and politicians like Hillary Clinton subsequently condemned the frog as a white supremacist, precipitating a veritable tsunami of additional Nazi-inflected Pepes. Furie was so distressed by this fascist fracas that in May of 2017, he killed Pepe off in a single-page cartoon strip, citing Pepe's irreparably tarnished image (Osborne, 2017).

Pepe was anything but dead, of course, because his life was never wholly Furie's to begin with. Instead, Pepe was the continuing creation of many participants. Participatory media scholar Ryan Milner (2016; see also this volume) articulates the social logics that breathe life into memes like Pepe. First, memetic media are multimodal, in that they employ a variety of communicative modes (i.e. text alongside image alongside audio alongside video). Memetic media are also collective, in that they reflect the participation of many individuals. Third, memetic media spread, in that they move between and across participatory collectives. Fourth, memetic media are reappropriational, in that they borrow stuff from other stuff. Finally, memetic are resonant, in that they connect emotionally with the people sharing. If these criteria are met, the media is memetic, regardless of whether the artifact in question is a silly picture on the internet or a new and interesting expletive overheard in a grocery store.

While each of these logics are integral to the Pepe meme, *spread* tells an especially rich story. The precise pathways of spread are, of course, different in each case, as no two memes follow the same networked arc. What remains constant, however, is the applicability of the three metaphors, mentioned above, that highlight how memes move online. In the process, these metaphors highlight how odd it is that we refer to them as singular, and in the process of that, highlight the fuzziness of the line between where "fun" memes end and harm begins. Sorry, Pepe.

PINBALL WIZARDS

The human steps to the machine and drops in a token, because that human has something to say to these balls. They slap at the ball launch, sending it hurtling into the case. The object of the game is to keep the ball from descending into the siphon of failures. To achieve this objective, the human must use mechanical flippers, controlled by pairs of flipper buttons, to ding the ball back to the top, ideally hitting prize locations that earn the human points and admiration.

This process describes how a particular meme, for example a cartoon frog who is not yet a Nazi, is launched by one individual, then—if the aim is successful—is accelerated forward by the flick (click) of a flipper (share button), particularly when there is a goal in mind (successful shitposting), sending the ball back into circulation, and exposing it to further pings. So long as contact with flippers keeps being made, the ball will continue to ricochet, all catalyzed by that initial launch.

For this metaphor to fully fit, however, we must enter the realm of theoretical pinballing. While it is helpful to think of individual flippers as individual sharers of content, they can also represent entire communities that, en masse, launch proverbial balls at this proverbial machine's display, and the proverbial displays of other proverbial machines throughout the proverbial arcade. Each flick of the ball is pregnant with that potential. But not just ball singular, balls plural. Balls being flippered, then exploding into clusters of replicant balls, zooming hither and thither through a room full of machines, in the process being chipped, reshaped, or smashed flat, before hurtling still forward. This constant pinging, constant dinging, of the balls that are most resonant, and are therefore hit most often, and are therefore able to ricochet most broadly, is how Pepe achieved his Nazi salute.

A STAND-UP GUY

We decide on Halloween that a funny and terrifying prop for our feminist dance party would be a life-sized, Donald J. Trump cardboard cutout. We can't decide what would be scarier: placing him in the kitchen, where everyone will be eating, or hiding him in the bathroom, where he will be least expected, and therefore most nightmare-inducing. Meanwhile, up the street, another "we" attached to another dance party, who happen to be members of the Republican party, decide on Halloween that a funny and patriotic prop for their party would be a life-sized, Donald J. Trump cardboard cutout. This "we" can't decide what would be Make America Great-ier: placing him in the kitchen, where everyone will be eating, or hiding him in the bathroom, where he will be least expected, and therefore most high five-inducing .

Memes are like a Donald J. Trump cardboard cutout: both singular (in the sense that I paid for this one single object for my one single party, which I am shuffling into the bathroom because objectively that is scariest) and plural (in the sense that there are tens of thousands of cutouts just like this one, because there are no original ideas for Halloween parties). Further, just like memes, the same exact Trump cutout placed in the same exact location, even annotated with the same exact caption ("Make America Great Again lol"), in identical tract homes on exactly the same holiday can mean entirely different things, all depending on who might be present. And this is to say nothing of what any of the cutouts might mean when displayed on different days of the year, on somebody's birthday, on Cinco de Mayo, during Hanukkah. Ten thousand cardboard cutouts, identical in size and shipping costs, with identical ink patterns, each serving divergent communicative ends, none of which are more correct than the others.

Or are they. Because the complication, of course, is that unlike cardboard cutouts of Halloween pumpkins, memes change over space and time—the result, metaphorically speaking, of being smashed in the balls by pinball flippers. And when they do, under exactly the right (or exactly the wrong, take your pick) conditions, the kind of polysemy described above can be foreclosed. For example, one would have a difficult time defending the position that you know what, I've thought about it, and I don't think Pepe the Frog stands for Nazism. Say whatever you want about how you're just trolling, or I don't know, something about free speech, but Pepe the Frog has been codified as a symbol of white supremacy, period, the result of its Nazi iterations replicating so quickly across so many online spaces that the remaining balls of "feels good man" have long been buried. Pepe is a unique case in that regard; but ours are very strange times. Until and unless similar symbolic lockdown occurs, multiple iterations of the same meme at the same moment in time can spur vastly different outcomes, intentions, and meanings, depending on whose party you might be attending.

A NOT SO PRIVATE AFFAIR

The basic assumption at each of these parties is that it's a private soiree, invite-only. To wit, within our metaphorical narrative, the organizers of the feminist party and Republican party both thought carefully about who they e-vited to make sure everybody attending would on the same basic wavelength; that they would know in what ways the Donald J Trump standee was meant to be a joke. This kind of party planning doesn't just sort *us* from *them*, it helps establish the bounded play frame as articulated by Gregory Bateson (1972), which establishes what gets to be interpreted as play, versus what has to be interpreted as serious. Within the confines of these two play frames, an attendee of the feminist party could proclaim that Donald Trump is very presidential and everyone would know to laugh, and an attendee of the Republican party could proclaim that Trump values the humanity of all men and women regardless of nationality or race and everyone would know to laugh.

That might be how it works at most offline parties. It might be how people think it works online, or at least, is how people would like it to work. But nope, on the internet, the very act of going to a seemingly private party, appropriately decoding the host's funny joke about Trump and the toilet, opens, and is designed to open, the front door to other attendees. It's not just that outsiders appear without warning. It's that, thanks to context collapse—the unpredictable comingling of audiences—you can't tell by looking when they have arrived. Oh and also, the privacy-protecting walls of the house have just fallen down, and now everybody at the party is standing in the atrium of the mall.

There is, in short, no such thing as a private party on the internet. Even when you're with your friends, even when the play frame is clear, those gates can always be crashed. More than that, with so many pinballs flying around, with so many spacetime travelling audiences summoned by the power of a like or retweet, there *are* no gates. The rejoinder that "no, I swear, I'm not a racist, I was just joking by posting that Pepe," thus becomes increasingly untenable. You might think you were invited to a private party, and that everyone is in on that joke. But when you're standing in the middle of the atrium at the mall, there's no way of even knowing whose guest you are, let alone whose play frame you're operating under.

CONCLUSION

These three metaphors aren't perfect, because they're metaphors. Really the most accurate articulation of memetic spread would be if you placed all three of them in a snow globe full of super balls, then smashed it against a wall. However, taken separately, pinball machines, cardboard cutouts, and private parties help underscore the exponential, asynchronous, caddywampus spread of memetic media. They also help illustrate how difficult it is to lock down the meaning of and audience for this spread, a significant concern when dealing with memes that evolve from innocent fun, for some anyway, to taunts or even fighting words, a la Pepe (RIP). The takeaway becomes, suddenly, much less innocent, and much less fun: as much as your memes might seem like playthings to you, they can be weapons just waiting to happen.

CHAPTER EIGHT

'Instagrammable' as a Metaphor for Looking and Showing in Visual Social Media

KATRIN TIIDENBERG

Over the past seven years, I've studied different social media platforms and apps, different groups of people and different types of visual content through different research projects. My participants say a lot of interesting things, among them, about looking and showing:

> *I remember looking at other people's sexy selfies on tumblr and getting curious about what I'd look like ... so I took some, and of course, when you do, then they kind of sit there and burn on your laptop, demanding to be let out. (...) So I posted, and it's become this weird dance. It's clearly about the attention, but not in the exhibitionist sense ... it's more of a dialogue*

In this piece,[1] I am interested in the situational elements that shape and delimit what people are doing and what they think they are doing when they are posting, liking, or hating on social media visuals, fro example selfies, or reaction gifs. Using Goffman and Bourdieu alongside the work of affordance theorist James Gibson (1979), I suggest that once we combine situational proprieties with affordances, we can understand the nuances of looking and showing on social media. Further, I propose "instagrammable[2]" as a metaphor for making sense of how social media

1 This is based on my invited talk at the Digital Subjectivity and Mediated Intimacies Symposium, at Coventry University in November 2018.

2 Instagrammable (also Insta-worthy) is a popular term used by social media users, influencers and journalists to mark something that "lends itself to being photographerd and posted on social media" (Wiktionary, 2019). In this piece I use it as shorthand for the articulation of the broad rules for success on visual social media apps (not just on Instagram).

affords different practices of looking and showing, but also for understanding what the "appropriate" ways of looking and showing on social media are.

LOOKING AND SHOWING

Looking includes noticing, which I define here as the culturally learned way in which we organize what we see (Carroll 2001). As John Berger (1972) said, we only see what we look at, so to look is an act of choice. He also said that looking is quickly followed by our awareness of being seen, for the "eye of the other" combines with "our own eyes to make it fully credible that we are part of the visible world" (Berger, 1972, p. 9). For him, vision is more reciprocal than spoken dialogue. This connects with core symbolic interactionist ideas about how reciprocity is inherent in actual and imagined co-presence, self-presentation, impression management and identity. In relation to the social media practices of looking and showing, this means that we look, but we also presume we are being looked at, which leads us to start showing (instead of just being seen).

This plays out in different ways and many of my participants over the years have expressed varying and contradictory experiences, attitudes toward, and perceptions about the practices of looking, or choosing to see, and showing, or choosing to be seen.

For example, a woman who posted sexy selfies to her NSFW (Not Safe For Work, sexually explicit) blog on tumblr said:

> *For me, posting sexy selfies is a way to reaffirm a part of me that isn't always apparent in my daily life. It's not something I do just to put myself on display. I'm reintroducing myself to a piece of me that has been buried under 20 years of marriage, 4 children, and the mantles of "wife", "mother", "neighbor", "coworker", and every other role I fill in my daily life.*

For her, showing seems to be a matter of self-reflection, affirmation and an introspective project of the self. Showing alters how she perceives herself.

Another of my participants on Tumblr said:

> *I decided, I don't even know why, to submit to a blog and when it posted … THE RUSH! I was hooked … I saw all these amazing images on this page and there was me included among them. (…) I definitely needed and wanted the attention. I do get off on someone else getting off on me, that is a HUGE part of it for me.*

She emphasized the value of being looked at as someone who belongs to a group of people, women in this case, who are being looked at in a particular, sexualized way. Instead of self-reflection and repair, sexual arousal from showing is elevated.

A man from that same study on tumblr confessed that his "showing" on social media was mostly coincidental, a way of paying his dues for being in a community.

> *I started out posting pictures of my female partners, my body was only in the shot incidentally (it is hard to have sex and take pix at the same time!) or as a "stunt cock," only there to highlight what the sexy woman in the picture was up to (…) I'm MUCH more a voyeur than an exhibitionist. I'm wildly excited by the blogs that combine storytelling—erotic or, everyday—with self-shots.*

His looking practices and preferences are more nuanced than his showing practices, and extend beyond just visual content. When looking, he likes his images in context. With a story.

Looking, especially looking at oneself, after having shown, and after having been looked at by others, can be experienced as therapeutic and transformative. This mother of two told me that after years of struggling with body image and eating disorders, her yumblr blog became a repository of evidence that she actually likes her body:

> *I post pictures of myself, where I like what I see. And the more pictures I take, the more things I find to like. And now, I have pages of evidence that I like my body. I've never in my life spent time trying to genuinely like my body. Only time trying not to hate my body. Those are very different things.*

On the other hand, looking can have the opposite effect. A young woman confessed to scrolling through Instagram several times a day, only to "feed herself" pieces of content that trap her into depressing comparisons:

> *I scroll through Instagram several times a day, stalking strangers, lurking in the Discover tag. I feed myself with others 'perfect lives' and its really all a comparison trap that makes me feel bad about myself. This if why I rarely post selfies. I would like to post more, but I never seem to think that the pictures are good enough. It's like a never-ending competition of who takes the greatest pictures.*

While these examples express the diversity of experience and motivations, the practices of looking and showing are patterned. They are guided by certain underlying assumptions and perceptions, which I think shine through in the metaphor of "instagrammable."

INSTAGRAMMABLE AS AN AFFORDANCE METAPHOR

What people think their devices, their social media platforms and apps allow and make possible shapes how they practice and understand looking and showing. The features, interface design, terms of service rules, community guidelines and policies of content moderation are interpreted in their own right, in the context of people's overall experiences, but also in the context of people's expectations of how the internet should work. Lately, these discussions are dominated by the concept of affordances. Broadly speaking, affordances mean possibilities for action.[3] And for

3 Affordance is a concept that was proposed by James Gibson in 1979, but usually texts regarding social media just mention him, then Donald Norman (1988), then maybe Ian Hutchby (2001a)

the purposes of the discussion at hand, "instagrammable" metaphorically communicates the affordances that social media has for looking and showing. It is those aspects of platforms and apps that we perceive as making it possible, even likely, for us to be able to perfectly capture and present our life as enjoyable, inspiring and jealousy inducing.

Given that we are talking about seeing and showing, I want to linger with James Gibson's concept of affordances. His ideas grew directly out of his work on visual perception, specifically, animals' visual perception of landscapes. Is this landscape walkable, climbable, sinkable, fall-to-your-deathable? Climbability and sinkability are not physical properties of swamps, cliffs and branches, but perceived in scale to the particular animal. This means they are perceived in relation to the particular creature's size, weight and anatomy. So, the perception rather goes—does this look like **I** will be able to climb it, will it carry **me**, will **I** fall to my death?

Gibson makes an evocative point that at the scale of humans and animals, the earth is flat and not spherical. Wherever we go, the earth is separated from the sky by a horizon that can always be visualized and experienced, because we touch a surface and experience that in relation to the horizontal plane. "The ground" as Gibson writes "is quite literally the basis of the behavior of land animals. And it is also the basis of their visual perception, or their so-called space perception" (1979, pp. 131–132).

In this sense, we perceive affordances through a series of figure/ground relations. Put into the language of metaphor theory, the process is metaphorical through and through; we are invited to take certain (and not other) actions because of what we perceive the object to allow, which is in turn determined in relation to us—that is, where we are, how we are situated. It is in relation to the horizon and the size and the weight of an animal's body that each animal makes sense of what is around them.

What is the horizon of social media? Well, maybe the internet is, or rather the old metaphors of the internet (cf Markham, this volume; Driscoll, this volume) that shaped everything later built on it. The matrix, the superhighway, the web. What did these old, tacit, currently invisible metaphors of the internet instill in our everyday perceptions? Perhaps the presumption that everything is binary. Yes, built from, stored in, and communicated via a binary system of ones and zeros—i.e. digital. But, also binary as in 'yes' or 'no'. 'Real' or 'not'. 'Good' or 'bad'. In the case of 'instagrammable' done 'right' or 'wrong.' But the old metaphors also highlight the networked nature of the internet. Billions of computers are connected to each

or William Gaver (1996) to swiftly end up with either danah boyd (2011) or Treem & Leonardi (2012) who proposed specific sets of high level (Bucher & Helmond, 2017) affordances for social media.

other and share a common language. That further suggests universal rules and norms – an appropriate (high speed) tempo of too much information moving too fast. You're in or you're out. You snooze you lose. The attention economy of instagrammability has a speed of its own, inherited, arguably, from the early metaphors of the superhighway or the matrix.

If binary, digital networks of fast-moving information that demand quick action and correct choices are the horizon, and specific social media platforms are the perceivable landscapes, then we are the animals running through these landscapes. In the Gibsonian world, we are perceiving the specific affordances of social media (e.g. how anonymous we can be, how editable or persistent the content seems) in relation to our characteristics as users, but also in relation to our needs, right? Because if I am a fox, a cliff may seem fall-to-deathable on the day I ate, but quite climbable when I've been hungry for a week. In my field studies, the words, in particular the verbs, which the participants use to describe their experiences of looking and showing, yield a tentative list of people's needs. Rather, they yield a list of behaviors and behavioral outcomes that emerge from trying to satiate those needs within those landscapes. In the repertoire of looking, we need to have an overview of what is out there, what is trendy, what is happening, to satiate our curiosity and to compare ourselves to others. We do that by *lurking* and *stalking* and *scrolling*. But we also judge others by *staring*, and interact with others through dialogue or what one participant called a "*weird dance.*" Last but not least, we look with desire by "*thirsting.*" In terms of showing, our needs include managing the impressions others have of us, which we do by showing ourselves *as* someone or something, and by showing *off*, but we also need to persuade and make claims by offering *proof* through photography's historic claims to truth. Finally, we need to tell stories, so we *illustrate* our points.

Between the horizon (i.e. the perception of the internet) and the needs (i.e. manage impressions, satiate curiosity) are the landscapes (i.e. Instagram or Snapchat) and behaviors (i.e. lurking, thirsting and showing off). Specific affordances (i.e. those that afford showing off on Instagram or thirsting on Tumblr) are the relational, connective tissue between the landscapes and the behaviors.[4] I suggest that the broader affordances that matter for showing and looking (i.e. what instagrammable as an affordance metaphor conveys), and which most social media platforms have in varying degrees are how (a) multimodal, (b) editable, (c) audienced, (d) persistent, (e) synchronous, (f) archived and (g) anonymous the content and the interactions seem. However, how we look and show in each platform, does not only depend on instagrammability as an affordance metaphor, it also depends on instagrammability as a normative metaphor.

4 To arrive at this, I relied on the logic outlined by Evans et al. (2017).

INSTAGRAMMABLE AS A NORMATIVE METAPHOR

We are not foxes in the forest. We are people online, so both our needs and our usage behaviors are shaped by our sociocultural conditions. There are many culturally, historically and politically informed rules, rituals and repertoires that shape showing and looking.

Looking and showing have always had abundant and complex additional psychosocial functions, but it seems more obvious in the age of ubiquitous internet and ubiquitous photography. Various online spaces and technologies invite, prompt, encourage, and discourage us from certain types looking and showing. Yet, each instance, interaction, each time we post, we are in a different situation, with its own proprieties. Affordance theory is too generalized to robustly explain how this happens.

To nuance the concept of affordances with sociocultural or interactional detail, I draw on Goffman's work on "Behavior in Public Places" (1963). Goffman's thinking helps clarify how we can see our social media practices as a continuous series of slightly different interactional situations. Using a somewhat ecological perspective, he elaborates how each situation is embedded in an environment of communication possibilities. It comes with a special set of rules that guide individuals when they are in presence of others, which is what he calls situational proprieties. Situational proprieties might govern our involvement in situations—how involved we are, or seem to be; whether we appear uninvolved, like lolling or loitering, which could be dangerous; whether we appear to be overinvolved in something, which is also suspicious; and whether we have appropriate excuses or "shields" to justify our un-, or overinvolvement.

I think there are aesthetic/ representational and moral/ political situational proprieties in the case of looking and showing on social media. Both prompt us to attend to some criteria for whether or not something should be shown or looked at. This is where I suggest that "instagrammable" extends, theoretically, from Bourdieu's ([1965] 1990) concept of photographability. Bourdieu emphasizes that photography is under collective rule. Even the most trivial photograph expresses not only the "explicit intentions of the photographer, [but] also the system of schemes of perception, thought and appreciation common to a whole group" (1990, p. 6). Any given social class at any given time, Bourdieu explains, considers certain objects, people and situations as worthy of being captured, stored, communicated, shown and admired—i.e. photographable. He claims that there is nothing more regulated and conventional than amateur photography. And it tells us a lot about broader social values and norms.

I suggest that "instagrammable" is just the metaphor we need to help us understand the meaning of an image *in relation to* one that is appropriate. A glance at popular media stories or blogposts about the criteria of instagrammability gives many hints about what "appropriate image sharing" is. These situational proprieties outline aesthetics and behaviors for image-based social media interactions. They also function metaphorically, in that they build an imaginary of what a social media image is, or at least, what it should be if you're doing it right (see Table 8.1).

Table 8.1: The do-s and don't-s of "instagrammability." Source: Katrin Tiidenberg

DO	DO NOT
post regularly, at peak times, but not too often (unless you meet a celebrity)	post on Friday and Saturday night, post too frequently, or too rarely
post your face, if you've "got it, flaunt it" (i.e. gym pics)	but not too many selfies, but also not too many pictures with no people on them, no Snapchatting your abs if you're a teenager
filter and edit	overfilter, and you have to avoid certain filters, and you cannot Instagram your Snapchat lenses
use hashtags (but if you're a teenager then only ironically)	but not too many, and never use #nofilter or #followforfollow
be nice, follow back people you know	beg for follows

Therefore, to decide whether or not an image and the situation is instagrammable (whether and image should be shared on social media), we seem to need to consider the aesthetic criteria of the photograph ("this is a good photograph"); the aesthetic criteria for the photographed object/subject ("this is a photographable body, woman, man, car") and the aesthetic criteria in context of a particular group/audience (this is a good photo or a photographable body in a community for body modification, versus in a community of expecting mothers). Finally, we also consider various moral criteria of the context ("nudity is not ok here, nudity is ok here").

CONCLUSION

Overall then, I'm proposing that affordances are a useful lens for making sense of looking and showing on social media. However, the analysis of "instagrammable" as an affordance metaphor and a normative metaphor shows that there is benefit in not stretching the concept too thin, or rather, not subsuming the sociocultural entirely within it. Situational proprieties of each particular instance of showing and looking in addition to (not instead of) an ecological and perceptual approach to affordances uncover a highly complex set of factors influencing how we make everyday, seemingly banal or practical decisions about how to engage in looking and showing. Analyzing 'instagrammable' as a metaphor for socially mediated looking and showing, but more so as an affordance metaphor and a normative metaphor, shows how entangled seemingly new forms of self-expressions are with historical norms, how predicated they are on older understandings of how the internet technologies work or should work, but also how situational they are. This highlights the risks of generalizing to a platform or an app ("Instagram makes girls depressed!") or to a practice ("being looked at is always disempowering"), when making sense of visuality.

SECTION 3

Ways of Relating

CHAPTER NINE

Growing Up and Growing Old on the Internet: Influencer Life Courses and the Internet as Home

CRYSTAL ABIDIN

As an anthropologist, I frequently travel to different cities to conduct fieldwork alone. After years of being perpetually on the road, all cities start to appear as mere permutations and combinations of pedestrian walkways, vehicular roads and railway networks, instigating in me bouts of disorientation and anomie. Between teasing out train maps and currencies, while retreating alone to yet another bedroom on yet another night, I go to the internet. I go to *my* internet. In there, I know the spaces and places and buttons and plumbing like the back of my hand. As the only constant experience in my life regardless of my geographical perplexity and inter-cultural fatigue, my internet is often my only continuous companion, my most trusted guide, and my home.

In a similar vein, many of the first-generation Influencers, whom I have been studying since the mid-2000s, often nostalgically refer to various spaces on the internet as their home, or sometimes a precious storage room. These pioneer batch of Influencers first debuted on blogs hosted on OpenDiary, LiveJournal, Diaryland, Blogger, tumblr, and WordPress that were popular in Southeast Asia, and subsequently moved on to more popular social media, but particularly Instagram and YouTube. Newer, shiner social media apps emerge every few months and the blogs where many Influencers first embarked on their now decade-long careers have been dwindling in audienceship, are dying out, or are being deleted en masse as companies go under. Yet, the few commercial lifestyle blogs (Abidin, 2013) that are still kept afloat hold special significance and productive purposes for first-generation Influencers. I see this in the romanticized tributes the Influencers pay to the sacred spaces of their usually-neglected blogs.

In this chapter, I consider how three pioneer-batch Influencers in Singapore regularly return to their old blogs to make sense of their relationship with the internet and of their prolific careers. Drawing on classic sociological theory on placeness such as 'matter out of place' (Douglas, 1966), 'place and space' (Tuan, 1979, 2001), and 'props and stages' (Goffman, 1956), this ethnographic essay reflects on the felt physicality and emotional materiality of the internet as a place (Markham, 1998, 2003). I argue that against the backdrop of the rapidly changing social media landscape, Harriet, Alexis, and Timothy experience and describe their old blogs as a home. The metaphor of home highlights how these Influencers experience their blogs as a grounding sanctuary where they feel safe to housekeep the less glamorous aspects of their careers, as an archival checkpoint to which they return to evaluate their histories and their progress, and as a panoptic room in which they have to be accountable to their earliest readers as family. My analysis adds nuance and a recent example to a significant body of work exploring how people consider and build home through such contexts as game environments (e.g., Nardi, 2009; Sunden, 2003), avatar based virtual worlds (e.g., Boellstorff, 2008); interactions with others in text spaces like chatrooms (e.g., Markham, 1998); in fan communities (e.g., Baym, 2000), and through blogging (e.g., Hodkinson & Lincoln, 2008).

APPROACHING USUALLY-NEGLECTED BLOG SPACES AS HOME

Harriet's, Timothy's and Alexis' stories are adapted from my larger study of internet celebrity culture in Singapore between 2010 and 2018. The incidents referenced here are taken from fieldnotes compiled through participant observation and digital ethnography on these Influencers' digital estates, and coded through a constructivist grounded theory-guided (Charmez, 2006) analysis. The larger anthropological project of long-term immersion follows the informants through digital spaces (Postill & Pink, 2012). I focus on the socio-cultural rhythms of what is considered normative or subversive in the Influencer industry at a particular moment in time, and the progression of Influencers' socio-political identity-making projects between and across older and newer social media platforms.

In the stories below, Influencers explicitly or implicitly refer to their usually-neglected blogs as 'home'. These feelings of leaving and returning to a blog are situated against the backdrop of the continuous emergence of newer social media platforms, each demanding that Influencers upgrade their skills, adapt to new digital environments, and learn to connect with new followers while retaining the congruence of their self-brand. Akin to Annette Markham's spatial metaphors conceptualizing the internet as a place (2003), for the Influencers studied, their blogs are a familiar site where they can: "wande[r]" through old archives and nostalgically review the growth of their careers while long-time followers watch over their progress at the origin site; "navigat[e]" through digital artifacts to curate a personal front to newer followers on newer social media as evidence that they were established icons in the age of commercial blogs; and "explor[e]" the public sharing of vulnerable feelings to reinstate follower affection and loyalty (Markham, 2003, p. 7). In the next three sections, I trace how Alexis, Timothy, and Harriet wander 'home' to their blogs to meet with loyal followers, navigate 'old props' in these spaces to curate different strategic fronts, and explore safe ways to 'take out the trash' as a cleansing ritual.

COMING HOME

Like many veteran Influencers who first debuted as commercial lifestyle bloggers, Harriet has all but left her blog for the more enticing and lucrative image-based platforms like Instagram and YouTube. However, she occasionally returns to her blog as a sanctuary away from these what she experiences to be highly competitive and aggressive new social media spaces.

In a series of blogposts between 2015 and 2018, each earmarking a moment of personal difficulty linked to an industry scandal or a romantic breakup, Harriet refers to her blog as the place in which she feels "the most comfortable." This is despite the fact that she primarily earns her income on Instagram, where she boasts over 160k followers, that she is a frequent guest star on several popular YouTube channels in the country, and that she also manages at least another half a dozen accounts on newer social media platforms.

I interpret Harriet's extended activity on other social media before her transient homecoming to her blog akin to how human geographer Yi-Fu Tuan (1979) analyzes returning home after traveling: "An argument in favour of travel is that it increases awareness, not of exotic places but of home as a place. To identify wholly with the ambiance of a place is to lose the sense of its unique identity, which is revealed only when one can also see it from the outside" (p. 411). In this way, the salience of Harriet's usually neglected blog as a special place that feels like home is established through the juxtaposition of her experience when she is 'away.' In this analysis, it is this nostalgia arising from having left her blog for the more lucrative social media platforms that continually reframes Harriet's return as romanticized comfort.

Acknowledging the remaining audience of her scanty and irregular blogposts as her "very first readers" and in all likelihood the most "loyal" of the lot, she thanks them for "watching over" her as she has grown up and "matured" from an adolescent into an adult before their eyes. This familiarity that she feels these readers share with her is crucial for allowing Harriet to discursively housekeep her emotional struggles on her blog, much more transparently than she would on her highly prolific Instagram account. And this is because, according to Harriet, her loyal long-term blog readers understand the social norms of her blog where transparency is valued, judgement is withheld, and catharsis is the intention. Just like at home, with close friends and family, there is an assumption of shared tacit norms, loyalty, and positive predisposition.

The feelings of comfort and safety and the values of openness and trust fostered in Harriet's blogspace are co-constructed between herself and her longtime readers. The blog is differentiated from her other social media spaces that are less imbued with value (Tuan, 2001, p. 6), and maintained as such because the group continuously assigns it "greater emotional charge" (Tuan, 1979, p. 409). For instance, her followers' comments demonstrate a general assumption that the content on Harriet's various social media are constructed and curated to some degree as this is "her job,", but they simultaneously maintain that her blog is the one place where she is more "real," more "genuine," and more "sincere," because of the disproportionate vulnerability she displays there. This ongoing social contract between Harriet and her longtime readers on her usually-neglected blog can be described as almost sacred, as Harriet says she feels "safe" enough there to share even her deeper, darker thoughts around depression and anxiety; something she would never address on her pristine Instagram account.

But there have been instances where Harriet's confessionals on her usually-neglected blog circulate widely across social media platforms, going viral among different audiences, and soliciting unwelcome guests at the doorstep of her 'home'. Comment wars unfold as visitors from her other social media platforms leave remarks doubting the veracity of her emotional breakdowns or the authenticity of her Influencer persona. "Are you acting depressed just to attract attention?" quips one commenter. "Yeah right, you look pretty happy in your last Instagram post though," ventures another. Without the tacit knowledge of her usually-neglected blog as a home, these visitors are unable to understand why Harriet's self-presentation there may differ from that on other platforms, but still be read as coherent and authentic by her long-term followers.

Using Tuan's discussions of the sense of place (1979), I suggest it is in these moments that the inhabitants of the 'home'—the longtime blog readers—"demonstrate their sense of place" on Harriet's blog by reaffirming their "moral and aesthetic discernment" in governing and maintaining the preciousness of this space (Tuan, 1979, p. 410). Through counter-comments and pushback in long threads, supporters emerge in defense of Harriet and her blog as a site for vulnerable self-expression. They mark off her blog as a place to be "defended against intruders" (Tuan, 2001, p. 4), against those who do not exhibit the felt values of the inhabitants who live there. In so doing they re-establish themselves as what Anderson (1991) would describe as a self-selected "imagined community" who virtually share the place as the 'home' of the "real" Harriet to whom only those who still linger on her usually-neglected blog are privy.

REARRANGING THE STORAGE ROOM

For other veteran Influencers who have progressed on to social media platforms, transient returns to their usually-neglected blogs serve as journeys back into the storage room where they hold the things they once used when they first made public their personal politics and values upon embarking in the industry. In my analysis of their actions and statements, they revisit old blogposts as an archivist would, reacquainting themselves with facets of their Influencer persona they have previously made public to reevaluate the coherence of their narrative.

Alexis was among the first bloggers in Singapore to receive monetary incentives for her blogposts through embedded advertising links and sponsored advertorials. Although she still maintains several other blogs on different platforms—alongside the Influencer staples such as Twitter, Facebook, Instagram, YouTube, and Snapchat—her original blog has not been updated in years. However, Alexis is fond of redirecting followers across her social media to old blogposts dating back as far as ten years to reference her long-standing ethics or stance on an assortment of issues.

Although she no longer monetizes her blog content as extensively as she used to, Alexis still uses her old blog to cultivate and strengthen her present-day Influencer persona. This is especially crucial given that her original Influencer self-brand was premised on being 'controversial', or her ability to generate scandal and channel attention towards herself.[1]

Specifically, whenever Alexis 'bandwagons' on or appropriates trending Twitter or Instagram hashtags to post outrageous content, and gets called out for being "just a troll" or an "opportunist" harvesting "clickbait," she barrages accusers with old blog links to underscore that being disagreeable and argumentative is her long-standing personality rather than a spur-of-the-moment whim. For instance, when same-sex marriage was legalized in the USA in June 2015, Alexis attention-jacked the prolific celebratory hashtags on Twitter and Instagram to repeatedly convey her disdain towards such unions. When American social media users who were surveying the hashtags called her out for "attention whoring," Alexis responded with links to old blog and social media posts in which she had expressed similar anti-same-sex marriage sentiment earlier. Yet, based on the June 2015 incident above, it is unclear if Alexis genuinely opposes marriage equality, or if it was staged

1 Building on the work by James B. Twitchell (1997) on "shamelebrity", I have elsewhere discussed similar negative-attention generation strategies as the commodification of shame and displays of weaponized shame (Abidin, 2016).

for self-publicity. Later on, in June 2016, Alexis uploaded several selfies on Facebook and Instagram depicting her attendance (and general revelries) at Singapore's annual pro-LGBT event Pink Dot SG. Her posts even included same-sex affirming hashtags such as "#isupportthefreedomtolove" and "#loveislove."

Using sociologist Erving Goffman's metaphor of the theatre, I analyze how Alexis positions her old blog as the storage room, from where she picks the digital artifacts—dated selfies, photographs, artworks, text posts, backlinks, and comments from readers—to selectively piece together what Goffman would call "background items" to "supply the scenery and stage props" for her next discursive assault (Goffman, 1956, p. 143). Alexis is a "circumspect performer" who is able to "adjust [her] presentation according to the character of the props and tasks out of which [she] must build [her] performance" (Goffman, 1956, p. 143). Depending on the material she decides to bring to the foreground and piece together, Alexis skillfully rearranges her existing props to stage different persuasions or appearances. Hence, like the performer on Goffman's theatrical stage, Alexis is unable to "begin" her "act" until she has curated an appropriate and congruent stage on which she is able to perform (1956, p. 13). Or, coming back to the central metaphor of home, Alexis continually modifies and modulates the content and tone of her posts across social media, posting contradictory viewpoints on different platforms, which she is later able to reconcile and reorganize to present specific (and potentially contradictory) narratives, akin to redecorating her home depending on the type of visitors who are on the way for a visit.

TAKING OUT THE TRASH

Usually-neglected blogs also surface when Influencers return to them as confessional spaces to tell 'their side of the story', especially when the text spaces of Instagram captions and comments and YouTube comment threads can be easily overrun by animosity from haters and (paid) trolls and bots.

Timothy has found himself embroiled in a string of Influencer scandals in his decade-long career. In one incident, rival Influencers sullied his professional reputation; in another incident, antagonistic followers were aggressively questioning his sexuality on internet forums; and in yet another incident, he was subjected to viral hate when it was revealed that he had undergone cosmetic surgery. In each of these instances, Timothy returned to his blog to address these accusations, repair his image, and reinstall follower loyalty in a manner than resembles anthropologist Mary Douglas' retreatment of dirt as "matter out of place" (1966, p. 36).

Douglas asserts that there exists "no such thing as absolute dirt" (1966, p. 2) but that dirt is merely matter that has fallen out of order and requires reorganization to be put back in place. In other words, the presence of dirt signifies that there is a normative "system" of ordering at work, and dirt is the "by-product of a systematic ordering and classification of matter, in so far as ordering involves rejecting inappropriate elements" (1966, p. 36). In an act of reinstating order, dirt has to be identified as transgressive, demarcated from other matter, then purified before being returned to the mass of matter (1966, p. 4).

Following this metaphor, I analyze Influencer scandals as the dirt that needs to be attended to and reordered, in order for the system to return to an equilibrium where only selective aspects of Timothy's life are on display, while others are kept away from the public eye. To reverse the backlash of unexpected exposé, Timothy engages in what could be described as housekeeping, by returning to his usually-neglected blog to post a confessional addressing the scandals, expounding on his feelings, and announcing his corresponding reactions. All of this mirrors the practice of sorting dirt back into its place.

Referring to the remaining readers of his blog as "long term followers" who know the "old" him, Timothy usually begins these reparation narratives by stating that he "owes" them an explanation, thus acknowledging their investment in his side of the story and their potential value in assisting in his reparation. He then addresses each accusation in detail, refuting some aspects with utmost insistence while apologetically admitting to others.

For instance, in one scandal, Timothy was called out for artificially inflating his statistics when he paid to use Instagram's 'Promote' feature to amplify the reach of a client-sponsored post. Timothy insists that he was not cheating as he had disclosed that the post was a paid ad and that there were no formal regulations against using his own money to "promote" the post through Instagram's proper channels as an added bonus for his client. But he also issued apologies for having to make this effort to secure the publicity of these recent posts, because he had not been updating his Instagram feed as regularly as needed with non-sponsored content to reel in followers more organically. Through these nuanced negotiations and boundary setting, Timothy seems to finesort his dirt, employing what Douglas refers to as "ideas about separating, purifying, demarcating and punishing transgressions" to "exaggerat[e] the difference" between practices that are "with and against" the order of things (1966, p. 4).

This practice of taking out the trash also demonstrates the networked nature of Timothy's social media persona. During these scandals, he would usually maintain a calm composure on his primary platform, Instagram, where he laboriously produces selfies that are conscientiously improved with photo-editing software and carefully curated for his highly stylized feed. While he may occasionally express some dissent and retort against accusations via the space of his Instagram captions, Timothy always frames these discourses in cryptic layers of code-switching such that his intended message may not always have been evident to the average follower. This "Insta-vagueing"—where often sharp messages are encoded in

Hallmark-esque ambiguous quotes and obscured quips whose double meaning would be lost on innocent audience members—makes it such that only those 'in the know' who possess the skills of social steganography (boyd, 2014) are able to cross-reference the hidden meanings against the networked capillaries of gossip, rumor, lore, and scandal among Influencers and dedicated followers. However, on his blog where he commits to self-reparation, followers are drawn in via long, thoughtful personal confessions and may be more likely to linger and empathize with him. This atmosphere of Timothy's blog again resembles that of a 'home' where inhabitants feel welcome and invited to linger, to exchange intimacies and exhibit more genuine layers of the self in a place that fosters these interactions.

GROWING UP AND GROWING OLD ON THE INTERNET

"Conceptualized as a space, the Internet develops architectures, boundaries, and multiple entry and exit points. Conceptualized as a place, the Internet comprises a socio-cultural milieu," writes Markham (2003, p. 7). Veteran Influencers who comfortably, nostalgically, safely retreat back to their usually-neglected blogs from their journeys onto other social media spaces exemplify this when they instinctively venture back 'home' to unwind, reaffirm themselves, or housekeep. Re-entering the blogs brings with it normative values, rules, expectations, and audiences to whom they are able to exhibit different facets of themselves. Considering the earlier and older technical affordances of blogs, this journey home also signifies a 'trip down memory lane' into a simpler time where Influencer commerce was less developed, less political, and more intimate and social. It is at 'home' in their blogs that they review and realign their values among the smaller and safer sociality of long-time readers, hone their skills and steel themselves before inevitably traveling to other spaces on the internet.

My experience of growing up on the internet is not too different from the journeys of Harriet, Alexis, and Timothy. Like Harriet who closes the door to different rooms in her home, as a compulsive cataloguer and curator of content, each of the twelve tumblr blogs that I run speak to different followers and mutuals who know me from 'way back' and chime in with forms of emotional support, even if these temporal and place-based notions of history differ across each blog. Like Alexis who rearranges the props in her home, as an academic who is active on social media, the types of data I choose to display across my professional and personal portfolios paint me in a different light with different personae. Like Timothy who takes out the trash during his housekeeping, as a highly empathetic person who has blogged extensively to cope with grief and loss, sorting out the grub and dirt in my emotional wellbeing allows me to assign bad feelings and thoughts into the right spots, their safe spaces, in order that I may be able to function properly in my daily life.

Yet in these moments of growing up on the internet and learning to be intimate with these places, in these places, and for these places, there are simultaneously these other newer and more foreign places on the internet that will always be incomprehensible to me. The feelings of belonging and attachment I feel to some places on the internet come with maturity—from growing up in them, just as the feelings of longing and loss I feel towards their impending deletion and obscurity come with age—from growing old in them. I can only hope that as I continue to grow old on the internet, the places that are dear to me will be conscientiously archived before their impending deletion, providing me with one map and guide of the spots that were once my home.

CHAPTER TEN

Remixing the Music Fan Experience: Rock Concerts in Person and Online

ANDEE BAKER

Fan A: 15 songs? Seriously?

Fan B: no, simply we have been most of the time with no feed

Fan A: I see—my mistake! …

Fan C: is there a final setlist?

Fan B: setlist on setlist.fm at this moment is surely wrong

Fan 3: Fire the focking feed Don. Problems here thanks …

Fan 8: Wild horses

Fan 7: anyone has a feed for 5 mins?

Fan 1: Not me. No feed.

Fan 6: me 2, problemos again

Don: lol

Fan 1: But hey, chat is fun!!

Don: marcello was doing great. Still 'broadcasting' but no one can connect. that's what happens in a stadium …

Fan 6: the set list sounds pretty good …

Don: well it was fun while we had it!

The above are two snippets of frustrated conversation among fans of The Rolling Stones as they try to experience their favorite band—not from the stadium, but from their own homes, some half a world away from where the show takes place. The first, with fans identified by letters, is from what is likely the oldest Rolling Stones fan board that is still online: "Heart of Stone" (HOS).[1] It was launched in 1994, has an international membership, and is run by a European who owns a data consulting company. The second, with numbered fans, is from what might be the newest online Stones community. Originally a spin-off of HOS, it was started by an American media designer and marketer in 2015, "Don," and is called "Paint It Black" (PIB)[2].

Figure 10.1: Mick Jagger and fans on screen. From London Stadium 2 concert, May 25, 2018. Source: Photo by Ben Cragg.

1 Names of fan groups and individuals have been changed to pseudonyms, other than for the photo credits.

2 The large fan board "Shattered" not included here, led by a U.S. financial counselor, does not generally follow shows in real-time or near real-time, but it does excel in arranging meetings between fans before and in-between shows, fostering social connections. Another board "Shine a Light" (SAL) originated by two men from N. Ireland and Mexico is very small and casual with much joking and few rules. It does post set lists and videos soon after they occur. While individual membership in Stones boards sometimes overlaps, most fans have chosen one primary group, their home base community.

I have been studying Rolling Stones fan communities for over twelve years (See e.g. Baker, 2014). For a long time, fans at live shows have let those unable to attend concerts find out what's happening at the show. As mobile phones became popular, fans would call or text friends during concerts to tell them the set lists as they happened. These friends would then post the setlists online, on discussion boards or social media platforms. The Rolling Stones staff later took up this task by posting each set list to Twitter. For the last few years, a recording and transmitting device called "Periscope" allowed fans to broadcast directly from the Stones' concerts. But how does an application that allows online concert viewing in real time affect fan experience? More specifically—how does this technology influence the fan experience of place?

Figure 10.2: "Keith Richards, onstage." Still photo from Periscope of Lucca, Italy concert, September 23, 2017. Source of Periscope and photo: Debbie "Tiger" Millsap.

HOS members have only recently learned to use the application Periscope. It allows them to hear and see, to an extent, the concerts as they happen and to discuss them on HOS in an asynchronous posting format. PIB has gone much further. The founder and administrator Don has arranged for real-time chats, with direct Periscope links to the shows, requiring no extra clicking on the part of participants sharing a single chat screen with the concert video. People also post standard videotapes of select songs as they become available, and even of the whole show, a few hours after the concert ends.

The process is not seamless. As the conversations above indicate, fans run into technical problems that glitch their ability to replicate the offline place (the concert venue) in their shared online place (the message board). However, when the technology performs, people can freely remix the information transmitted from fans at a concert. When good feeds coincide with a good performance, the shared online space is filled with gratitude and good-natured banter, akin to that happening among a group of friends visiting a live show.

Figure 10.3: "Mick Jagger onstage." Still photo from Periscope of Lucca, Italy concert, September 23, 2017. Source of Periscope and photo: Debbie "Tiger" Millsap.

Fan D: The mighty Linda Lowe on Periscope: [www.pscp.tv]
Fan E: Being spoiled rotten is the life for me, if only everything could be this good … 2 amazing periscope feeds of my favorite band, It takes me awaaaaay
Fan F: Enjoy it. Just enjoy it.
Fan G: Mick has poured out everything. You never know do you you never know your luck he says. That harmonica of LARS (Like a Rolling Stone), one hand, moving, incredible.

Don: I'll put a little notice on the homepage and the forum tomorrow
Fan 1: Merci!!
Don: de nada
Fan 2: Perfect
Fan 3: fantastic don
Fan 4: THANK YOU Don … I so appreciate you doing this for the show. As usual, got caught up with fans Tweeting me … LOOKING forward to the next time I can devote to the entire show …
Fan 5: Thanks Don. Great job as usual …
Don: Fan 2, don't be a stranger!
Don: glad to do it
Fan 1: And Letty, don't be a Guest!!
Fan 1: Don, thanks again for all you do!!

Each Stones fan board has its own culture and technologies. At HOS, fans had to access the Periscopes indirectly, from links posted to Facebook or other Periscope locations. Their conversations are asynchronous, and thus mainly about technical matters of accessing a Periscope. On PIB, which allows live chats during concerts, the conversations range from banter and complaints about technical issues to critiques of individual performers, and evaluations of the show as a whole, including the live audience's response.

Fan 10: learning norwegian, munster?
Fan 9: go choir
Fan 9: ha ha
Fan 9: Ronnie is tight
Fan 12: Hva?
Fan 10: ronnie is on fire too
Fan 9: sing sing
Fan 9: Nice guitar
Fan 10: kjenne du til levetation band?
Fan 9: cheers
Fan 10: skål
Fan 9: ha ha ha
Fan 11: It's far away but Keith is on fire
Don: they sound great tonight
Fan 11: they're rocking
Fan 6: had a great time, thanks, all, see ya at the next one, most likely! …
Fan 11: It's _awesome_ that the people streaming thanks from *us* for sitting at home
Don: no joke
Don: it is a joy to follow the tour from home …
Fan 13: Excellent Show Tonight. Jura had a great periscope going

Figure 10.4: "Crowd facing stage." Still photo from Periscope of Zurich, Switzerland show, September 20, 2017. Source: Periscope and photo from it by Debbie "Tiger" Millsap.

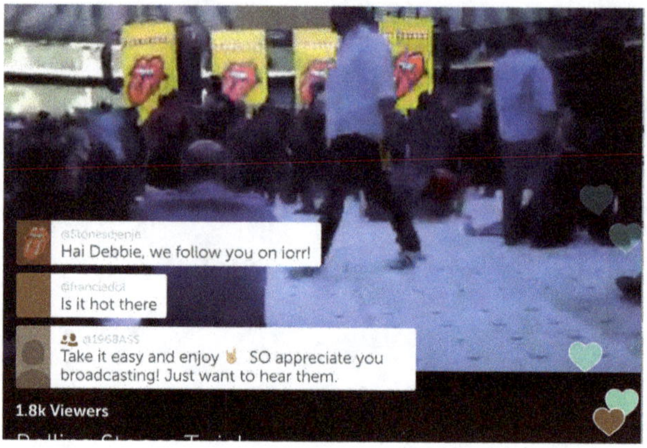

Figure 10.5: "Pre-show crowd, facing stage." Still photo from Periscope of London Twickingham show, June 19, 2018. Source: Periscope and photo from it by Debbie "Tiger" Millsap

For at least two decades, internet researchers have argued that online versus offline is a flawed distinction. In 2012, Nathan Jurgenson called this flaw a "digital dualism," claiming that outdated conceptions unnecessarily reified and separated the two realms of online and offline. The enjoyment of music fans seems to cross the boundaries easily these days, with the actual sound and some of the sights appearing in real-time from localized venues to fans around the world. Most would still appear to want to "be there" live, but the chat set-up with Periscope of the PIB fan group provides built-in companionship during a show. A group of people can talk together to compliment or denigrate the performances, without disturbing other fans. No expense or discomfort is experienced.

With the advent of Periscope, more fans have joined the online memberships of PIB and HOS, at least on show days. Perhaps the trends are more common among young people who may want to stay on their phones, even forgoing driving a car until later in their lives (see e.g., Lipman, 2012) On the other hand, recent evidence from a study of 1,000 Australians suggests that people who attend music concerts in person feel better about themselves than others (Weinberg, 2017). In any case, fans of the Rolling Stones are remixing their places for loving music, not blurring the boundaries between online and offline as much as braiding the two together in context specific ways that meet people's needs.

CHAPTER ELEVEN

Chronotope

CATHY FOWLEY

Today [1] I [2] entered the past [3],

an old-fashioned pink page appeared on my screen. In the middle, on a very small white rectangle, I typed my name —my real name—and a password that came to my fingers as if I was typing it every morning and every evening.

We came in, looking for people Looking for answers, Looking for ourselves, and through words we found

<KateDU> somewhere
that makes me feel comfortable

A place where I can sit back, relax, and talk to friends about anything and everything.

1) This multi-voiced poem is composed from past and present words of the users of women2women (W2W), an online community founded by Eva Shaderowski and Sue Boettcher in 1997. At the time, Eva said: "I'm really excited by the fact that more and more women are getting online. What I'd like to see is a true representation of women reflecting the population. 50% women is my goal. And I do think we'll get there someday!"

I used posts, chat transcripts and emails, as well as present discussion with the women who remain and are part of a Facebook group. This piece includes voices of some of the women who were part of the initial group and who died. These words are shaped to illustrate Markham's (1998) framework: if members used the internet as a tool to find someone, something, a community, friendship, the site became more than a place, it became a "home."

Here a place that is firmly
entrenched in my heart?
Home …
</KateDU>

<Tzales> I am the grandmother
figure here. I used to be a nurse.
But my feet hurt
</Tzales>

<Zanne>A place to share,
A place to learn,
A place to love
</Zanne>

<Circe> I wanted to find a place
where people talked
about things that really matter like
coming out of the cold into a
roomful of wise, intelligent, funny, nice
people (3).
</Circe>

<Jigsy> But it seems like this is
where I can come and talk about
things I can't talk about
</Jigsy>

<Betty> This is a place
I can speak my mind,
say what I am thinking
sort of sort things out
</Betty>

<Terri> this was one place I could
open mouth
—insert foot
and still come on the next day
to share, learn,
and laugh so, so much.
</Terri>

This was the word the members used about their/our site/place, filling it with emotion. As with family homes, the place also became a way of being.

2) I am one of them, I lived in our "home" for 10 years, on and off, like an older daughter studying in college. The metaphor of place was laden with emotion and story, our pink place given a resident color as well as the title of Home. This inscribed the storied everyday interaction into a tradition of women's diary-like writing, where secrecy (privacy?) is part of the narrative (Radner, 1993). The emotional resonance of the home place in this case also links to Markham's third metaphor, of the internet as way of being. Several of the women voice their relief at being "themselves," removed from judgement or labels, in a space removed from their habitual social space, a Foucauldian heterotopia (Foucault 1984).

The story of this group of women is bounded in place and in time: it happens in a place which, like a home, can be left and can be lost. It happens in time as well, with a beginning, a middle and an end, although it does feel like a time outside time, finished yet permanent, and I see this as a story, as a chronotope (Bakhtin, 1981).

3) "Don't write about us," they said then. "This is home, this is where we can be real and honest, it doesn't belong anywhere else. This is our haven." "I am not writing about us," I said, "I am writing about young people in my thesis."

<Wren>
Here
being me is okay (4)
My life is richer.
</Wren>

And yet time passed
And home changed
Rooms within rooms
Safe

<Pixie_Charlotte>I am so grateful
for this secret place where
I could come today (5)
</Pixie_Charlotte>

We lost
[KateDU] one morning

[OldMD]some days later

<person>… and then all of us
reacted to that loss
by virtual silence ….
</person>

<andre> It's still hard
for me to come here
and know
she isn't here
</andre>

"Please do write about us," they said now, "we will help you. Take our words, you are welcome. The pink place is gone, the only way to keep it alive is through memory and writing. We used to write a lot, for and to each other."

4) Wren writes about her hesitancy in taking her first steps in the "pink place," her fear that she will be ignored, as she was in other discussion forums echoing Annette Markham's quote of MacKinnon's (1995) phrase "I am perceived, therefore I am." Wren's shyness influenced her choice of name, Wren, a small bird. But after her first post was acknowledged and welcomed, she relaxed into being herself, funny, whimsical. She came to see herself as the long-lost cousin of the family. She is not the only one to voice her feeling of acceptance and that she can be "herself." KateDU, a strong and outspoken woman, also voices her relief in being able to be "who she really is."

5) Within the Pink Place, there were many discussion threads, which we saw as "rooms," or places to talk about specific topics, if we could be disciplined enough—which did not always happen. Each long-term member also had a journal for reflections on their own lives. There too, visits often happened, as in this exchange between Terri, KateDU and RBurtone:

Kate: Sorry about using your space Rose, but Terri NEVER puts her info in HER space

Terri: <sigh> going to my very own place now.

Rose: Hey use my space anytime, whatever works

Our "pink palace" has gone quiet

<PJMac> It's kinda lonely (6)
around here …
</PJMac>

We have to move If only

<wren> we could find a web space
to have our own little
private pink garden with a
gateway to allow visitors
</wren>

But we lost so much, and somewhere,
in a room

<tzales> It becomes harder and
harder for me to sit
with my feet down here at my desk
</tzales>

Maybe we could stay, in empty rooms

<early>we can prune away the old,
perhaps to the attic
</early>

<betty>I know I can always come
back to my second home
Here where all of you are
I would like to stay here too (7)
</betty>

The pink wallpaper faded
Old-fashioned, dated
We lived on with our memories
The ghosts of our friends
still talking to us

(6) The community changed over the years, attracting mostly older women who felt other digital environments could be confrontational. It became more of a safe space for older women to talk about their everyday. None of us had known each other in our offline lives, we were separated by geography, by time and sometimes generations. A core group of active participants gathered around specific discussions and journals, linked by strong ties of friendship. As time passed, some meetings were arranged, visits planned as part of holiday trips. I met Andre and Circe in Paris, then Terry and another member in Los Angeles. Rose travelled to Texas to meet Terry and Tzales. As time passed again, however, some women left the group, and after the death of two of the most active members in 2009, women2women limped on until 2011 when the remaining women migrated to a Facebook group, which is still used mostly to touch base during pivotal events in the women's lives. Our place, our home, tucked away in a remote corner online, was at last abandoned and we moved to the ready-made corporate place, where we created a small and overgrown walled garden.

7) I feel that there, I could be a part of who I am, a part which has no real place in my other world. We all took on new roles, cousin, head honcho, resident grandmother, grasshopper learning how to see age. Annette talks about people who "focus on the expression of self and others through the text," says that "for these users, online technology is a way of being." But these were days when we wrote ourselves into being, and like memoirists, chose the thread of the story we wanted to tell.

<Early>Since we can
no longer talk on the phone,
and the IM on this site
is silent from you,
When I think of you
missing you so much,
I come here (8)
</Early>

Sometimes Tempers flared
Loss lingered
People disappeared
One by one

8) After KateDU and OldMD died, members gathered in their journal spaces, and did so for years. In 2011, two years after Kate's death, Circe posted in a general discussion: "Joc's problems at home—she goes to Kate's Place to talk." Pixie_charlotte (Joc's W2W name) acknowledges this herself, within her post: "not ready to post about it in my own journal yet." Tzales approves: "Yes Joc, this is a great place for you to come and share with us." This wonderfully illustrates the importance of the internet to provide, "meaningful places where things happen that have genuine consequences."

CHAPTER TWELVE

Ecologies for Connecting across Generations

ANETTE GRØNNING

How might an ecological framework help us understand life in the 21st century? In what follows, I draw on a narrow slice of the life of two families in Denmark, each crossing three generations,[1] to talk about the continuous accomplishment of building and maintaining family life in the digital age. Even as these everyday interactions could be considered quite mundane, they create overlapping networks of information flow and feedback through a variety of digital interfaces, using multiple digital artefacts. If viewed through the lens of biological systems theory, we can see how these everyday activities sustain homeostasis, or relative balance. In this chapter, an ecological framework enables me to focus on the way individuals and media co-exist. How personal digital tools are used and how mothers and daughters, fathers and sons live. More specifically, the idea of *a personal ecology* helps elaborate the way three generations connect and negotiate their relationship through digital artefacts. Denmark is among the most digital countries in the world (International Digital Economy and Society Index, 2018). Only four percent of the Danish citizens (between 16 and 89 years) have not been on the internet (2018). Since 2001, Danish citizens have been subject to forced digitization, driven by the authorities via services like NemID for receiving digital mail from authorities and signing into services (Tassy, 2018). The two different, yet typical Danish families described in this chapter, illustrate that for them internet

1 The empirical insights come from two focus group interviews, conducted by email with six Danish citizens (two times three generations, three females, three males) over four and six months, respectively.

has become a part of, and a tool to sustain their personal and familial ecologies. The internet is a way for them to be a family and as they live in media, rather than with it (Deuze, Blank, & Speers, 2012), it's a bit like fish live in water, rather than with water.

Based on my long digital conversations[2] with the (two times three) family members born in the 1920s, the 1960s and the 1990s, I found that Karen (mother), Charlotte (daughter) and Matilde (granddaughter), used the internet to enact and sustain their relationships, and nothing of their family relationships remained external to media. For the second family, Poul (grandfather), Anders (father) and Christoffer (son), this is a more complex question as they externalize the media they use as something they visit or use momentarily, but at the same time they find their digital tools essential to and inseparable from their everyday lives. For both groups, it is clear that digital media are woven in and through this lifeworld seamlessly.

ECOLOGICAL FRAMEWORKS

While many theories of ecology have been developed in relation to social processes, the basic ideas align with a core systems theory premise that all elements of systems are interrelated, that all processes are dynamic—continually organizing or structuring a system, that structures can seem to be stable, which is simply a state of relative balance or homeostasis, and that evolution occurs as changes in the basic state or 'attitude' of the system. Changes in any part of the system influence all other parts.

Ecological models have been applied to conceptualize the interrelated networks we occupy and traverse in digital landscapes and how we use digital artefacts in interrelated networks (cf. Meyrowitz, 1985; Raptis et al., 2014). An ecological framework helps us lay out macrostructures and the microprocesses of complex systems. Larsen & Sandbye (2014) offer a clear starting point, defining ecology as "the science of the relationships between living creatures, their social interactions and the interactions between them and their surroundings" (p. xxx). Since ecologies are defined by patterns of organization, the science of exploring these relationships is enacted not by looking at what the ecology is, but by focusing on what is happening. When applied to studies of media or digital ecologies, we then focus on what information does (Bateson, 1972), what media do (McLuhan &

2 With the women from April 2017 to August 2017, with the men from April to October 2017. The interviewing style was more conversational than classic semi-structured interviewing as we all wrote to each other, resulting in a longitudinal digital group conversation with days of silence and days of conversation between the family members and me.

Quentin, 1967/2007; Postman, 1992) or what digital media or digital objects do (Fuller, 2005; Redström & Wiltse, 2019).

Building from the definition of digital ecology offered by Raptis et al. (2014), I suggest that anything we might call a *digital ecology* will be defined by how we mark the boundaries around a certain pattern of activities around and with digital artefacts in a social (media) network. In everyday use, the design, the features, the affordances, and the user become weaved into an interconnected *personal digital ecology*. In other words, our personal ecology consists of a set of digital and non-digital artefacts and through activities we become nodes in a network with ourselves and the surroundings. The activities are structured by the user and by the artefact (e.g. software, app). We may experience different digital ecologies as we engage in various activities (at work, with family, among friends), but all of them are part of our own personal ecology we try to create homeostasis, or relative balance in.

MICROPROCESSES OF NETWORKED ECOLOGIES

What the family members actually do can be thought of as the microprocesses of their personal and familial ecologies. Take the practice of digital conversation. Digital conversation connects people with other people and their surroundings. Digital conversation practices happen on and with the internet, which from this perspective is primarily a collection of tools (software) that enables connectivity between spaces (both geographical and digital) and link personal space and time into relational personal ecologies. During an average weekday, we participate in a huge number of different digital conversations with our family, friends, colleagues and others through our mobile phones, tablets or computers. These digital conversations may be short or long, open or closed to others and include content in very different forms (Grønning, 2018). Fundamentally, the digital conversations enact and sustain our relationships and create our ecologies.

In the following, I describe the microprocesses within the personal ecologies of three generations of two families: a mother, her daughter and granddaughter and a father, his son and grandson.

Family 1: The female trio

The grandmother, Karen (born 1925), is a retired psychiatrist and a heavy digital communicator, partly because of her hearing impairment. She takes part in many variations of digital conversations, both within the intimate core of her digital personal ecology (with her family and closest friends) as well as in the more semi-private institutional sphere of her digital personal ecology (home banking, digital consultations at her GP, shopping). The daughter, Charlotte (born 1962), is trained as a nurse and works as a health manager in a municipality. She is available for digital conversation 24/7 and uses email to contact her mother and Facebook Messenger, text messaging, phone and email to get in touch with her daughter. The granddaughter, Matilde (born 1994), is studying to become a teacher (pedagogue) and uses e-mail to communicate with her grandmother and Facebook Messenger, text messaging, phone and email to contact her mother. All three of them are active on Facebook with hundreds of friends and active posting behavior. They all live in Denmark, each, on their own, and not in the same town.

Family 2: The male trio

The grandfather, Poul (born 1937), is a retired general practitioner who takes part in text messaging with his wife and in telephone conversations once a week with his son, but does not enter into many other online conversations. He prefers analogue conversations through physical meetings with friends and family. The son, Anders (born 1965), is trained in economics and works as a managing director in an international, private company. He talks on the phone with his father and uses Facebook Messenger and the phone to contact his son. The grandson, Christoffer (born 1995), is studying business administration and uses the phone to communicate with his grandfather on special occasions and Facebook Messenger or text messaging to communicate with his father. They call each other in case of an emergency. The email is used primarily for formalities and when they forward emails from others. All three of them have a Facebook profile, and the grandson also has an Instagram profile. They all live in Denmark, Poul with his wife in a small town, Anders with his wife and their youngest son in another small town, and Christoffer on his own in the same small town as Anders.

MALLEABLE SPACE

While members of the same family—for example Poul (grandfather) and Christoffer (grandson) may define an experience of digital conversation and their spatiality differently—Poul as a gigantic vacuum full of noise, Christoffer, depending on the platform, as an intimate space akin to face to face interactions, neither family and none of the members contest the centrality of the technology in the digital conversations that sustain their familial ecosystem.

Focusing on the spatial scale, the digital tools both expand and shrink geography. On the one hand, the space expands when Christoffer and Matilde are communicating 'on the go'—from the bus, the train or even the toilet. There seems to be no sense of place, in the words of Meyrowitz (1985), they could be anywhere and everything is immediately nearby. On the other hand, the geography shrinks when Karen prefers to write from her desktop computer at home although she has an iPad and a mobile phone. She turns the computer off every evening at bedtime and on first thing every morning, marking a boundary around her activity. She situates her digital space physically and temporally. She has to be at home in a certain room to feel comfortable and able to enter the digital space. Likewise, Poul states that he prefers to communicate from his computer situated in his home but at the same time he connects his phone to the burglar alarm to keep an eye on his dog (described as a family member) when he is away from home:

> *The mobile today is an indispensable good for me. It provides a sense of security if something unexpected happens away from home, is an easy and smart payment method, holds a gps when you get lost, replaces pencil and notebook, contains photo app. and a scanner and connects to our domestic burglar alarm, so we can even see what the dog is doing.*

Poul's experiences of geographical space in one brilliant sentence: when you get lost you can find your way. For Poul, maintaining a constant, mobile link to his personal ecology allows a sense of personal security, while for Karen the link is anchored to a time and a geographical place. Karen is in daily contact with her daughter, Charlotte, through email and the inbox is part of her safe space at home where she feels good. Karen knows that Charlotte is there for her. Charlotte explains why:

> *I believe deeply that I have to be reachable for others. I was outraged when one of my peers, she told me that she turns off her phone at night and therefore hadn't noticed that her grown-up children had called. I am available for my mother and my daughter day and night.*

Anders and Charlotte switch between the computer, tablet and phone and they both tend to think that they have too many emails (at work) and prefer to get away from the inbox(es) when they are off from work, so they swim into Facebook (Messenger), Instagram and Snapchat for private (even if passive or one-sided) digital conversations. Anders considers himself "a passive voyeur" of Christoffer's Snapchat stories where he—in his own words—gets a "flash from Christoffer's life," primarily directed to friends. Here, Christoffer could mark an explicit boundary by not letting his father connect with his Snapchat account but as long as the father stays a passive voyeur, Christoffer lets him swim around there. The three women stress that they enjoy the asynchronicity of the digital conversations, in particular, and they appreciate that they can leave messages without feeling that they are disturbing or interrupting each other. Concurrently, visual connectivity seems very important across the generations and corresponds with the fact that our society has, in general, become more visual (Larsen & Sandbye, 2014, p. xvi). Pictures keep the connectivity alive and create a deeper kind of closeness. The family members circulate photos from many different situations. Receiving pictures and other visual material is perceived as a form of 'being there' as it turns the communication more present and alive. In this way, visuality is bridging the boundaries between here and there—blurring or erasing the geographic distance. You feel that you are there, as Karen states:

> *I am more into, what is going on. As an example, I have just received some pictures from my brother [who lives] in California, showing how they are cutting down one of the big trees in the garden. On that, I can see how they do it, who is cutting and I can see parts of the house and what it causes of changes.*

PEOPLE AND DEVICES

The moments of digital absence and perception of these offer insight into the personal ecologies of the two families. Being without digital devices and social media, life has become unbearable. Anders states: "I am massively dependent on my mobile phone and email and I get withdrawal symptoms if the phone or PC/email doesn't work or is stolen or if I have left the phone at home." In the same way, Karen finds it "(…) nigh on catastrophic" if her computer goes down: "I really don't know what to do without an internet connection. Today, my situation is more or less the opposite of 'don't teach your grandmother to suck eggs,[3]'" she points out. She explains that now she learns about the technological artefacts (and a lot of other things) from her daughter and her granddaughter whom she raised and educated earlier in her life.

And the daughter, Charlotte, told me this story:

> *My phone broke down this summer. Within an hour it had used all the battery and could not be recharged. Thank God, on a working day, so the IT Department quickly got me back with a replacement phone, but I thought well enough about how panicky, I really thought it was. And I even have an iPad with network connection, but the idea that I was not on the phone was scary. It is an incredible development—and not necessarily for the better, because we have become so time-controlling and it can also cause concern to a much greater extent than before. For today, we expect to receive an SMS or other sign if you expect to be late. In the past we just waited and then at some point the explanation for the delay came enough.*

Beyond devices, images deserve being mentioned as important digital artifacts. As mentioned, being able to communicate visually is highly important to the informants. Individually, they say that they use pictures to document and to remember

3 "Don't teach your grandmother to suck eggs" is a Danish idiom meaning "Don't offer advice to someone who has more experience than yourself." Here, the point is that the grandmother finds that she has taught her daughter and her granddaughter so many qualities during their childhood and adolescence—and now they teach her back and invite her into their digital networks (ecologies).

their daily life, and collectively, they share pictures of family members, links, screen-shots and pictures of funny stuff they see around them. The pictures expand their memory and enhance the closeness between them. Karen says "[p]ictures make the communication of the digital life more present." Matilde states that things "(…) become more real if you send a picture." She mentions an example where she sent a picture of her sunburned face to her mother instead of just writing the information to her.

Matilde points to the fact that the digital communication sometimes expands interaction: "I think, that often, we write something we would not have said." This brings a new kind of closeness to their community and makes it stronger. They feel that if they need to, they can always contact each other about almost anything. Charlotte explains: "(…) the digital has replaced it, but on the other hand increased our contact extremely much. Maybe even too much." and later she adds: "It is such a kind of "now and here" communication that does not necessarily require answers." They feel close. Here, distance enhances closeness (Chayko, 2017, p. 12), and all three women describe the digital space between them as a strong community. Matilde adds: "We have the opportunity to keep each other updated about our lives." She states that she misses her mother and grandmother less because of the close digital relationship with them.

The digital artefacts the families use comprise family members' personal ecologies, which overlap or interrelate into the family overall ecology. When we are alone, we do not necessarily organize our practices in the same way as when we are swimming together with others or trying to invite others into our water. Same activity but different marking of boundaries. Matilde chooses email to connect with her grandmother, something she would never do to connect with her friends. Karen prefers written contact because of her hearing impairment. Christoffer calls his grandfather, Poul, on the phone, something he rarely does to connect with his friends. When Anders finds that digital communication helps to keep the "close relational pulse going" between the physical meetings and the phone calls he is both part of his own personal ecology and part of the personal ecologies of Poul and Christoffer (and others). Using digital artefacts create overlapping networks of information flow and feedback based on the personal ecology, preferences, routines, etc.

MALLEABLE TIME

Being together asynchronously is important to the family members, as Charlotte points out: "The beauty of all digital communication is that it does not require that there is one at the other end simultaneously, but can be answered when it suits the individual."

Matilde explains:

> *Digital communication is not bound by time and place. It is fantastic, but it is exactly what makes our society a bit crazy, I think?? It has become so popular that we sign up for fitness—so we can decide when we will exercise. We write messages over the internet—so you can decide when to reply. You can take an online study—then you can choose when you want to study. It is very convenient that you do not disturb, for example, when children have to be tucked in or something else, but I also think it causes/induces our society become a weird mix of "doing what you want when you want"—hmm is it healthy for us?*

As time is a relevant feature in contemporary social relations, time and temporality is relevant as an object of analysis (Markham, 2013b). As she notes, internet technologies make time a malleable construct (2004); it is shrunk and expanded or extended by features of platforms, but also manipulated by people to suit their purposes, often without being noticed (Markham & Stavrova, 2016, p. 235). Time is highly relevant to interaction and at the same time it has become almost irrelevant—or disrupted.

When Matilde goes out with her friends, her mother follows her digital footsteps. When Charlotte wakes up in the middle of the night, she can see that Matilde has been active on Messenger at 3 AM. In that way, she is able to follow when Matilde is doing something. Thus, the tools are co-constructors of the ways in which we choose to communicate with each other and challenge our idea of connectivity in everyday life (boyd, 2014, p. 11). The email, the chat message and the text message become institutionalized tools for digital conversation shifting time, space and connectivity. This set of institutionalized tools also takes a swipe back, at analogue conversation that changes gradually in a simultaneous process. Matilde mentions an example with the photo album which is no longer circulated physically but digitally, changing both structure and content of the coffee visit after holidays.

Thus, the timeline feature of various social media platforms, as well as the platform owner's algorithmic intervention into the time of the timeline (i.e. Facebook's Edge Rank algorithm that picks the most popular of 'your memories' and asks you to post them again, thereby constructing a 'memory' in your digital ecology, or Instagram's visual archive that expands time) expand our way of thinking about time and memory and also become part of our personal ecology. If we miss an event or in other ways fall out of the timeline which would be an imbalance, we can easily catch up and reestablish the homeostasis as part of our personal ecology. Sometimes the reminder of missed activities (feedback) comes from ourselves, sometimes it comes from the technological features as when you receive a message from Facebook or Twitter telling that you have missed a lot of updates since your last visit. Furthermore, the tool's ability to convey social cues about the user and about the context is an important part of the connectivity's opportunities and restrictions (see also Baym, 2015).

When the grandmother, Karen, was young, she sent her parents a 'Sunday letter' every week with updates about her life. When the daughter, Charlotte, was young and moved from home, she made a 'Sunday phone call' to her childhood home every week. And now, Charlotte is available 24/7 and she can track Matilde's footsteps through digital tools such as Facebook and Messenger. In this respect, contact between the three generations has developed from a fixed momentary full connection initiated by the youngest social actor to a ubiquitous quasi-full connection initiated by the older social actor. Similarly, in family 2, Anders calls his father once a week, Thursday or Friday, on his way home from work, something he has been doing for many years. Anders also tries to call Christoffer and Christoffer's two brothers but finds them difficult to reach by phone: "My success rate is only one in five."

Across generations, connectivity has developed from 'no news is good news' to 'no news (updates) is bad news' as we constantly, potentially, leave traces of ourselves online which our nearest and dearest can search for and follow. On one hand, this constant digital connection makes the question of time superfluous, on the other hand, it makes the question of time more important than ever. The fact that we, potentially, have both asynchronous and synchronous digital contact 24/7, ascribes more power to the absence of digital contact. Potentially, this indicates a new kind of relation to time as time both seems to disappear and not disappear through the possibilities of digital contact. The potential constant contact weakens the time without explicit contact. A clear indicator of shifting temporalities and the need for immediacy.

CONCLUSION

I have drawn on a narrow slice of the life of two families in Denmark, each crossing three generations, to show how an ecological framework might help us understand life in the 21st century. As emphasized by Deuze, Blank, & Speers (2012) the shift from 'living with media' to 'living in media' marks an ontological shift. Digital ecologies are not places, but relationships. Users may experience different digital ecologies as they are engaged in various activities, but all of them are a subset of their own personal ecology. Each of us draws on different parts of the digital ecologies to compose our own personal ecology, not freely, but based on the affordances of the different tools combined with our way of interacting with them within the overall ecology.

The ecological view invites attention to relationships between people, devices and perceptions. On an analytical level, personal ecology as a perspective highlights how we mark the boundaries around a certain pattern of activities and with digital artefacts. Swimming in and out like a fish alone is one thing and when we are alone we do not necessarily organize our practices in the same way as when we are swimming together with others. Sometimes same activity but different marking of boundaries. Matilde chooses emailing to connect with her grandmother, something she would never do to connect with her friends. Christoffer calls his grandfather on the phone, something he rarely does to connect with his friends. On the internet, Charlotte monitors (follows) her daughter via Messenger and Poul his dog via the app for his burglar alarm, both to feel secure, creating new connections within the ecology. In everyday use, the design, the affordances, imagined or technical, and the user weave this *personal ecology*.

The view of people as 'communication nodes' suggested new ways of thinking about relationships in a globalized world of mediated interpersonal communication (e.g. White & White, 2005). The concept of personal ecology takes this thinking a step further and underlines that each of us has our own personal agenda including tools and activities (and the perception of these) beneath (or within?) the overall digital ecology. We are floating in and out of our own personal ecology, into other personal ecologies, creating a new kind of overall ecology—all of the time trying to create homeostasis, or relative balance, in the system. This new kind of overall ecology swings back to our personal ecologies, therefore constantly moving.

CHAPTER THIRTEEN

The Unavoidable Place: How Parents Manage the Socially Mediated Visibility of their Young Children

PRIYA C. KUMAR

The birth of a child marks the beginning of a period of "snapshot significance" (Chalfen, 1987, p. 89). Out come the cameras to capture coos, smiles, steps, and birthdays, but also some of the tantrums, tears, or even toilet activities. Parents display these photos on walls and albums and send them to loved ones—as physical objects mailed in envelopes, as files attached in emails, and, increasingly, as images posted on social media. As soon as they enter the world, children develop a presence, even a social life, online. How do parents think about this process? How do they conceptualize the mediated presence of their young children?

Parents must make profoundly complex choices about the mediated presence of their children, but my interviews with new mothers suggest a certain normalization of this complexity. For most people, posting pictures on social media is a mundane part of everyday life. They make choices without necessarily noticing their intricacy. They experience the practice as inevitable, perceiving the internet as an "unavoidable place." Here, the internet is more than a tool for transmitting or containing information, but not quite a way of being in which self, technology, and everyday life collapse completely and seamlessly. The mothers I talked to are still aware that they're performing an identity online. In this vignette I seek to illustrate how parents implicitly accept responsibility for managing their child's socially mediated visibility (Pearce et al., 2018) and harness various social media features to do so in ways that align with their beliefs.

In 2013–2014, I interviewed 22 new mothers as part of a project on parenthood and digital photo-sharing (Kumar & Schoenebeck, 2015). This piece focuses on the stories of Brianna[1] and her then four-month-old daughter, Abigail, as well as Marina and her then 10-month-old son, Cooper. Both women lived in the U.S., worked outside the home, and used social media. For Brianna, the "inevitability" of her daughter entering Facebook caused frustration. For Marina, bringing her son into social media helped her contribute to the professional success of her best friend, a popular YouTube vlogger, as well as share his pictures with family abroad. I describe how these women managed their child's socially mediated visibility and how they articulated their everyday choices regarding their child's mediated presence.

STRATEGICALLY LIMITING VISIBILITY

The potential visibility of her child on Facebook weighed on Brianna during her pregnancy. "It made me uncomfortable … people who I hadn't spoken to in 20 years knowing her name and knowing what she looked like," Brianna said. Yet this was not a straightforward issue of privacy or mistrust of the internet. Brianna used the internet as a tool to email pictures of her daughter to her parents. When it came to social media, and Facebook in particular, Brianna didn't want her daughter present in a place populated by people Brianna wasn't close to.

"My original plan had been to keep her completely off of social media," Brianna said. But when she did, "a lot of people were complaining that I wasn't posting photos." She bought her parents special frames that display the digital photos she emails them. Still, "my mother is constantly hounding us to put photos up. And she wants her family to see them. All my aunts and uncles and everyone on Facebook," Brianna said.

A few weeks after Abigail's birth, Brianna's sister-in-law posted a picture of the infant on Facebook without asking. "I was frustrated with it," Brianna said. "It highlighted for me the inevitability of the fact that [Abigail] was going to be on Facebook." Feeling like the pressure would never yield, Brianna created boundaries to limit her daughter's visibility (Pearce et al., 2018). "There was no way I was going to completely be able to keep her off [Facebook]," she said: "so I wanted to try and limit it as much as I had control over it." Brianna created a list of close family, best friends, and people who had met or would meet her daughter (about 15% of her Facebook friends) and changed the settings so only this group would be able to see the baby-related content.

When Abigail was two months old, Brianna posted an album of 10 pictures. Two months later, after more pressure from her friends and family, she posted a picture of Abigail's toes in the sand. "I like the idea [that] the only the people who

1 All names are pseudonyms.

know what her face looks like every day are the people who actually see her face every day," Brianna said. Yet her ambivalence persisted. "I'm still uncomfortable with her being on [Facebook] at all. Like, I don't love the fact that I put those 10 pictures up."

Brianna felt that she was "responsible for shaping [Abigail's] online presence before [Abigail] had any sort of control over it." This prompted Brianna to think about "allowing [Abigail] to create her own presence." Brianna also challenged the notion that a baby automatically belongs on a mother's Facebook profile. "It's not her Facebook. It's my Facebook," she laughed. "Yes, she's a big part of my life, obviously. But, I think that my Facebook should be about me and the things that I'm doing … If we take a family photo, then maybe that can go up there because that's me and that's my life. But the point of my Facebook isn't to document her life. It's to document, to the extent I want, my life."

Brianna's conceptualization of Facebook as a place for self-expression, as well as her desire to grant Abigail the agency to shape her own presence online, led Brianna to see Abigail's visibility as something that she needed to limit and protect. "For some reason, I feel more private about her than I've ever felt about anything else in my life," Brianna said." I kind of want to keep the baby stuff to ourselves … I feel like my job is to protect her from being on the Internet as much as I can."

Brianna's sentiments might seem fairly straightforward, but they surface overlapping tensions and contradictions that speak to the complexity of one's choices about mediated presence. Brianna discusses her own private feelings about Abigail as well as protecting Abigail's privacy. She then makes a claim about the nature of the Internet as a place one needs to be protected from. She also makes a point to distinguish her own self-expression from the presentation of her daughter, which makes a claim about the function of a Facebook profile.

EMBRACING A MANAGED VISIBILITY

The day after Marina gave birth to her son Cooper, she texted her best friend, whom Marina described as a "YouTube star." The best friend "got really excited, called me crying, and she said, let me know when I can make this public," to her hundreds of thousands of YouTube subscribers and Instagram followers. Marina, who frequently appeared in her friend's videos and photos, had created Instagram and Twitter accounts to support her friend's career. "My followers … they're all her fans," Marina said. "And I post cute pictures of the baby because they love the baby. And I'm OK with that …. If it gets her more likes by these kids, then I'm going to do it. Because it's her career. And you know, she's my best friend, so obviously I'm going to help her in any way I can."

When Cooper was seven months old, he and Marina joined the best friend on a trip abroad. "And she had been vlogging and of course we were in all of her vlogs, because it was her daily life," Marina said. "You know, cutting us out would have been more difficult than just having us there." Marina's best friend made a living by performing her life online, and Marina accepted that this friendship involved her and her son's participation in the friend's online presence. Marina's comfort also stemmed from her feeling that her friend had "a very family-friendly YouTube channel," making it an appropriate place for her son to appear.

Cooper's presence on Instagram and YouTube benefitted Marina's best friend. Marina also posted pictures of Cooper on Facebook, and his presence there benefitted her family. "I'm doing it for my cousins who I don't see every day. I'm doing it for my aunts and uncles in Australia who might not ever meet him," she said.

Compared to YouTube, which Marina perceived almost as her friend's workplace, Facebook was more a way for family members to "see each other's children grow up." Yet Marina openly acknowledged that she carefully managed how she presented Cooper on Facebook: "I want [friends and family who see Cooper on Facebook] to know him as the baby that I portray through phone calls," Marina said. "And when I talk about him, he's, like, he's the happiest, most smiley kid I've ever met .... When they hear stories about him, they want pictures that coincide with those stories. So I would never put up a picture of him crying, because I wouldn't call 'em and be like, oh my god, he just threw a tantrum ... I want him to be seen as a happy-go-lucky kid."

Marina described her son as "the most important thing in my life." For her, this translated into him belonging on her Facebook profile. "I'm that mom that if my profile picture isn't of my baby, I have to have him up, him up somewhere. Or else I feel like a failure," she said. While this might be read primarily as a claim that Facebook is the place to present Marina the Mother, Marina herself interprets Facebook as being the place to document her child's life. "I don't have a baby book for my child. You can call me the worst mom of the year. ... [But] I have a modern day baby book. I can go back to my Facebook profile and tell you the exact day that Cooper took his first step. I could go back and tell you the exact day he crawled. And ... Cooper can look back and look at his life. You know, that's something that I never had for my childhood," Marina said.

In Marina's sentiments, like in Brianna's earlier, we see contradictory claims about the internet, particular platforms, and their functionality for children's mediated presence.

NAVIGATING THE "UNAVOIDABLE PLACE"

When Marina and Brianna were children, family pictures sat in an album, on a mantle, in a wallet, or on an office desk. In the early days of email, photos went from one computer to another. Now, they often go from a smartphone to a social network site, making children present and visible on social media. The images do not independently fly from phone to Facebook, instead needing a human actor to choose to upload them. Nevertheless, the mothers I studied see social media sites as "unavoidable places" for their young children.

Instead of deeply questioning this inevitability, parents take on a responsibility to manage their children's socially mediated visibility (Kumar & Schoenebeck 2015). How they do so differs based on their perceptions and interpretations of the technologies as well as of their role as parents. For Marina, Facebook, YouTube, and other social media functioned as tools for self-presentation as well as ways of being a best friend and mother. She embraced bringing her son Cooper into this unavoidable place while remaining attuned to her impression management goals. Brianna also saw Facebook as a tool for self-presentation, but found it at odds with her desire to maintain privacy and to give her daughter Abigail the agency to control her own digital presence. She begrudgingly brought Abigail into this unavoidable place in response to peer pressure, but only after creating boundaries to limit Abigail's visibility.

Cooper and Abigail are part of the first generation to grow up with a digital presence from birth. Soon, they will begin charting their own path through socially mediated visibility, offering a promising line for us to think about the internet as a *tool*, a *place*, a *way of being* or something entirely different.

SECTION 4

Ways of Becoming

CHAPTER FOURTEEN

Trans-being

SON VIVIENNE

Lately I feel more confident. It might be starting testosterone or a shift in the way I think about myself. My head-and-body-space. But I'm not impervious to paranoia and 'dysphoria'. I know some people don't 'get it' and I guess I should expect that I might lose friends and make enemies. (2016)[1]

As a researcher, I am inspired by how Markham questioned some assumptions of traditional research: "that the researcher can and should separate the planning from the doing and presenting of research; and that the researcher should present research projects as if they were a sensible linear process, when in fact the linearity is made sense of retrospectively" (Markham, 1998, p. 78). In accordance with this self-reflective stance on the ways we make meaning, in this chapter I articulate the impact my research *has had on me*; the ways my presentations over the last couple of years have 'transitioned'. Explorations of privacy management strategies became conceptual explorations of congruence. All the selves I've been became entangled with pseudonymized contributions from the gender-diverse storytellers that I work with. Coming out online as 'non-binary' has affected my physical body and the way I think about its boundaries. Non-linear fragments of personhood, made sense of retrospectively.

1 All unattributed sections in italics that follow are excerpts from Vivienne's creative writing and blogging practice' so that is established as a chapter style, but happy for you to make final call on this if you or publisher prefer that each excerpt is attributed to (Vivienne, blog 2016)

It's no surprise to me that the blurring of binaries in gender identity have become more visible courtesy of the internet. I wonder whether co-incidences of non-binary ways of being—neither male/female nor online/IRL nor authentic/incoherent—could be an opportunity to understand the complexity of continuums? Can we posit *'trans-being'* as a new framework that simultaneously constitutes the 'post-gender' and 'post-digital'? These ways of being evolve from and yet are imbricated with what Markham originally referred to as 'life online' (Markham, 1998).

> *Before the internet I was a timid boyish looking child perched on the lip of a wheelbarrow, man-spreading if you will, while my mum gardened. Prompted by this old black and white photo, I recall the joy of inclusion in a bigger boys' baseball game. I still have the faded green Bonds t-shirt that stretched across my nub-less pre-teen chest.*

When we scratch away to reveal the underlying roots of 'digital tools' or 'digital places', we see code; binary series of 1s and 0s (see more in Horst & Miller, 2013; Negroponte, 1995). Despite this, the endless replication of that code in different patterns, distributed across different platforms, transforms binaries into a multitude of potential pathways that transgress any singular gendered way of being. We don't see the code, so it's easy to forget it's there. Platforms like Snapchat and Tumblr, and even stand-alone blogs, manifest as fluid spaces that are actually composed of networks of living human beings, bytes and bots. As Markham notes in 2008, time, and more specifically, the *malleability* of time and space, is a feature that emerges when we superimpose the networking of the internet with digital traces; points of data combine into endless variable interpretations. Meanwhile platforms experiment with temporality in explicit ways (for example Snapchat messages that are only briefly available before disappearing or Facebook time-hop offerings). These afford playful circulation of multiple, enhanced selves.

Markham's framework of *tool, place*, and *way of being* only works to describe this potential if we collapse the three categories and consider how the digital and physical, and the past, present and future, enmesh. I prefer 'space' instead of 'place' here, because rather than invoking a finite, bounded frame, 'space' allows for absence, and an internet that beckons us towards empty spaces waiting to be filled. There's so much potential in the digital, to constitute and reconstitute the self, simultaneously everywhere in fragments, present at multiple moments. In *'trans-being'* we can focus more on the 'augmented realities' that emerge through these processes and entanglements. This is our contemporary way of being.

Yet even as it helps us to defy certain binaries, many of the ways the internet has grown and been shaped shove us backwards, reifying myths that we can be identified; that first impressions count; that facial recognition is definitive; and linked public data sets make us into whole, legal, single citizens. Within this push/pull of forces, I find myself. I found myself. And I am finding myself.

A confession: I patrol the boundaries of my identity inconsistently. While I'm supposed to have strong preferences about pronouns sometimes I let it go …

There are so many unknowns. Like whether I am perceived as 'male' or 'female' in a new workplace and city. And what if I don't get an interview anywhere because I insist on non-binary 'they/their/them'?

When I'm insistent, and people fuck up, then apologise, I feel the need to comfort them. Regardless, I am alert to uses of 'he', 'she' or 'they'. Mostly, I am happy for gestures of acknowledgment and am not easily offended. Sometimes I slip when gendering myself.

Sometimes it feels weird to re-inscribe myself (see 'double-voiced speech', Bakhtin, 1970) with 'they'. Not because it's grammatically incorrect but because sometimes it's inaccurate; it is not what I remember being. In the past tense, I was 'she' and when I quote people who are speaking of me, I often slip into how I think they must see me. On the other hand, 'they' invokes multiple aspects of my personhood—a responsible parent, a reliable employee, a crazy thinker, a cringing child lacking self-worth.

The continual reification of some notion of truth, of a unitary coherent identity, seems to be related to the persistence of the false but alluring binary of online/offline, which in the mid-1990s might have been understood as a more profound distinction between 'virtual' and 'real'.

I have an androgynous appearance and a non-binary legal identity. I have a passport, with an X, in lieu of M or F. When I travel across national borders, I am conscious of where I fit or belong, and questions that extend to my citizenship and legitimacy as a person. How can I present as gender-diverse in places where there is no legal or digital recognition of non-binary identity?

We are well past the postmodern turn where relativity and uncertainty dismantled some long-held traditions about the solitary or central self. Queer theory, and more recent iterations of transgender scholarship, goes some way towards explicating not just the abstract or theoretical, but very lived possibilities of multi-sited 'incoherent' performances of self. This has resulted in finding new labels to highlight what qualifies the self, such as the relational self (Gergen, 2009), fragmented self (van Zoonen, 2013), situational self (van den Berg, 2008), distributed self (Stevens, 1996), and networked self (Papacharissi, 2011).

Riki Wilchins is a transgender scholar and gender activist who is credited with coining the term 'genderqueer' and leading various advocacy groups including 'The Transexual Menace'. In a provocative editorial commentary, written for 'The Advocate' in 2017 Riki ask, 'Is Trans Over?'. They describe a conversation with the parent of one of a new generation of young people who use non-binary pronouns:

… she was discussing her son, who she explained was nonbinary and used them/they as pronouns. I asked how long they had been transgender, and she replied, "Oh, they're totally straight and male

> *with a girlfriend—they just hate male/female categories and says that gender binaries are so over." … My first response was, "Oh, my God—we've gone too far!" But upon reflection, I realized a profound shift was taking place, and a fundamental question was being posed…. if I identify as "they" and "them" and have no desire to change my body or wear any sex's clothes, am I nonbinary, perhaps even genderqueer? Am I cisgender? Am I still "trans?"?* (Wilchins, 2017)

In this spirit of emergence, I can enact a multi-sited sense of self, which is enhanced by how social media works to build discrete places (platforms) where I can invent, perform, present, and otherwise remix my understanding of myself and others' understandings of me. Conceptually, I also love the creative challenge of bringing together contradictory representations of self within a single frame—a 'complex' profile pic.

Figure 14.1: Incoherent/Coherent Self. Source: Photos by Son Vivienne

In Figure 14.1 numbered 1–11 from left to right, I'll briefly describe the context of each shot in the profile pic.

1. My work office floor, the last time I wore 'femme' shoes (shiny flowers) and celebrating application for an early career researcher award
2. First glasses (pink and purple) glimpsed through my fingers (foreground 'v' for victory)
3. Looking decidedly hung-over and sharing a photo of new haircut (covered in hoody) by SMS
4. PHD graduation and ex GF/best friend
5. Calm screen shot and real view in office
6. Uncomfortable femme representation in sister's wedding, many years ago (making mum happy)
7. Sleeping alone
8. a 'surprising' still from an animated sequence in trailer for 'Bent not Broken' documentary
9. (bottom left corner) lunch with a prospective GF when son was a baby
10. loving reading uninterrupted
11. (bottom right corner) an intentionally obscure bathroom sequence in which I begin intimate experimenting with 'transition'

This eleventh picture made its way into an exhibition for a research theme that I co-convened titled 'Technologies of Memory and Affect' (Vivienne & Barnett, 2017). My daughter was horrified.

> *Mum, you have your vagina on display in public!*
>
> *Where?*
>
> *(She points)*
>
> *Oh, that's actually my arm-pit!*
>
> *(Rolls her eyes *as if that's any better …*)*

So, while the internet facilitates multiplicity, this way of being has not yet transformed institutional frameworks for defining being, or a being, in singular tense and concrete form. Despite being legally non-binary I am required to contradict myself when I fill in forms that only offer male or female. Private parts, revealed in public, are still embarrassing. Incoherence is still stigmatized.

Outside of the self, gender transition most often sits within medical and legal frameworks. It is situated as a reactive response to gender dysphoria (adjudicated by psychiatrists, counsellors, endocrinologists and surgeons) and perceived in finite terms whereby transition is undertaken permanently and across a clear gender binary. These boundaries are rigorously policed to the extent that access to hormones, surgery and legal protections may, in some places, only be awarded to those who have a demonstrated track record of living daily life (for up to two years) as the opposite gender to that they were assigned at birth (often referred to as the 'real world test').

Even as I observe the permeability of gender-boundaries, there's a persistent cry for consistency and, since the rise of the reputation economy and self-branding, *authenticity*. These forms of identification call for a one to one mapping of a person with a singular truth.

Yet policies on gender transition are inconsistent (varying dramatically from state to state, both in the US and Australia). This is partially because categories of 'male' and 'female' are defined differently according to psychological, medical, legal and social perspectives. Unsurprisingly, non-binary gender identities pose multiple challenges for education, health services and citizenship globally, making categoric definitions (and slippage between them) matters of urgent significance.

The uneasy binary of online/offline, digital/physical has neither been erased nor embraced. Even as we continue to distinguish between online and offline as socially distinct places, most of us are forced to prove the truth of our existence digitally. In the UK, public services have been digital by default since 2014. In Australia, free medical treatment is contingent on providing physical (yes, hard copy!) evidence of a digital record. In Estonia and Denmark, all public services are centralized and digitally connected, requiring citizens to maintain a digital profile. While the benefits of having records of illness and medications compiled and easily accessible may be obvious, so are the potentials for abuse and discrimination and marginalization. One can't travel beyond national borders without linking the physical body to a digital identity and thereby generating further data via airport security scans.

> *The Director of a leading transgender advocacy group offers me an anecdote. They describe a 'masculine presenting' community advocate, often dapper in a three-piece suit, that we both know. This advocate was travelling to the US with their wife and child. The border security officers did not believe the 'F' in their passport and consequently took them aside for interrogation. Thankfully, the quick-thinking co-parent, confronted with separation of the family unit, encouraged the child to keep the advocate company … and eventually the child's plaintive claims to 'mumma's' attention persuaded border security to 'believe' their gender identity.*

My informant tells me that another trans-masculine presenting person had been made to remove their packer (or prosthetic penis), in full public scrutiny. Later a high-profile transgender academic tells me that we shouldn't be fearful (or paranoid) about border control. We can request a pat down rather than the body scan. Border security will assign a male or female officer to undertake this intimate scrutiny according to either perceived gender OR the 'M' or 'F' that is legally inscribed in one's passport. I wonder whether I can request a non-binary security officer to match my body?

> *When I approach the body scanner, I eyeball the guy who has to choose the pink or blue button. He determines the anatomical body type that my body should conform with. I part my legs and reach my arms in the air, thinking of the non-compliant 'X' in my passport.*
>
> *My body, spread-eagled and under surveillance, loosely corresponds to the 'X'. I smile to myself but try not to look suspicious. They are searching for weapons. Luckily, I don't have a concealed phallus (this time). Guns, penises and patriarchy.*

A body of scholarship that emerges largely from psychology outlines the pervasiveness of 'irresistible' first impressions. Ability to determine mood, authority and correlated trust via snap judgements of facial features influence everything from choice of sexual partner through to popularity of presidential candidates and has a long tradition in evolutionary science and the study of physiognomy. Ramifications of facial recognition technologies and A.I are equally profound, especially when biases that preference white men are promulgated through use of big data sets that draw on dominant western norms.

Meanwhile an increasingly large body of internet scholarship explores the potential to navigate personal and political *differences* online, aided by the non-linear structures of platforms like Tumblr and interlinking of digital spaces beyond the parameters of specific platforms. For example, the potential for prospective employers to stalk social media accounts is frequently presented as a risk, with accompanying educational rhetoric around selective self-representation and 'cleaning up' profiles prior to interview. This work anticipates stigmatization of contradictory aspects of self (for example someone who loses control drinking or imbibing drugs will, apparently, not be a reliable employee).

While Goffman originally pointed to the ways that we may intentionally sculpt performances of self for front-stage and back-stage audiences, Hogan develops these ideas to discuss the ways platforms also curate identities on our behalf. He argues that:

> ... self-presentation can be split into performances, which take place in synchronous "situations," and artifacts, which take place in asynchronous "exhibitions." Goffman's dramaturgical approach ... focuses on situations. Social media, on the other hand, frequently employs exhibitions, such as lists of status updates and sets of photos, alongside situational activities, such as chatting. (Hogan, 2010)

I have built on Hogan's framework of curated exhibitions of self (as mediated by technology) to consider the possibilities of *intentional* curation, as a sort of hack of identity categories that blurs boundaries and celebrates multiplicity and fluidity.

Four years ago, I started working with a group of trans and gender-diverse people in Adelaide, South Australia, on a project called *Stories Beyond Gender* (see further details of the initiative in Vivienne, 2018). Every month or so a small group of self-defined gender-diverse people met for creative workshops that explored digital self-representation and creative activism. We shared stories about transition, non-binary gender, and strategies for coming out and/or confronting transphobia.

We experimented with platforms like Tumblr, Facebook and Twitter, played with various tools and modes of storytelling (prose, poetry, face paint, video, dress-ups and memes). I delivered workshops in two regional centers and set up profiles for all participants on a stand-alone website where we continue to share our work-in-progress (www.storiesbeyondgender.com). I ran a Trans*World Café during the Adelaide queer culture festival, 'Feast', to facilitate sharing of experiences between gender-diverse folk and their families and work colleagues. In November 2017 the initiative wrapped up with an exhibition and launch of a zine. The 'born digital' artefacts of our lives were received in an atmosphere of excitement, celebration and tears. The zine continues to make its way via handbags and backpacks, onto coffee tables and into reception areas and lecture theatres. The zine exhibits and disseminates fragments of our gendered selfhood (see Figure 14.2).

Beyond surveillance by machines and systems, self-surveillance plays a large part in how embodied and digital technologies interweave to produce new ways of

Figure 14.2: Stories Beyond Gender Zine. Source: Son Vivienne

'trans-being'. In the following I reflect upon my first announcement of gender-exploration online.

> *Once I release personal information online, I have no way of knowing who has read it. After sharing the blog link on Facebook, I become even more aware of the ways that timeline algorithms have effectively guaranteed that even the most vigilant follower may miss an update. Because I no longer know who knows what, I become hyper aware of my vocal pitch and facial hair.*

This hyper awareness is an agent [character] in my own performance of self, filling in gaps or making presumptive leaps when I cannot see the Other with whom I'm presumably interacting. This informational space is an entangled mix of materiality, anticipation, and embodiment. When previously I'd assumed that no-one would notice changes in my body and voice, now I felt they were scrutinizing me, looking for changes.

With the aid of multiple modes of digital self-representation and replicability (see Figure 14.3), I reinvent, tweak, and creatively, iteratively interpret myself. Becoming non-binary happens in interactions with others, but also as a by-product of the code that enables a remixing of the elements of the self. How can I feed these surveillance regimes, in my mind and in the world, alternative data sets, through creative hacks?

The top left image in Figure 14.3 is the welcome splash page of my blog and professional website 'Incite Stories'. Via tabs you may navigate through excerpts of my media productions, academic articles and blog posts both scholarly, and

Figure 14.3: Multiple profiles across platforms. Source: Photo by Son Vivienne

intensely personal. Doing so requires some time and personal investment but reveals a complex set of insights into potentially contradictory and embarrassing aspects of my personhood. My Tumblr blog meanwhile reveals my obsession with creating multiple and abstract visual representations of my being. Twitter reveals my uses of the platform—largely re-tweeting ideas that I find provocative at academic conferences. Finally, LinkedIn reveals my ambivalence towards both the platform and self-promotion. I have a small cohort of 'connections' (just over 200 compared with 500+ on Facebook) and, despite the fact that I am currently looking for work, I have not invested in 'premium' membership. In intentionally bringing these diverse representations together in a single frame I reveal a more complex self than any single space, regardless of how many fragments a single platform may contain. This is because each platform accommodates, and is curated for, distinct yet potentially overlapping audiences.

What issues do I deem too complex or too contentious for public blog posts? Some material discoveries are carefully framed (like the armpit-vagina, which is itself framed within other images as distraction) and selectively revealed to particular audiences. I note how, in some ways, it appears easier to curate these self-representations through careful consideration of digital words and images. There is always the potential to be caught out by an unintended viewer or their ill-informed interpretation, but these alerts offer opportunity for further discussion and recontextualization. My digital selves are multiple, easily replicable, distributed through time and space but also malleable. Not that my body and incarnate being is entirely opposite or different, but my body is almost always more spontaneously manifest. And offering context for every possible interpretation of me, is simply too time and energy consuming to sustain.

> *I am me right here, now, in front of you. I might make an effort to perform according to how I think you will receive me, but I can't control what you think of me. Since testosterone, I don't really care what you think of me.*

However, without my digital traces and imagined, future inscriptions, I would not have access to curating these experimental 'ways of being'.

Willingly and intentionally curating contradictory, complex and potentially stigmatizing aspects of self requires both degrees of resilience and privilege. It calls for attention to the strengths and skills that can emerge from adversity. It can re-frame trouble and/or bad times, creating value where there was none, allowing insight to emerge out of discrimination and oppression. Here I have argued that it is not just trans* people who can benefit from celebrating fluidity and multiplicity. Together, across boundaries that will always be transgressed, we embrace personhood that is neither online or off, male or female, mainstream or marginal. Beyond the remix of differences, we anticipate opposition with self-surveillance and hacks that counter singular coherence—we are 'trans-being'.

CHAPTER FIFTEEN

Popular Music Reception: Tools of Future-Making, Spaces, and Possibilities of Being

CRAIG HAMILTON AND SARAH RAINE

INTRODUCTION

Since the original publication of *Life Online* (Markham, 1998), internet use has become what Hine (2015) summarizes as embedded, embodied, and everyday. Websites and messageboards, once experienced as definitive spaces, are now connected with other platforms. Notions of individuality and agency have become entangled with processes of corporate data collection and analysis (Amatriain, 2013; Lynch, 2016). Algorithms loom in our everyday lives, enacting their role as gatekeepers of consequence (Tufekci, 2015, p. 16).

These developments are particularly apparent in the field of popular music, where technologies are everyday, data infrastructures culturally 'ordinary' (Liu, 2016), and data collection 'nestled into the comfort zone' of many people (Van Dijck, 2014). The growing importance of, and commercial reliance upon data by and about listeners (see Thompson, 2014; Webster et al., 2016) invites us to revisit questions of how audiences derive meaning from popular music, and how scholars can understand the processes and conditions involved with this. How are listeners negotiating this shift in their everyday lives?

Returning to Markham's original work, we contend that digital music technologies have travelled a path from 'tool', to 'place', to 'ways of being' since 1998. In this chapter, we consider the use of music listening technologies as acts of agency that can be understood as a process of conscious '*future-making*'. This process includes '*speculative, deliberate*' tool use, and allows us to suggest additional metaphors to describe people's everyday engagement with internet technologies. We suggest the terms '*space*' and '*possibilities of being*'. Each is difficult to conceptualize as any engagement with an imagined, speculative future occurs within platforms and systems driven by commercial and algorithmic logics: in other words, the '*speculative, deliberate*' tool use is never completely controllable.

THE HARKIVE PROJECT, DIGITAL TECHNOLOGIES, AND MUSIC RECEPTION

In order to understand the changes in popular music outlined above from the point of view of the everyday user, *The Harkive Project* (www.harkive.org) has been gathering stories about everyday music listening since 2013. This online, crowdsourced project asks people to describe how, where, and why they listen to music, and explores our relationships with formats and technologies, and how these provide routes to meaning. Stories are submitted on a single day each year through a number of online channels and range from short tweets to long-form essays (Hamilton, 2019). Together they form a corpus revealing a myriad of practices occurring at the intersections of popular music reception, technology, and everyday life. We define music reception as the way 'people receive, interpret and use music as a cultural form while engaging in specific social activities' (Negus, 1997, p. 9). This allows us to consider engagement with music not only as (commercial) consumption, or the physical, embodied act of listening, but also as the experiences surrounding discussing music with others, reading about artists, or reminiscing, which now often take place within interfaces where 'data capture, analysis and outputs are integrated' (Rieder, 2016). We suggest that these activities are acts of music reception occurring as everyday 'ways of being' through digital interfaces and connected devices. Listeners are communing with their digital selves through the use of digital music interfaces/services/devices.

MUSIC RECEPTION ACTIVITIES AS 'TOOL,' 'PLACE' AND 'WAYS OF BEING'

The metaphor of tool—which Markham further elaborates (in 2003) into ideas of conduit, extension (prosthesis), and container—illuminates how technologies of music reception become useful and are used. Conduit implies movement: how things, people, and music get from A to B. We may consider the *Spotify* or *iTunes* (or similar) interfaces, as well as ubiquitous, connected devices such as the smartphone, as conduits through which large catalogues of music travel from

A (rightsholders, producers) to B (users, the self). The metaphor of extension helps us think about the abundant catalogues now available to listeners via these services, but also contemplate how the 'digital self' is negotiated and managed within online interfaces. Yet, music technologies are a "significantly more complex process than simply bundling, sending and receiving a package" (Markham, 2003, p. 6), which invites us to move towards Markham's metaphor of 'place'.

Here we can envisage discovering music through *Spotify*, searching for old vinyl on *Discogs*, or engaging in conversations about music with friends on social media as online 'places,' where 'one can spend time wandering, navigating, and otherwise exploring' (Markham, 2003, p. 7). However, to understand 'place' we need to think not just of architectural boundaries (on/offline, in/out of the *Spotify* interface) but also of 'a sense of presence with others' (Markham, 2003, p. 8). The emergence of large-scale data collection activities and their outcomes have shifted how we conceptualize the self and the other—both now encompassing numerous iterations of digital selves. The following extract demonstrates how the respondent engages with digital others via numerous platforms, with others in 'real life', and also with a version of their digital self through the interface of a 'personalized' streaming service.

> *Start the day with a look at Twitter, catching up with the people I follow. I see that Jah Wobble has posting a YouTube video of an old piece he did with Eno and then I'm down the rabbit hole for the foreseeable, clicking on related stuff. I love the way people have used YouTube to archive obscure music, and before long I'm listening to private press psychedelia of the early '70s, Japanese post-punk/freejazz,… Later on, I listen to a few favourite MP3s with my wife via Winamp. In the late evening I turn to personalised streaming radio.*

Based on the example above, we can argue that internet technologies of music reception have reached what Markham described as 'ways of being', where individuals' relationships to technologies become enfolded within their everyday routines, almost going unnoticed as either tools or places. The focus for users is no longer on the technologies concerned, but instead on the expression of the self (and engagement with others) through technologies.

Over the twenty year period that began with the emergence of Napster and MP3 technologies—which coincided with Markham's original publication—and through the incremental (although comparatively rapid) establishment of new forms of distribution and consumption via downloads, and then access/streaming models, the centrality of data collection and analysis has been established. The ways in which the self is conceived, managed, and expressed through dynamic digital interfaces under these new conditions are an intriguing area of enquiry. In what follows, we engage with *Harkive* reflections to offer a speculative update of Markham's original metaphorical model for explaining how people engage with and make sense of the internet.

TOWARDS A SPECULATIVE UPDATE OF MARKHAM'S MODEL

The Harkive Project respondents engage in music reception that attempts to influence their future listening experiences. Relegating or pushing particular songs through replays, for example, informs future playlists *and* an imagined, future self that may manifest both as an embodied listener receiving automated recommendations, and as a digital self through public profiles indicating one's musical taste and activity. This future engagement is made possible through what could be called an 'entanglement with practice' (e.g., Gillespie, 2014). As described in the following example by a participant, explicit and implicit logging of preferences through digital interfaces helps guide activity as yet only imagined:

> *... for my commute I usually set my phone to play music in a random shuffle manner, from song to song. This has an added bonus that actually quite a sizable portion of my music collection I've never actually heard before—so it's as good a way of making new discoveries as the traditional way of listening to the radio! In order to log what I've heard, I use the iTunes star rating system on each track as it plays _ basically one star indicates I intend to delete the track ... from the library, two stars puts the album or the artist at risk of deletion, three is my basic default of yes, I like this, four is an indication of 'So, this is interesting'... and five stars is a log that the track is a definite favourite with me.*

By engaging with music in this manner, individuals are not so much drawing upon, or creating memories. Instead, they are creating an experience that enfolds digital monitoring and the logging of preferences to inform activities they engage in once 'back' in the 'real world' at some future, imagined point. However, to what extent are respondents aware of and comfortable with communicating with their future digital selves like this?

Although popular music is largely created and disseminated through processes of capitalism and mass production, it is simultaneously elevated through shared discourses of value that have become central to explaining and justifying (Potter & Wetherell, 1987) one's musical taste and listening activities (see, for example, van Eijck, 2001; Hennion 2001; Ruud, 1997). By engaging in music reception through online platforms, the meaningful experiences of the musical self and others are translated into data and then subsequently offered back to the individual/group, who attempt to make sense of what these engagements mean in relation to shared discourses of taste and identity. 'Music to drive to' or as a 'curated' soundscape to one's morning coffee purport to offer a personalized experience, but the ability to connect listening to social media platforms also facilitates public showcasing of identity and musical taste. And all of these processes feed algorithms with data.

Speculative and deliberate: tools of future-making

We suggest that some listeners are engaging with the algorithmic assemblages and interfaces of digital music platforms in a '*speculative and deliberate*' manner. Some listeners become familiar with the algorithmic systems and the ways in which their actions influence their present and future listening. In the context of Markham's framework—the internet as a 'tool' becomes apparent again in a new guise. This new 'tool' offers avenues for both present *and* future agency, but requires a personalized understanding of how platforms function as 'tools' in the present, of the platform(s) as 'places' that can be influenced by listener action, and how these tools/places become enfolded into one's 'ways of being'. We suggest that this kind of listener engagement with platforms is best described by a metaphor of '*future-making*'. Across platforms, likes and dislikes, plays and skips, opinions and critique are displayed to present and potential future others via the public broadcasting of activity, the conscious management of a new facet of one's desired digital self.

Further to the above, the '*speculative and deliberate*' actions of users are disrupted by the influence of algorithms and other technological/commercial assemblages. Increasing personalization and a considered engagement with options to influence algorithmic processes offer new tools for engagement with future listening, ultimately leading towards '*possibilities of being*': a future, imagined self and potential future listening experiences. The following example serves to illustrate this idea:

> *The final musical act of the day is to sync the iPod to iTunes which then communicates my latest plays to the Last.FM website to eventually be published, league table style, to my Twitter and Facebook accounts. I will imagine my networks will ooh and ahh at my adventurous, intelligent and oh so credible choices of excellent music. Or mostly ignore the guy who publishes pretty meaningless statistics of musicians that they've neither heard of or care about.*

We acknowledge, however, that these speculative processes of future making involve tensions between what Gillespie (2014) calls 'editorial' and 'algorithmic' logics: the aims of large corporations to sell and maintain subscriptions jarring with listeners' intentions to influence the music they will hear in the future, and the value placed upon music as a meaningful element in identity construction. It is at this point in our tentative update of Markham's original model that the creation and maintenance of an individualized and knowable '*space*'—in which users can exert agency and control through these '*tools of future-making*'—emerges. This 'space', however, can only ever be partially realized within listening platforms organized through externally produced and controlled algorithms; it is permanently in flux, always imagined. Here we can consider the differences between space and place in terms of De Certeau's (1984) conception of constant negotiation, or in Lefebvre's (1991) theorization (utilized effectively by Prey (2015)) of the tensions between abstract, lived, and social space. *Harkive* respondents constantly negotiate these tensions in numerous online services (often simultaneously) as they dexterously switch from one digital service to another. This complicates our understanding and requires a theorization that is able to take into account the multitude of locations that contemporary listeners find themselves (and their digital selves) within.

Digital listening as tool-place-ways of being

In the following examples, we can first of all see respondents engaging with technologies in ways that highlight how the levels of tool/place/ways-of-being 'collapse.' Distinctions between technology, everyday life, the self, and others, fall away. The first respondent below uses playlists stored within their Spotify account on one level as a 'tool' to negotiate their morning routine, but simultaneously describes the 'usual ADHD scramble' that suggests Spotify is a familiar, everyday 'place' (personalized through the creation of numerous playlists) to which they can turn for suitable music to enfold into their everyday routine, thus becoming 'ways of being'. The second respondent displays a similar multi-level engagement, and in finding themselves 'tired' of their available music subsequently allocates the selection task to an aggregated list within the Songza interface. This, too, is on one hand suggestive of 'tool' use, but simultaneously indicative of everyday, enfolded familiarity and trust in the curatorial efficacy of a digital platform that highlights how systems ('tools' and 'places') of this kind have become enfolded into everyday 'ways of being'.

> *my morning commute was soundtracked by the usual ADHD scramble amongst Spotify playlists on my iPhone, throwing up Ian Dury & The Blockheads, Hiatus, Public Enemy and Ghostface Killah & Adrian Younge*

> *Even later, still at work: After having 'Mandatory Fun' on repeat for most of the day, I needed something low-key to get me through the rest of the day, but I was tired of all my current playlists. So it was time for Songza. Today I chose the 'Blogged 50' playlist and it delivered as usual. Found some great new tracks & artists to check out. This playlist got me all the way through my drive home as well*

People responding to *Harkive* appear to have dexterously taken to an everyday, mundane use of systems of this kind, indicative of an increasing familiarity with and 'domestication' of digital and internet technologies (Baym, 2015). However, it is in the manner that respondents are equally exhibiting a similar degree of familiarity with the more recent technologies of data collection and analysis that allows us to move towards our speculative update of Markham's model.

Digital listening as 'tools of future-making'

Harkive respondents demonstrate a level of familiarity, agility and trust in terms of engaging in everyday communication with digital abstractions of their music reception practices. Furthermore, they are engaging in activities that can be read as attempts to replicate the algorithmic/computational work of recommendation systems. For example, the respondents below describe management of their abundant music collections through the use of interfaces and cloud storage services that render music they 'own' in terms of music provided by services via 'access' models.

> *Pretty much all my listening these days is via my 160GB iPod, but as it's hard to remember everything that's on there (currently over 25,000 tracks), here's what I do … every so often I compile a list of albums to listen to, mostly ones I've bought since my last list, but supplemented with old albums I've recently been reminded of, ones I think deserve another listen …. that list is my "Bible", and what I concentrate on listening to, until I've listened to everything at least 3 times, then it's time for a new list!*

> *…listened to my music, held on a server (over 800 CDs worth) and played on a Logitech Radio in a random way… In about an hour of music heard some Blues, some Latin and various old early 60's pop tracks… plus one or two tracks of African music—I have catholic tastes! I'll be listening to more as I work on the PC again this evening—but probably played through a tablet, connected to music centre and playing from 'Google Play Music', which accesses my collection as well—and a very good system it is—makes interesting playlist suggestions too.*

The engagements above are seemingly performed by respondents because they have the potential to influence both future listening and the 'version' of the future digital self that may be visible to others. As Magaudda (2011) observes, in a 'circuit of practices' the material objects of music consumption are now no longer just vinyl, CDs, radios, and stereos, but also multi-function devices, and online services, all of which create new and diverse pathways to meaning. In the following example, we can observe echoes of precisely this. The respondent exerts their agency through a variety of digital, analogue, online and offline modes of reception—each of which are to varying extents visible to others, including to data-collection mechanisms—that in turn will inform both construction of digital selves and future listening possibilities via automated recommendations.

> *For my commute I listened to the new Slow Club album 'Complete Surrender' on Spotify. Tuesday is 6 Music day on the office radio so I get in and switch that on which will be playing in the background all day. After lunch I popped on the Alvvays album which was streaming in advance of release on NPR.org. After that… it was back to 6 Music on the office radio again. 3:30pm… checked out the new Lykke Li video for 'Gunshot' on YouTube. This was swiftly followed by the La Roux album which was streaming directly from the artist's official site. Back to Spotify to listen to playlist 'Top of The Poptastic 2014' compiled by pop blogger @Poptastic.*

However, the conceptual, future 'spaces' we suggest users move towards are only partially influenced by the speculative actions of the user. While the speculative actions of future-making can sometimes influence future listenings and digital selves on public display—a form of Gillespie's 'editorial logic'—at other points these actions can also be overridden by the 'algorithmic logic' of the very same platforms. Listeners paradoxically become enfolded within the latter through their deliberate and speculative use of technology as 'tools of future-making' via attempts to carve out their own, unique 'space'. The manifestations of digital selves we see in the following example are thus simultaneously 'real'—in the sense of being imagined by and engaged with by users—but also fluid/abstracted via respondents' use of and/or attempts to replicate the functional operations and outcomes of algorithmic assemblages.

> *I spent the morning working from home with Spotify to keep me company. Chet Faker's 'Built on Glass' has been sat on my 'New stuff to listen to playlist' for a while so I put that on. It's later moved over to the Good stuff 2014 list. The 'New stuff' list is usually populated from within Spotify these days, via Spotify's New Releases page … Sometimes recommendations creep in and, when they do, it's via Twitter.*

We suggest that Markham's 'ways of being' are complicated by the speculative and imagined nature of user attempts to engage with a future, as well as a present, and this is especially so since the process can never fully be under the control of the user—despite the advertised rhetorics of personalization and control offered by platform operators. These actions therefore can be understood to construct only 'possibilities of being'; actions that may or may not influence desired, future listening experiences, and that may or may not contribute successfully to the construction and communication of a desired digital self.

CONCLUSION

In this chapter we have proposed a new application of Markham's 1998/2003 model that takes into consideration the ways contemporary music listeners are engaging in 'speculative and deliberate' actions for future-making. The snapshots of digital listening as narrated through the stories of *The Harkive Project* provide a useful way of exploring a particular, crucial moment in the development of music reception as a cultural and commercial activity.

Following a movement from the unknown to the known, from a novice to an integrated, knowledgeable user in Markham's original model, the use of listening platforms as 'tools of future making' represents an engagement with a new and unknown future of lesser and greater possibilities. Action is always speculative; its outcome desired rather than guaranteed. Our reading of the *Harkive* narratives suggests that respondents are comfortable in communicating with their present and imagined future digital selves (both real and abstracted), and that this is becoming a central, conscious, and seemingly reflexive element of music reception activity. The opportunities to influence their own future listening practices, or in Markham's words, 'to gain a certain measure of control from technology' (1998, p. 114), are simultaneously made possible and precarious by the interconnected capabilities of audio and social media platforms.

CHAPTER SIXTEEN

Co-becoming Hybrid Entities through Collaboration

MARIA SCHREIBER AND PATRICIA PRIETO-BLANCO

When we first met at the "Visual Cultures, Visual Methods" summer school in Aarhus in September 2012, we immediately felt a sense of connection: two female PhD students, each around 30 years-old, both struggling to get by financially, with similar research topics. We were also both influenced by our German academic experiences—highly specific ways of working, very thought-accurate and nitpicky. And as academic nomads we were each used to being on the move and mobile, skilled in managing to maintain digitally mediated relationships since the beginnings of the Internet. We initially kept in touch through Facebook, but as we bumped into each other at various conferences over the following couple of years, we finally started to intentionally collaborate on work in 2014. Through shared conference travels, AirBnB stays and glasses of beer, an academic collaboration and a friendship began to develop, both online and offline.

In this contribution we reflect on our collaborative practices through the framework of the internet as a "Tool, Place, and Way of Being" (Markham, 2003). We address what Markham calls the "interweaving of technology and human in context, both acting as agents within social structures" (ibid., p. 10) in our own practices, teasing out how "the construction of identity, place, boundary, and meaning is thoroughly negotiable and ad hoc" (ibid.). Similarly to the dramaturgy of *Life Online*, we start each stage/phase/dimension/layer/aspect with a brief vignette or an example, and go from there.

TOOL—EXTENDING THE REACH

We rarely meet face-to-face. Patricia was previously living in Galway, Ireland and currently lives between Belfast and Brighton in the UK, while Maria was originally based in Vienna but lived in Berlin and Melbourne for a while, before returning to Austria. We meet in computer-mediated and networked environments: "Within this general framework, the Internet can extend one's reach, expand the senses, and collapse distance by decreasing the time it takes to get from point A to point B, informationally speaking" (Markham, 2003, p. 3). We started out just alerting each other of events and opportunities e.g. calls for papers, job postings, mainly via E-Mail. Retrospectively, this "transmission of information" was much more than "simply bundling, sending and receiving a package" (ibid., p. 6). These intermittent but stable exchanges created a sense of union among the two of us, enabling the emergence of a common ground (Malinowski, 1923/1965, p. 315); an understanding facilitated by tacit, intersubjective knowledge and embodiment (Mannheim, 1982, p. 243). A few months after our first E-Mail exchange, we were becoming friends—and without actually realizing it, we were building a trans-European peer-support-group and place of solidarity in a precarious labor situation in the context of increasing neo-liberalization of higher education (Arnold & Bongiovi, 2011; Faucher, 2014; Courtois & O'Keefe, 2015; UCU, 2016).

Ever since meeting in 2012, our engagement with each other has been shaping our academic identities, which, in turn, have continued to develop into a distinctive entity—an assemblage of Maria+Patri+Internet, the emergence of which we will describe in this piece. Over time, our similarities have allowed us not only to surpass geographical distances and time, but also to extend our inquisitive and analytical reach beyond the limits of our own individual personas. Mannheim's sociology of knowledge reminds us that "there are modes of thought which cannot be adequately understood as long as their social origins are obscured" (1955, p. 2). His work invites us to read our collaborative experiences as conjunctive, meaning they emerge from the common ground established by connections, relations and bonding moments. Our common ground is constituted by our shared German academic background, similar assumptions and ways of using E-Mail and social media, a shared interest in visual communication, as well as our non-native use of English.

Although online communication is often framed as a diminished or an emotionally and socially impoverished form of face-to-face communication (Baym, 2015, p. 57), empirical studies on the topic have demonstrated that even minimal digitally mediated interactions, can have a great impact on emotional relationships and on a sense of belonging (Kaye, 2006; Prieto-Blanco, 2010; Prieto-Blanco, 2015; Schreiber, 2016; Wulff, 1993). We have used a range of different media and apps to communicate with each other, and in the process, our collaborative practices of solidarity and peer-support became quite diverse. Based on our own example we propose that scholarship seeking to understand the complex ways people relate to each other needs to stop asking what mediation does to communication and start asking what people do with mediated communication (Baym, 2015, p. 67; Prieto-Blanco, 2016a; Schreiber, 2017). In our case, we built a variety of communicative contexts, and did so through different modes and with the help of different media as analyzed below.

Once we started to collaborate on papers and panels, we began using both real-time and time-delayed forms of communication. Most of our work has taken place in the second mode. For example, one of us starts creating text in a document, the other then comments and adds material; a back-and-forth ensues as we comment on comments, add to additions, etc. At some point in these editing processes, the documents become messy and have to be sorted out in person, or as close to 'in person' as we are able to achieve. Difficult and complex parts in the process of co-writing a text are discussed via Skype, which allows us to talk and type at the same time, offering a broader range of social cues and modalities of communication. We have discussed aims, arguments, narrative flow as well as style issues in the video-conferencing mode. Notes are taken while we talk, sometimes using a pen and a piece of paper, other times on Google-Docs. However, once we agree on a list of action points, we almost always go to Google-Docs. It often happens that both of us move there immediately after video chatting on Skype, but it also happens that action points get carried out individually, in a time-delayed mode, and only then entered into the shared Google doc. Working on Google-Docs means amending the text itself. This platform allows us to do it *on the fly* and it also enables contributors to see, live-track and keep a register of changes made by each other.

Choosing a specific medium, or tool in Markham's terms, refers back to meeting our need for a concrete kind of conversation or for a specific level of communication. Planning and scheduling work and meetings, as well as personal exchanges, primarily happens on WhatsApp. At times, conversations of personal nature take place on Skype. Remarkably, the tool that started our collaboration, E-Mail, has retained its relevance when it comes to sharing and forwarding professional and institutional information that comes from "outside."

A range of related theoretical lenses are helpful to explain our use of internet as a tool. On one level, our communication takes place in various *modes*—textual, visual, auditive, video and mixed (Bezemer, 2012)—it's quite common for us to be chatting on Skype to clarify an argument, all the while taking notes with a pen on paper. Further, this multimodal communication can happen in live or delayed-time. A closer analysis of these modalities reveals that we attach specific forms of interaction to concrete media. Viewed through the conceptual lens of affordances—understood here in a relational sense, as they both enable and restrain concrete communicative practices (Hutchby, 2001b; McVeigh-Schultz & Baym, 2015; Wright & Parchoma, 2011; Zillien, 2008)—we notice that what app or platform we chose to use is guided by our perceptions and previous experiences of what kind of self-expression and representation it affords. WhatsApp conversation does not allow us to "speak" at the same time, but a Skype call does. This leads us to choose Skype over Whatsapp when we need to discuss an idea at length, figure out the next step in the research process, share thoughts about recent scholarship one or both of us has reviewed, etc. A Google document allows us to introduce various layers of text production in parallel. We edit and comment properly edited academic text via the comment function, thereby expressing what we like or dislike, asking each other questions, praising each other and assigning tasks. The platform affords plenty of layers of meta-text-production in real-time through both the chat window and the commenting function (Figure 16.1). However, when it is time to submit a co-authored piece of writing, we move to Microsoft Word and E-Mail.

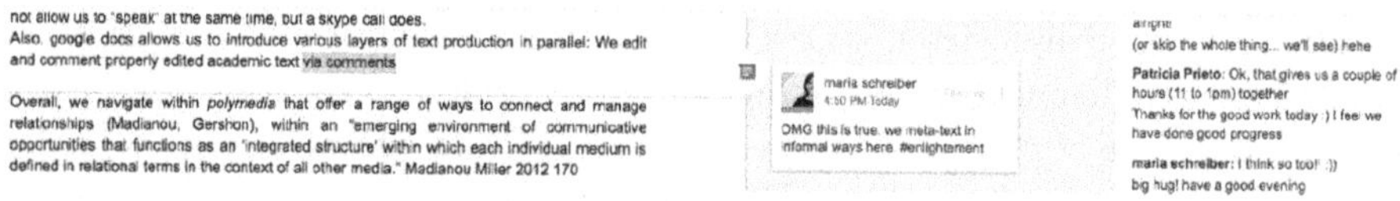

Figure 16.1: Meta-text-production. Source: Maria Schreiber and Patricia Prieto-Blanco

Overall, our process of co-becoming Maria+Patri+internet takes place in "an 'integrated structure' within which each individual medium is defined in relational terms in the context of all other media" (Madianou & Miller, 2012, p. 170). Thus, the internet is a flexible tool for our conjunctive engagement. Specific apps, platforms and devices are chosen based on their modes, affordances and position within our shared polymedia environment to indicate the kind of communication that will follow. As Gershon notes: "over time, the medium chosen for sending the message comes to signal what the message might contain, and how the conversation through that medium might unfold" (2010, p. 401). At any given moment, we can choose between, for instance, having a two-hour Skype discussion or quickly exchanging text messages, and we make those choices based on the aims and objectives to be attained through the mediated conversation, perceived affordances of the constellation of softwares and hardwares, as well as on the time and infrastructure available to each of us at the given moment.

PLACE—SURROUNDED

"Through the design, control, and play of information across contexts, personalized worlds can be created, organized, and enacted." (Markham, 2004, p. 10)

In 2015 our ad hoc collaborative working modus became a hurdle. Our work was scattered in various online 'places': diverse E-Mails, Dropbox folders, Clouds and Google-Docs. The multimodal character of our cooperation was overwhelming. We had exhausted the affordances of options at our reach and felt the heavy weight of the chaos on our shoulders. It was difficult to find specific information and we would become agitated by how scattered our collaboration was. It was at this point that we decided to employ a new mode: a shared folder in Google-Docs. At that time we had started to co-edit a special issue for the postgraduate MeCCSA journal *Networking Knowledge*, so it made sense to call that new folder "patri and maria—editorial room" (Figure 16.2).

Although our goal was to simply and effectively store our collaborative work in progress, we have retrospectively realized that the metaphor we chose is quite telling. The name of the folder represents our digitally mediated presence (Villi, 2015), our shared ownership of the content, but it also creates a virtual place. The form and purpose of this place allows for interactions similar to those carried out in a physical space. We populate the editorial room with articles and information for each other, using folders and sub-folders. In the process we leave traces of our actions. Our presence is automatically recorded and shared. "patri and maria—editorial room" has become more of a shared office than a shared folder. All we need to do to enter our editorial room is to double click on the folder icon, and we will be standing in front of a virtual shelf with files structured in projects-folders (Figure 16.2):

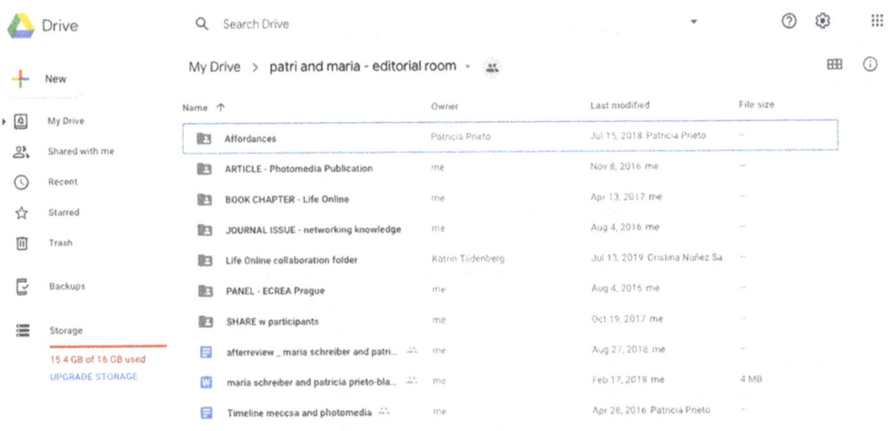

Figure 16.2: "Patri and Maria—editorial room." Source: Maria Schreiber

Our shared place is always online and offline at the same time. If we want to be in a shared digital place at the same time, this has to be scheduled. However, having this place makes life as early career researchers in precarious conditions of employment in higher education (see Nadia Hakim-Fernández's contribution in this volume) possible. Current structural conditions of extreme competition for mostly part-time, fixed term or zero hours contracts pose fundamental problems for knowledge creation and dissemination at a global level. We are part of a working "elite" who has no choice but to live and work in a bohemian way: few permanent ties (if any), available to work anywhere at a moment's notice, ready to move to the other side of the world for a (precarious) job. Being a junior academic these days means to be available anywhere anytime, which means our devices have to always be with us, slowly but surely becoming part of our academic personas. Our working spaces are not tied to geographical coordinates or walls but to the technology that enables connections and exchanges. We carry our shared editorial room with us.

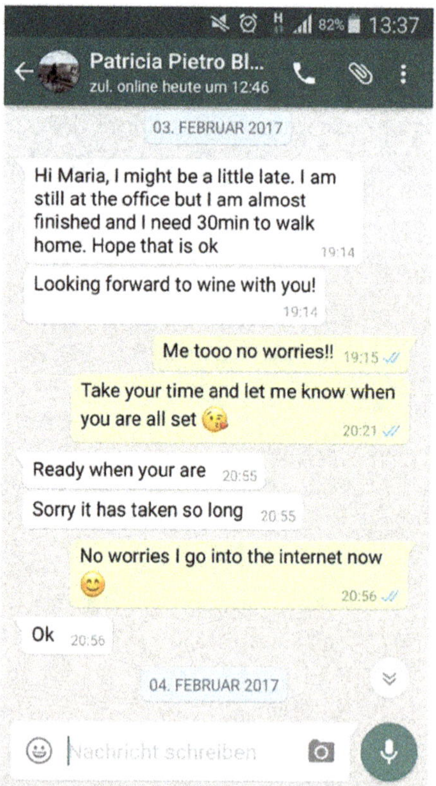

Figure 16.3: Physical and mediated spaces entangled. Source: Patricia Prieto-Blanco

In a WhatsApp conversation (Figure 16.3), Patricia lets Maria know that she will be a bit late for a private Skype date—she gives her current location ("still at the office") and the anticipated time of arrival at home ("I need 30 min to walk home"), describing how she moves through physical space. About an hour later, Maria lets Patri know that she would be ready to Skype once Patri is "all set:-*"—the kissing smiley expresses intimacy, empathy and patience. About another half an hour later, Patri is "Ready when you are" and apologizes for everything having taken so long.

In this conversation the entanglement of physical and digitally mediated spaces is striking: In a WhatsApp conversation, different physical locations, but also conditions and states of being "ready" are negotiated in the form of metacommunication—actually preparing another kind of and another space for communication—a Skype chat. This is also clearly marked with Maria's ironic statement that she goes "into the internet now" while she is of course already online with her smartphone using WhatsApp. A change of platforms but also of devices—from smartphone to laptop or computer—is perceived and framed as a change of the level of intimacy and directness. From WhatsApp we move to Skype, which is our place for real-time conversation.

WAY OF BEING—INTERTWINED

As Markham suggests (2003), practice and process allow for the Internet experienced as a tool to slowly evolve into it being experienced as a shared place of interaction, and ultimately ways of being. Skype and its real-time live-chat with video is probably the software enabling most "social cues" and therefore seems most similar to face-to-face interaction (Miller & Sinanan, 2014). What is it to us? Through Skype, we share views of our bedrooms, offices and holiday apartments. We share new haircuts and bruises and clink glasses to successes (Figure 16.4). We only Skype if we have time—and space—in the sense of a quiet room, with no other people present. Video-conferencing both enables and demands the physical and intellectual/emotional sharing of time and space. We seek and inhabit the place thereby created. We co-construct and appreciate its privacy and intimacy. We talk on Skype when we write a text. We also have moments of silence and reflection. Our academic persona resides in there. In being intertwined with each other in concrete spatio-temporal dimensions, we reinscribe our individual identities and make some sense of our profession. Skyping allows us to "dialogically and recursively constitute each other simultaneously" (Markham, 2003, p. 11), and yes, we use the brand as a verb.

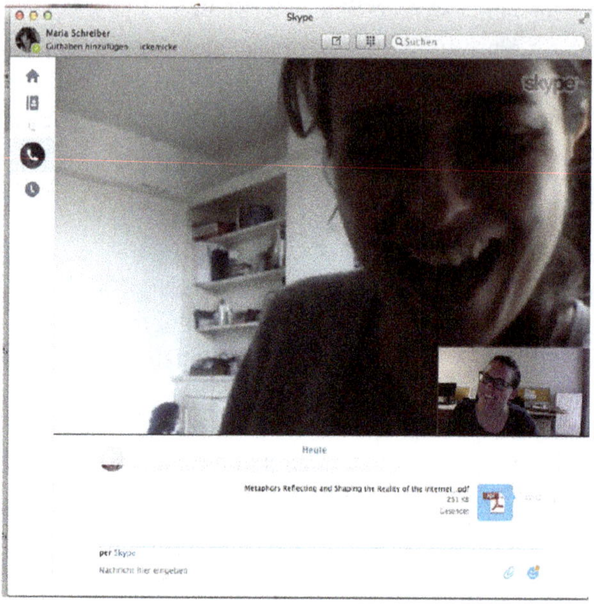

Figure 16.4: Video-mediated Intimacy. Source: Maria Schreiber

Yet, as everyone who Skypes on a regular basis will know, its affordances (and glitches—as Nadia Hakim-Fernández demonstrates in her chapter in this collection) shape and constrain conversations in particular ways. The video-conferencing modality is demanding in terms of time, space, as well as intellectually and emotionally. Some people compare it to having a cup of coffee with someone (Prieto-Blanco, 2016b), but we dare to say it is more intense through its operational surveillance (the default mode shows close-up shots of both interlocutors) and perceived exclusivity in terms of use (when video-chatting, nothing else matters). And there are times when we do not feel like being seen by anyone (see

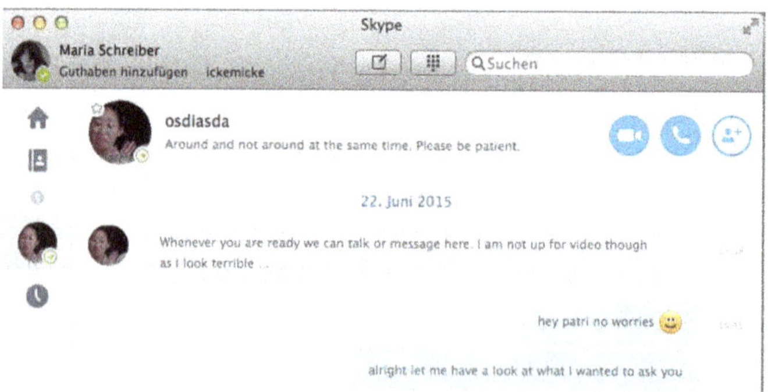

Figure 16.5: Screenshot of Skype conversation. Source: Maria Schreiber and Patricia Prieto-Blanco

Figure 16.5). In those occasions, the "continuous malleability and transformative potential" (Markham, 2003, p. 11) of our intertwining is negotiated via Skype and its modalities. We turn to text-chat and interact in a more outcome-oriented way, which while productive is clearly not our preferred mode as it allows for simulation (Kittler, 1988, pp. 63–64) rather than affording a way of being.

As we move through space, platforms and software, we learn to incorporate them into our professional practices. For both of us, these non-human components participate in the construction of practices and places of scholarship. They allow us to be and to be together in certain ways: multimodal, mobile, precarious, etc. In our experience the non-human objects like smartphones or software are hybrid actors (Latour, 1991), which enmesh or are enmeshed in our collaborative practice. As Markham writes, "Technology does not hold a position as object outside the agency of the human. Rather, the categories are collapsed, to varying degrees. [...] Technology disappears as a separate construct in everyday life because it is a transparent way of making sense of the world." (2003, p. 10)

CONCLUSION: HYBRID WAYS OF BEING

We propose to expand our perspectives from thinking about hybrid *actors* to thinking about hybrid communicative practices and relationship*s*. The example of our communicative exchanges via various platforms make visible that our relationship and interactions are diversified and have developed as we relate with each other and with various media. Rather than looking at Maria+internet and Patri+Internet, the hybrid communicative entity we are interested in is "Maria+Patri+internet." This entity is dynamic and in continuous transformation, its parts are ever-changing and evolving (see Figure 16.6).

Figure 16.6: Sketch of Visualization: Metaphors of how we relate to each other through tool, place, way of being together. Source: Maria Schreiber and Patricia Prieto-Blanco

When we first started connecting online with each other, our shared understanding and use of a constellation of hardware and software was that of information delivery. E-Mail was our tool of choice and those intermittent but long-term exchanges (paired with some offline contact) allowed us not only the potential to extend our reach, but propelled us to seek alternative constellations by which we could mediate our presence. Social media became this new constellation. We saw traces of each other on Facebook and Twitter, sometimes live, sometimes with a delay. There were places for us to meet. The brevity and frequency of those encounters forged the outline of our presence in each other's lives. We were together while apart. Then, we started to collaborate.

Working together was our aim, the malleability of internet our arena. We intuitively explored tools at our disposal and places where to collaborate. We created our own personalized combination of Google-Docs, Skype, Whatsapp, E-Mail and social media. Through our process of inhabiting "patri and maria—editorial room," we became entangled with each other and with our always malleable constellation of hardwares and softwares. We practiced research in there. We developed an academic identity in there. The synergy of our work together, and of us working together thereby gave rise to something else, a way of being that may be described as post-human, or perhaps as cyborg. We "are wary of holism, but needy for connection—[we] seem to have a natural feel for united-front politics, but without the vanguard party" (Haraway, 1991, p. 151) and we "are not afraid of [our] joint kinship with animals and machines, not afraid of permanently partial identities and contradictory standpoints" (ibid., p. 154).

To summarize, we understand "tool, place and way of being" not only as metaphors or modes of a *life online*, but also as stages or dimensions of a process through which collaborations and relationships can be transformed and become more intense. This does not only pertain to the relationships between human and non-human actors, but also to the entanglement of specific humans with each other and with non-human actors. Digital, networked media are entangled with our communicative practices as they enable a transformation from loose connections to a professional collaboration and friendship, a relationship becoming closer, more intense, more attuned.

CHAPTER SEVENTEEN

Interview with Artist Cristina Nuñez

Cristina Nuñez is an artist and a social activist. She started taking self-portraits in her early 20s as a form of self-therapy. During the past decade she has used her own experience to create a unique workshop methodology called The Self-Portrait Experience (SPEX) and conducted these workshops all around the world. The workshop is for artists, photographers, therapists, leaders, university students, prison inmates, people with various diseases and the general public, and Cristina aims to help them to learn to convert their vulnerability and emotions into art. In 2013 she started her ongoing net-art project *La Vie en Rose*, on video, performance and web, with the real goal of finding her perfect partner. This is a conversation between Annette Markham, Katrin Tiidenberg and Cristina Nuñez on the ways of being a photographer and the photographed in the era of ubiquitous smartphone cameras and internet connection.

***Kat and Annette:** Building on your experiences with self-discovery and self-healing via photographic practices—how would you describe living in the world of ubiquitous photography and ubiquitous internet?*

Cristina: When I started taking pictures of myself in 1988, digital photography and the internet were not available to me and there were no social networks. After spending a childhood feeling invisible and lonely, and teenage years as a heroin addict, I desperately needed to be seen by others and relate to them. But I wasn't ready, because I felt wrong. While I worked with my then husband on his fashion and portrait photography, I used a camera to take self-portraits as a private dialogue with myself, never showing my pictures to anyone. This practice, along with years of psychotherapy, allowed me first to become an artist and professional portrait photographer in 1994, and second, to open up to others.

In 2004 I realized that my practice could be useful to others, so I started building my method and teaching self-portrait workshops. I had created my first website in 2002 for my professional work, but it wasn't until I joined Flickr in 2005 and Facebook in 2008 that I started to publish my self-portraits on the internet. It happened to be the right moment, because I was feeling 'right'; excited about my discoveries, feeling I had a mission to accomplish and therefore ready to communicate my practice to others. Since then, the internet has been a tremendously positive tool for me to be seen, create a powerful channel of communication to others and thus divulge my methodology, organize workshops, get into interesting projects and attract the interest of the press. I have become quite 'famous', mostly in Italy and Spain, thanks to the Internet and social networks. I have been able to hold online workshops with people from the US, New Zealand and even China, some of whom have become best friends, although we've never met in person.

At the same time I often surprise myself by believing—or hoping—that the work that I post online will be seen by a wide audience, and then immediately disappointed after realizing that, if I'm lucky, only 200 or 300 of my 5000 Facebook friends will see what I post. Compared to the time 5–7 years ago, I feel it is now more and more difficult to be seen and get clients for my workshops, there are just so many interesting images online.

So, the ubiquity of digital photography has affected me, and my work, in many ways. On the one hand, digital photography considerably increased the competition among photographers for jobs in magazines or advertising. This helped me to give up on commercial photography, and start building my method and workshops.

On the other hand, the selfie phenomenon (cf. Tiidenberg, 2018b) made me feel that as an artist, I had unconsciously foreseen something—as artists sometimes do. But what people were doing was so different from my practice, that it stimulated my research. I needed to understand why so many people were taking pictures—and what kind of pictures—of themselves and sharing them. I remember in 2007, years before the selfie explosion, my teenage daughter showed me self-portraits by a friend of hers, Matthias, who photographed himself (see my blog article: http://selfportrait-experience.com/2013102teenagers-self-portraits-matthias/ with his phone, while living through hard times. He was the one who asked me to organize my first self-portrait workshop for teenagers, which I did, in 2008.

Figure 17.1: Self-portrait in Mauthausen (1995) Source: Cristina Nuñez.

Kat and Annette: *Would you say that photography is a tool for you and others to express, explore and reframe how they see themselves and the world? Or perhaps the internet is a place wherein this type of an experience is possible? Or is ubiquitous photography rather a way of being? Does this ubiquity afford a particular relationship with photography, the self and self-presentation?*

Cristina: Exactly, yes to all. Digital photography can be a tool for me and others to express, explore and reframe how we see ourselves, the other and the world, and how others see us. This allows us to work on our place in the world: what do we expect in our relationship to society, and how can we build our own ways of relating to ourselves, others, the society. These processes are rocketed by the ubiquity of the internet and the fact that photographic self-representation has basically become a common language. Therefore ubiquitously shared photography can become a way of being, although this doesn't mean that it should become like a drug you can't do without. There are many moments you don't share. There are moments you don't photograph.

In order for the tool to work and provide new insight, however, it is necessary to leave space for unconscious expression. I really believe in not deleting the ugly images, for example. I think we should be interested in them—they might help us honestly explore our inner life, especially the most difficult emotions.

In my experience with my own and other people's "ugly" self-portraits I have discovered that sharing intimate or emotional images on the internet can provide an immediate sense of relief and empowerment. First, because you give them away, they are not yours anymore; second, because through you, other people can start seeing themselves, and maybe start their own self-discovery process; and third, because sharing and the fact that they become useful for others helps you accept them, to see their use.

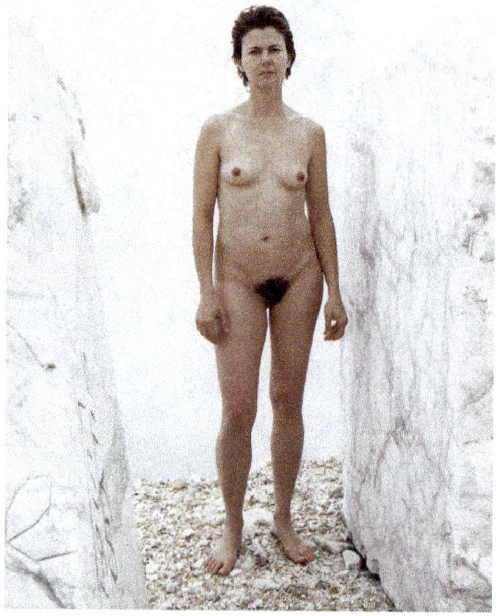

Figure 17.2: -5°C self-portrait (2004). Source: Cristina Nuñez

Kat and Annette: *A lot of your work is about emotions and emotional stimulation, if we were to suggest that networked photography is a tool of emotional stimulation for you and your collaborators, how would you respond? What about framing self-photography as a way of being emotional in a (visual) culture, which on the one hand, yes, has widely accepted these practices, but on the other, heavily regulates the kinds of self-presentations that are 'allowed' to different people?*

Cristina: Yes, networked photography can be a tool, which enables emotional expression. This presumes communicating our inner/intimate life with undefined and unknown others, which provokes emotional responses, among them possible rejection. Our visual culture has widely accepted some versions of these practices. There are many examples of therapeutic photography since perhaps 2013–2014, and a small scale explosion of young artists creating impactful but 'cool' images of themselves crying. However this crying is offered as an artistic gesture, without an apparent aim of personal disclosure, or link to any particular discourse.

Analyzing these practices and the feedback (or lack of feedback) I get of my work, I am aware that even in contemporary art world there is no real freedom of self-representation. Emotional self-disclosure has to be aesthetically framed to shield the public from the artist's life. I was once told by a curator: "you should solve your problems before showing them to the public." After all, contemporary art is still led by white, middle-aged and very wealthy men, who are certainly not interested in artworks that convey boundless emotional expression. And I am particularly interested in what's rejected.

Kat and Annette: *Let's talk about your project La Vie en Rose—what do you think sets apart what you do from what, for example, Susan Sontag was doing to examine what people do when faced with other people's pain? Is there anything particular about networked photography or photography shared on the internet that is different from, for example, analogue photography?*

Cristina: In her book "Regarding the Pain of Others," Susan Sontag thoroughly examines all aspects of our relationship to photographs, mainly in the area of photojournalism that depict excruciating pain and suffering caused by war or other kinds of violence, usually in faraway places. She doesn't establish differences between analogue/digital or printed/networked images. Even if my work is about another kind of pain, emotional pain, most of her thoughts can be applied to my practice as well, because she is studying human reactions to the expression of suffering.

During in the second half of the 20th century, humans have experienced so many shocking images via photojournalism, and somehow have gotten used to them. Today, online, some people seem to need to display intimate images of a closer pain, the emotional pain everyone has to face, one moment or other, in life, and which can become even more unbearable to others, because you cannot avoid seeing yourself in them.

As Sontag wrote: "uglifying, showing something at its worst, is a more modern function: didactic, it invites an active response. For photographs to accuse, and possibly to alter conduct, they must shock." This statement applies to my work very well. If we have got used to shocking images of war (it is perceived as far away from us, cannot happen to us), then, in order to shock, we need to share emotional pain, which usually means having experienced rejection.

I once displayed my Higher Self series—of people expressing difficult emotions in the studio—in a "Portfolio Promenade" in a Birmingham Photography Festival. People strolled by the tables as if strolling by the seaside, probably to have a nice pleasant moment looking at beautiful images. Most people, who approached my table rushed off to the next one, turning their faces to avoid seeing too much. Only two people in three hours stopped by, and stayed for the whole afternoon, talking to me.

Figure 17.3: Higher Self Portrait. Source: Christina Nuñez.

Kat and Annette: *Do you think the internet has any particular affordances for expressing pain, but also for meeting or rejecting other people's pain? And if it does, what would be the best metaphor to describe it?*

Cristina: If you publish personal emotional images on your Facebook wall, people will comment, trying to cheer you up, or claim that you shouldn't be posting things like that there. If you post those same images on a Net Art platform, giving it an aesthetic frame, you get seen less, people find it hard to comment, but the artistic medium tells the viewer that this is an art project with a concept and a purpose. So, if the artist is expressing emotions, the viewer knows that there is a purpose, that this makes sense. In my case, I use my real life, my pain, my desires, so there is a strange situation: this is art, but this is also real life.

I recently showed an excerpt of my project *La Vie en Rose*, of myself in a real moment of deep despair, at an event, and asked for open critique, as this is part of my PhD work. Most of the immediate reactions were extremely critical, almost aggressively so, but after the event, several people came to congratulate me. The critique called my work banal, claimed it didn't touch, or that I should only present myself as empowered and never a victim. Yet, this critique came from a place of some sort of stimulation, as one of my critics said, "it was disturbing to see things that she would never ever show to others."

This is extremely interesting, because I have recently realized that the unconscious aim of my work is to make conflicts emerge. Conflicts become power relationships, and some people, when you show them extreme vulnerability, they will attack. I have a hunch that my work could function as a very quick way to spot people, who have power strategies in relationships and, who cannot cope with feeling vulnerable. This means that it can be quite explosive, but if well used, a powerful tool for social activism.

CHAPTER EIGHTEEN

Trans-constituting Place Online

KATIE WARFIELD

> *"I feel like I'm trying to cling to a wet slippery fish that is wriggling to return to the water."*
> (Annette Markham, *Life Online*, p. 19)

I love this sloppy wet and tactile metaphor. Perhaps above anything in *Life Online*, I love most the messy material and affective anecdotes that Markham includes in her rich ethnography: Chinese food boxes splayed in her office, what Terri Senft describes as "computer butt" after eight hours in front of a screen, the physical discomfort of waiting for a response from an awkward interview subject, the tossing and catching of virtual balls and eating of virtual ice creams. I like so much these material-affective descriptions because after working with young people who share images of their bodies on social media platforms, I see the same importance of the metaphors of *place* and *being*—what I'm aligning with *matter* and *affect*—even today, 20 years later online. And the thing that perhaps holds most true to me is not the distinctiveness of concepts of place and being, but rather their messy, slippery, wet and entangled nature. Being online is not a matter of hard edges and clear boundaries; it's a matter of slippery squishiness, boundary and border traversing, entanglement and chaos, inversions and instability. And that's probably why I love it so freaking much.

I'm inspired by so much in *Life Online* that writing this paper was like trying to wrestle with a theoretical jellyfish, as Justin Lewis (1991) calls it. Keeping the theme of slipperiness and jellyfish in mind, I wanted to focus on one oily concept in this chapter: I want to talk about *place* in particular and in relation to *tools* and *ways of being*. I want to pick up on Markham's metaphor of *place*, adopted by herself and her participants, to describe *being online*. I want to splatter my slippery chapter here onto her metaphor of place. I want to moisten the categorical edges of the seemingly distinct categories of place, tools and ways of being—the three dominant metaphors in her book—and discuss how, with the groups of young people I've worked with over the past few years of studying self-presentation online (what I prefer to call *selves*-presentation), the internet, when it comes to social media, *becomes place* via an entanglement of social media *tools* and *ways of being*. I'm not saying, straightforwardly, that place = tools + ways of being. To me, these concepts are not *co-constituted*, rather they are, to be cheeky, *trans-constituted*. In other words, *place*, *tools*, and *ways of being* are all entangled and inseparable and become (momentarily) within given radically unique situated moments.

Why *trans*-constituted instead of *co*-constituted? I'm not saying that the notion of co-constitution is wrong or incomplete. Rather, trans is my preference, and I see the prefix trans as doing two things: first it points to an ontological shift in our orientation to studying digital subjectivities or *ways of being online*. Second, it points to the theoretical territory of transgeographies, which I want to suggest in this piece, constitutes an important field that informs social media studies broadly.

First, the prefix *trans* points to an ontological reorientation (not my own, but carried on the tongues of indigenous scholars, queer theorists, and most recently feminist new materialists[1]) in thinking about digital subjectivities. It is best understood in contrast to the typical prefix of 'co,' which signifies coming together, mutuality and sharing. To me, there is a kindness to co-interactions. As has been examined and explored by many theorists, when young people interact online, the process is messy, complex, bumpy and perennially in a state of becoming. The concepts of place, tools, and ways of being do not come together in equal measure across cases, and they do not remain static and fixed concepts across platforms and over time. The prefix trans signifies moving across, moving beyond, and reaching on the far side of conceptual categories to push and query their boundaries and ontological edges and fixity. Tools, places, and ways of being are *a priori* entangled and they *become*, momentarily, out of the innumerable complex forces that make up contextually specific moments. Trans rejects clear and static categories and sociological equations of how things come to be online, and instead focuses on the more slippery, varying, and complex processes of *becoming online*. Could this prefix also be a political provocation? Sure: what I'm suggesting is that the processes involved

1 By feminist new materialists I refer to the core theorists of Karen Barad, Rosi Braidotti, Deleuze and Guattari, and Donna Haraway who among other goals, ontologically orient towards queries of becoming above questions of being. For an overview see Introduction chapter in R.-J. Ringrose, Warfield, K., and S. Hassan-Zarabadi (2018).

in becoming online are not straight (forward), cis-, or fixed. Becoming online is fundamentally queer.

Second, the prefix trans emphasizes concepts emerging from transgender theory broadly, and more specifically in this piece, *the becoming* of place online. Transgeographies places special consideration on the lived embodied experiences of space and place, often via narratives, of transgender and gender non-conforming people (Browne, 2006). Although transgeographies mostly narrates the experiences of physical built spaces (cities, streets, malls, etc.), the narratives of my various participants on various projects often described being online as Annette Markham's participants did more than 20 years ago—as if it were a *built space*. Participants would use various terms to connote this, such as a "safe place" or "a home" or equally in more conflicted situations "a place I don't want to be" or a "hostile environment."

In what follows, I first clarify the concept of transgeographies in thinking about the becoming of selves online. I then draw quotes, interactions, observations from five years of studies with women, men, trans and gender non-conforming young people I've worked with in various capacities to show the parallels between offline studies of transgeographies and online experiences of youth from my research. The empirical work I draw from in this paper also moves beyond categories as I will draw on three different empirical studies I've conducted: a phenomenological study of young women and selfies; a questionnaire to trans and gender non-conforming people on Tumblr; and a co-writing project with my friend and trans activist Courtney Demone. I weave slippery empirical narratives to show how the experiences of my participants working in and through social media places are extremely similar to the experiences of trans folks working in and through the built spaces within transgeographies. I suggest that the field of transgeographies, can help scholars grapple with, not just how trans and gender non-conforming people become, unfold, and unfurl their multiple and changing ways of being online, but also how all sorts of people of varying intersectional identities become, in similar ways, online.

Transgeographies, as a field, offers much to the intersections of social media, gender, identity, and experiences of space and place. Broadly speaking, transgeographies emphasize the importance of examining the material and experiential relational shaping of bodies, space, and environments for transgender and gender non-conforming people (Browne et al., 2007; Doan, 2010; Hines, 2007; Nash, 2010). Transgeographies emerges from trans theory but is not simply interested in the experience of trans people in space but more broadly in the material-affective interactions of the becoming of gender, bodies, and space. Transgeographies is not simply interested in representations and social construction, but "also in the *real* fleshy lived materialities of bodies" (Johnson, 2015, p. 5), where the autobiographies or auto-ethnographies become the complex narratives fulcrums of the becoming of selves and bodies, within varying spaces and audiences, among varying discursive forces. Among many of its other benefits, transgeographies theory bolsters the importance not only or primarily of the discourses that operate in *places* online, but also the *materiality* of built place (in social media contexts, the affordances and interface) and the *affective registers* or visceral bodily feelings that run through and are entangled in places, both online and offline. This could be beneficially applied to the study of any way of being online.

In an autobiography of her embodied experiences of different public spaces while transitioning, Petra Doan (2010) explains that for her, "the experiences of particular situations that we obtain through our bodies both shape and are shaped by the public and private spaces in which they occur" (p. 638). Similar to what has been proposed by Elizabeth Grosz (1995) in regards to feminist spatial theory, transgeographies argues subjectivity involves a mutually constitutive relationship among bodies and environments. Transgeographies draws on the work of feminist phenomenologists (Alcott, 2006; Stoller, 2000) to propose that embodied experience is both natural and cultural as opposed to predominantly cultural as post-structuralism might propose. What is important is the epistemological validation of the importance of the felt and embodied experience of gender (Browne et al., 2007). This is why phenomenologically informed narratives and first-person accounts of gender experience are so valuable for transgeographies, and also why, more particularly, the first-person accounts of people's embodied experiences in place and space, are of central importance (Nash & Bain, 2007). These narratives, then, often reveal the discursive negotiations of gender, the personal experiences in and against public spaces, and the embodied affective experiences in those places.

I find this attention to at once the discursive and material forces, and the felt/affective sense of self really important in observing the construction of selves in online spaces. In my early studies of young women and selfies, I was fascinated by the embodied indicators used by young women in the process of assessing, critiquing, editing, and selecting "good" selfies. Some choices seemed to be clearly discursive: many young women tossed out photos that didn't present themselves as what they determined to be beautiful, pretty, or thin. Some choices seemed clearly material: a technological glitch like poor lighting or a blurry photo was rejected while equally good lighting and a nice material background were celebrated qualities. But there was also an embodied and affective register to the selection of a good selfie. The self that was to be shared online had to have an "a-ha" quality. Something punctum-like, to refer to Barthes, something that seemed pre-reflective. Those photos that did not have that quality were described as "cringy" or "icky" and often immediately deleted. Those photos that did have the proper affective value were celebrated with "YES!" or, as one girl exclaimed: "This is it! This is GOLDEN." As much as I tried to explore and find the clear edges of what determined this illusive perfect selfie for these participants, I could not. But I would describe it as this. It was not recognition that the self on the photo was a good and separate representation of the person photographed. Rather it was a moment wherein the photo became affectively relevant. It was a moment where the photo gained a sort of prosthetic opening and connection to the participant's sense of self. And it was that affective connection and entanglement that permitted the photo to be shared and released on social networks as a proper representation of the participants momentary sense of self.

On top of this, the process of the becoming of the selfie was also a fascinating negotiation among these various forces that revealed the becoming of and challenging of boundaries in the becoming of digital representations of the self in different places online. For instance, I'm thinking of a woman I'm working with, with whom I sat as she moved from preparing a photo for Snapchat versus Instagram. She had originally planned to take a photo for Instagram and in the process would reflect on her image, play with her hair, fix an eyebrow, toggle back to other photos she'd recently posted on Instagram, return to her process of image taking and continue to curate her look. She took a few photos before I asked her if she would post the same image to snapchat. "Oh, no way" she said. I asked her if she would take a photo for Snapchat for me. Immediately she changed the style of her hair. Making it a bit messy. She looked over her shoulder at her position in the room. She chose to lay down against a desk as if she was in class and bored. She played around with much more goofy facial expressions: fatigue, boredom, sticking out her tongue. "On Snapchat I'm more casual" she said. "You can post anything to Snapchat. You don't have to be perfect." The curation was just as involved in her Snapchat production but the form and expression of self was of a completely different style than for other platforms. The medium, the platform, the space shaped her becoming through the image production. It wasn't a matter of one or another of herself she was photographing being more or less authentically her. It was a matter that the material (platform, lighting, position, body), discursive (performance of self, performance of gender), and affective forces (humor, feeling) coming into play through the pinhole lens of the camera were different in this particular moment than in the one a few moments back.

Following this complex entanglement of discursive, material and affective forces, within transgeographies, gender expression, and subjectivity broadly, is also importantly spatially and temporally situated. Agency is delocalized and dispersed. Rather than space affecting gender expression uni-directionally, and rather than people shaping the collective experience of space in a given environment uni-directionally, "the performance of gender in space not only shifts with each performance, but in a very real way each performance also changes the space in which it is performed" (Browne, 2006). It is important to note that in this encounter with space, gender identity doesn't shift, but gender expression does wherein some built spaces enable an expression of both gender identity and desired gender expression and some spaces may disable expressions regarding one, both or the desired relationality between (Doan, 2010). In short, place can enable or disable being. And beings seek out other beings' interests, values or ways of being, and in turn shape and create places in order to collectively be.

Recent research in Internet studies has shown how online identities are modulated (AKA identity modulation) according to and along with the platform affordances on a given social media site (Duguay, 2017). Speaking specifically about the ways LGBTQ social media users negotiate the intensity and visibility of certain aspects of their identity online, Duguay suggests that such negotiation is at once a matter of personal self-disclosure via communication and the manipulation of a platform's affordances. Identity modulation has been illustrated by the increasing number of studies specifically on Tumblr to show how the specific platform affordances—either intentionally or unintentionally designed (Wittkower, 2016)—permit a creatively malleable environment for trans people to productively express themselves.

Within my own work I remember noticing this with a cohort of trans and gender non-conforming people I worked with on Tumblr. When I asked them to describe what it was specifically about Tumblr that made it a better place to share images of themselves online, people revealed the complexities of negotiating the visibility of certain parts of their selves in certain places above others. One participant said that certain people on Facebook and Twitter didn't know that they were trans but on Snapchat and Tumblr they don't have to worry about people like conservative relatives and friends they may know and come to face in offline spaces. The platform culture that has emerged on Tumblr seemed to encourage the becoming of diverse ways of being for this cohort of trans and gender non-conforming people. Further to this, the fostering of more ways of being encourages the space to grow as a "safe space" of sharing diverse ways of being. Another participant said, "I post selfies on tumblr a lot though because it helps me feel connected to other users as a person, and it's an ego boost if I get a lot of notes, and I feel like I can be more authentic and attention seeking with mostly strangers rather than people I know irl. It's also just part of the culture of the website." In comparison to other platforms, another participant suggested Tumblr as a place they need now in becoming their identity—that the people and place serve specific needs in terms of their situated subjectivity at that moment in time: "The reason why I take selfies has a lot to do with accepting myself in what body I'm in, and I really only want to share that journey with other trans people … tumblr is where I can access a network of other transgender people. I'm not really interested in showing a network of 'real-life' friends that part of my journey right now."

Further, gender expression is not only *modulated* alongside space, but it is also deeply influenced by the observers, audiences, and communities within a given space: "I recognize that my gender performance is simultaneously modulated by the observers of my gender as well as the spaces in which we interact. These modulations do not shift my own sense of gender, but they do shape the visibility and impact of my gender performance" (Doan, 2010, p. 648). Here it is important to note that the forces through which identities are enabled and disabled offline in built spaces and online are often through a combination of discursive and affective intensities. Actions such as 'gender policing' occur when "gender enforcers" call out an individual's non-conforming gender expression and "then act to sanction that violation in as public a fashion as possible" (Doan, 2010, p. 640). This public shaming operates along discursive gender norms and affective registers where affect is seen as "visceral forces beneath, alongside, or generally other than conscious knowing, vital forces insisting beyond emotion—that can serve to drive us toward movement" (Gregg & Seigworth, 2010, p. 1). Affect in this case can also work against movement or to restrict action of movement, as in the case of gender policing where the "gender outlaw" is made to emotionally suffer as a result of their normative gender transgressions.

This has also been proven to be true in studies of online communities where people strategically make public or private certain aspects of their identities based on the imagined or real audiences online (Livingstone, 2008; Marwick & boyd, 2010;). Several scholars have examined how the more public and the larger the audience an individual has on a social network, the less personal and intimate people's posts tend to be (e.g., Papacharissi, 2011). Jean Burgess (2006) uses the term "vernacular creativity" to describe the everyday practices people adopt to craft and shape their self-expressions in creative and playful ways. What runs through all these creative processes of self-disclose is a thread of affect or also the underlying affectively-influenced reasoning where these vernacular artists disclose and safeguard parts of their identity because of the fear of reactions by imagined audiences.

I most clearly listened to the experiences of violent gender policing when I co-wrote a book chapter with my friend and trans-activist Courtney Demone. Courtney gained wide-spread viral celebrity when, in 2015, she decided to share a series of topless photos of herself on Instagram to see when the platform would censor her breasts—at once deeming her to "pass" as female but also invisibilizing her chest as therefore sexual and pornographic. Although this was the popularized story, her coming out story is a complex and ongoing series of online and offline deeply embodied experiences of becoming. Courtney posted a coming out video to YouTube in 2013, a process she said was extremely scary because it was "as if she was sharing a piece of herself with the world." The video garnered critical reception in the comments section and was subsequently copied illegally from YouTube and shared on 8chan, a platform that is notoriously hostile towards trans, gender non-conforming, queer people and people of color. When Courtney and I wrote her narrative, the slippery boundaries between online violence and offline confidence and psychological trauma were invisible. The comments on 8chan forced her to take down and police her own coming out video on YouTube. Subsequently she carefully negotiated which platforms to share images of herself, saying she never trusted a given platform was a safe place. Similarly, she told me about first coming out in public and walking the streets of Victoria in a dress and makeup her girlfriend had helped her prepare. She narrated how she had to negotiate which streets were safe or not and which streets were too visible with too many gazing pedestrians. She used very similar language when describing the slow processes of coming out online: choosing certain venues over others on specific platforms. Once those platforms seemed safe, she moved to what she felt to be more visible and public platforms. I am constantly intrigued by the similarities with which online and offline places, ways of being, and tools are negotiated.

This chapter is not intended to prove that transgeographies is a field of inquiry for all aspects of social media studies. What transgeographies does offer, and what the prefix trans orients us towards, is the study of the complex processes of becoming without losing ourselves in a desire to clearly see, and normatively establish, what "being online" is all about. There are just as many ways of being online as there are beings online. Studying ways of being is studying a very slippery jellyfish. An orientation to becoming turns our gaze sideways. It queers our gaze. It looks less at the people and more at the processes in play by which beings become online. These forces include material forces like online affordances and offline built environments. These forces include discursive forces, which may be those related to gender, race, sexuality, ability, class, age and more. These forces may also be affective and relate to radically unique bodily resonances we experience in technologically mediated encounters. An orientation to trans-constitution is an orientation to all these forces. It's an orientation towards complexity and movement. It's an orientation towards the beauty inherent in all of our processes of becoming.

SECTION 5

Ways of Being With

CHAPTER NINETEEN

Facebook as a Wormhole between Life and Death

TOBIAS RAUN

I interviewed Camilla[1] on a Thursday afternoon in her home in a small town of Denmark. She had just come home from her job as a sales assistant, and greeted me with her partner in their single-family house. Camilla and I went into the living room to talk while her partner started preparing dinner. I explained to her that my research was an exploration of what mourning online is like for people, prompted by my own experience of loss and sporadic postings about it on Facebook. I had made a publicly visible request about looking for participants who had actively used Facebook as part of their mourning process, and a mutual acquaintance had shared this information with Camilla.

Even though Camilla had not been interviewed before and my explanation of the process seems fumbling and overly pedagogical to me now as I listen to the recording, it was not difficult for us to find rapport. Camilla opened up immediately, and started talking about her mother's death three years ago, followed only two years later by Camilla's sister's death. They had both abused alcohol and Camilla's mother had suffered from COPD.[2] Camilla's sister's eating disorder-related illness had escalated when their mother died: "She just couldn't come to

1 Camilla is not her real name, but a name I chose for her among the twenty most popular names in Denmark. She is in her thirties. The interview was conducted on March 26, 2015.

2 Chronic Obstructive Pulmonary Disease. An umbrella term for lung diseases where one for instance has difficulty breathing due to long term smoking.

terms with her death."[3] Camilla herself was especially affected by the death of her sister as they had a very close relationship where they "confided in each other—told each other everything."

In the aftermath of her sister's death, Facebook became an immensely valuable resource for Camilla. Specifically, her sister's Facebook page. "I feel closer to her when I'm writing on her wall," she had told me in an email exchange before our in-person conversation. During the interview, she elaborated:

Camilla: When I'm sitting and looking at my sister's profile or writing something, I feel closer to her than when I'm at her gravesite.

Tobias: So, in a way Facebook feels more like her gravesite to you than her actual gravesite?

Camilla: Yeah, or more like her. That's at least how I feel. With my mother, I feel close to her at the gravesite.[4] When I am there, I'm like, that's mum! Because with her I cannot log onto Facebook and see pictures of her or … But with my sister I feel closer to her when I'm on Facebook.

I was intrigued, yet puzzled by the way she repeatedly emphasized and privileged Facebook as a channel to connect with her deceased sister. I wondered what this feeling of—or psycho-emotional investments in—Facebook as a telepathic or metaphysical dimensionality entailed. What might Camilla teach me as a media scholar about current experiences of being online, about mourning, and contemporary understandings of communication across the threshold of the living and the dead, bodies and machines? I set out to pursue these questions inspired by Annette Markham's early work *Life Online: Researching Real Experience in Virtual Space* (1998). What Markham explores in this self-reflexive ethnographic book is what it feels like to be online in the early days of the internet, offering a set of metaphors to describe the experiences of the interviewees. Clearly, many things have changed since Markham conducted her studies. What metaphors are most relevant in relation to the evolving practice of mourning with or through social media as described by Camilla?

It is broadly accepted among scholars of communication that internet has become ubiquitous for most people in the Global North. It is something we live in and with (Deuze, 2011, p. 138; Hepp, Hjarvard, & Lundby, 2015, p. 319); or as Markham presaged—a way of being. Within a life lived with/in this ubiquity, the metaphors of tool and place still have a lot of explanatory power. However, Camilla's persistent talk about getting "closer" to her sister through Facebook also

3 This quote and all the following are from the interview I conducted with Camilla. It is also my translation from Danish in this and all the following quotes.

4 For an investigation of online mourners sharing of photographs of the grave site see Raun (2018).

suggest that a feeling of presence beyond the grave is an essential part of her experience. I argue that this goes beyond the metaphors of tool and place. Facebook hereby becomes something else and more—it becomes a wormhole.

A TOOL FOR CATHARSIS

The metaphor of the internet as tool is described by Markham (1998) as focusing on "information transfer" (p. 145). When we think of the internet as a tool, we think of it as a communication medium that facilitates interaction and is thus comparable to other kinds of media (telephone, writing a letter, etc.). It "can extend one's reach, expand the senses, and collapse distance by decreasing the time it takes to get from point A to point B" (Markham, 2003, p. 3). In sum, the internet "extends our physical capacities" (Markham, 1998, p. 213). But does it also extend our physical existence? Reading Markham's early work, I cannot help but think that it presupposes living, breathing human beings. In recent years, we've seen more and more services for post-mortem digital interaction emerge,[5] and more and more people using the internet to connect with their deceased loved ones (e.g. Bell et al., 2015; Christensen & Sandvik, 2015; Kasket, 2012, 2019). The internet has become a tool for creating one's afterlife. In this vein, Camilla uses Facebook as a tool to communicate with her sister, as a medium that transfers her thoughts and feelings to her. According to Camilla, Facebook renders other kinds of communication channels redundant. In the aftermath of her sister's death, Camilla underwent therapy, where her psychologist asked her to write a letter to her sister as part of her grieving process, but as Camilla tells me: "But, that's what Facebook is for! It's not necessary to write her a letter." When I ask her if she has engaged in diary writing she replies: "That's where I have used Facebook, to get it out." Hence, for Camilla, Facebook works as a tool for interaction beyond the grave and for cathartic release:

> *I just feel that you get it all out, that you are alleviated somehow when you write in there [Facebook], ahhhhhh, I mean then you get it out instead of just keeping it inside all the time. Ahhh now it's out [she draws a sigh of relief and makes a bodily gesture of being unburdened.] It may sound stupid but it's like a compulsion … it's a relief—it sounds silly, but it is a relief.*

5 These websites and internet apps designed for users to plan and prepare for future digital interactions that will occur after their death is the focus of Paula Kiel's PhD study. As stated: "digital platforms such as www.deadsoci.al, www.lifenaut.com and www.liveson.org, open up new possibilities for post-mortem forms of interaction that potentially allow an active participation of the dead through digital media. For example, by allowing the dead to "send" emails, "post" on social media networking sites and even "engage" in conversations" (Kiel, 2016). See also Kiel's *TED Talk*: https://www.youtube.com/watch?v=zfQBCi-6d3E

Camilla's perception and use of Facebook have changed after the death of her sister. She tells me that she did not spend much time checking and posting things on Facebook before, and that she initially thought of it as shallow and unimportant: "Well, Facebook was just Facebook to me before." In line with broader cultural discourses around Facebook, she thought of it as a broadcasting channel for insignificant and self-centered trivialities. But this all changed when her sister died. She is surprised by her own shifted perception—and not least use, as she did not anticipate that Facebook would be such an important and crucial channel of communication with her sister:

> *I didn't believe that I could use Facebook for that. I didn't think that I would. But it has just come automatically, somehow, I think .... err, I have never thought about it as a possibility before—not at all.*

She is now spending much more time on Facebook, visiting her sister's profile page almost daily, checking her pictures, and if anybody has written on the page. She tells me that she usually writes to her sister from her own profile, tagging her, but if she has a "personal" message for her sister, she writes on her sister's wall. When she is having a hard time or the loss feels unbearable, she writes on her sister's wall. In other words, Facebook is immensely valuable to her. Even if some might find it strange that a dead woman's profile has a post-mortal life of its own, constantly reminding the extended network of friends about her birthday and posts that she 'liked' years ago, Camilla is reluctant to shut down her sister's account. At the time of the interview (March 2015) Facebook had publicized the option of memorializing profiles of deceased people (launched in February 2015 in the US), but it was not launched in Denmark until the summer of 2015. When we spoke, Camilla seemed to welcome the idea of turning her sister's profile into a memorial page, but confessed to being afraid to make changes in the settings, lest things would disappear or continued interaction would be impossible. She was especially worried about the possible loss of her sister's images.

A WORMHOLE

Beyond a tool for catharsis, Facebook also offers Camilla a place where to meet and talk to her sister. Camilla's persistent use of a speaking "I" that addresses a "you" in her posts indicates that for her, Facebook is more than just a one-way broadcasting channel.

Camilla: I feel that I get to talk to her openly [on Facebook] when I write something, contrary to when I talk to her on my own where it takes place in my head.

Tobias: And what does this openness entail or do?

Camilla: I feel that she listens more somehow. I feel that she can hear or see it in one way or another. That's what I feel. My use of Facebook enables me to get in touch—or to have contact with her, not least because I can see her [because of the photographs of her on her profile]. That's not possible here [offline], well, yes, sort of, but not in the same way. So, it's more open—she can hear me, whereas here it's closed.

Tobias: So here [offline] it is more a conversation with yourself?

Camilla: Yes, yes, with myself, yes, it's more just me, whereas Facebook, that's where I can talk with her—out loud, where I feel that she's going to see this—and she can hear me.

Camilla experiences Facebook as a place where she goes to be—or communicate—with her sister. She describes Facebook as an "open" communication channel, whereas talking with her sister offline, in her head, is closed. Her use of the words "open" and "closed" seems to describe the level of interaction or dialogue made possible between her and her sister. And yet, "open" also suggest the ability to access a liminal space between life and death that the sisters can co-inhabit. When talking with Camilla I get the sense that she experiences Facebook as a kind of telepathic channel that allows access to alternative dimensions of time, space, and affects. A metaphysical tool-place. A wormhole.

Camilla's use of Facebook to speak with the dead resonates with a longer history where the advent of new technologies is interlinked with a desire for and belief in contact with the afterlife, propelled by the invisible, immaterial, spherical essence of electricity and with it, wireless communication. Media such as the telegraph, the telephone and radio were believed to bring messages from the afterlife (Sconce, 2000). Similarly, the experience of looking at a photograph or watching a film has frequently been described as watching and being watched by specters (Barthes, 1981; Derrida & Stiegler, 2002). In that respect, the "ghost […] has always occupied an important place within the machine" (Blanco & Peeren, 2013, p. 201).

SCROLLING BACK AS LIFE SUPPORT

According to Camilla, Facebook offers a unique connection with her sister. She has virtually lit a candle for her mother and her sister on Mindet.dk[6] [memory in Danish]. But the experience is different:

6 Mindet.dk is a website designed specifically for mourning. It is described by Christensen and Sandvik as: "On this website, participants perform their grief by designing online memory spaces for their loved one(s), displaying photographs, poetry, stories, and expressions of grief and longing. They mark red letter days and difficult times by lighting online candles for their child and they express empathy for others by lighting the same kind of candles for other people's loved ones" (Christensen and Sandvik, 2015, p. 58).

> *[Mindet.dk] helps me, as I am giving them this candle, but I don't in any way get closer to them, not at all, nothing like Facebook. Facebook is something else because, again, there are pictures of her [name of the sister]. She was [interrupts herself]—this one was her profile.*

Other sites might help Camilla with her grieving process, but they do not facilitate contact. Facebook is the place where Camilla feels her sister's presence the most, which both enables and intensifies the sense of being co-present or in conversation with her. Although her sister might not literally respond to her posts, it nevertheless feels as if she is present. It is this feeling of her presence that give rise to a feeling of closeness.

In *Life Online* Markham also touched upon a sense of presence, quoting interviewee Scooter who states how the Internet makes him feel "connected to something outside myself" (Markham, 1998, p. 16). Questions of presence center on the complex ways in which people feel—or don't feel—that life online is real. Markham elaborated on her own feelings of co-presence with other users—of being there, despite the obstacles and poor quality of the interface (codes and commands). A feeling of presence arises from the interactivity with other users and automated systems, from people typing themselves into being in a co-existing here-and-now (op. cit., pp. 89–114). As the internet becomes more ubiquitous and more mundane, it feels less like an alternative space we can escape to, and more like an everyday mode of self-presentation and sociality that we are constantly requested or even pressured to partake in. Furthermore, it is less a text-driven internet, characterized by disembodiment and identity-play, where "one can be anyone or anything simply by describing oneself through words and names" (op. cit., p. 35), but more a visually-driven internet with an increasing demand to cross-check, authorize and match the profile to an offline identity. It seems to be exactly this ubiquitous everydayness of Facebook, the integration of profile to a formal identity that holds the promise of connecting Camilla with her sister. It is through the huge amount of 'digital dust' left by her sister on Facebook, that Camilla feels her sister's presence.

The affordances and use of the Facebook Timeline play an important part herein. Facebook has retroactively organized Camilla's sister's status updates and photos into a narrative biography (Van Dijck, 2013, p. 204). Camilla emphasizes the importance of photographs, but not in and of themselves. Rather it is the dynamic context of the Facebook timeline—the text her sister anchored them in, the comments from her extended network of friends, the time, date and place of upload registered by the automated systems—that is essential for the feeling of presence, closeness or 'thereness'. Her sister's timeline hereby functions as a 'life support', keeping her alive as if she were in a coma. This is why Camilla cannot close her sister's account. It is not enough just to download the photographs (which she has already done). They need to be there, in this particular context, where the sister herself has told, shared and recorded her life. It is the ability to scroll back through her sister's Timeline that contributes to Camilla's sense of presence. For Camilla, scrolling back brings the past to the now, those who are gone to the present.

CELESTIAL PRESENCE

The metaphor of tool and place do not quite capture what seems to be at the core of Camilla's experiences. What I want to forefront is Camilla's feeling of her sister's celestial presence in her Facebook profile. Facebook is more than a place—it works as a kind of wormhole, allowing her to access a universe of its own with her sister. Facebook is also more than a tool of representing someone who is not physically present (Markham, 2003, p. 4), but rather "*is her*." It is this sense of vibrant co-presence that is most important to Camilla in her use of Facebook to mourn her sister:

Camilla: What is important to me is that I feel that I talk to my sister when I'm writing to her [...] So the response from other people doesn't mean anything to me [...] Well, it is sweet that people post a heart and tell me that they are thinking of me. It's nice of them and all that. But that's not the reason why I write—NOT AT ALL [...] Again, when I write to her I don't think about the fact that others are also able to see it. I don't feel that's the case.

Tobias: So, you kind of feel that it is a private space that the two of you have?

Camilla: Yes

Tobias: Even though you know that [Camilla interrupts me]

Camilla: Yes, that there are others, who are able to see it. I just feel that I'm close to her when I'm there. Then it's just me and her, right? Also because I can see that there aren't any others who post on her profile besides from when she just died [...] So somehow I feel that it's just me and her together in there.[7]

Camilla is not alone with these experiences. (see also Bell et al., 2015; Kasket, 2012, 2019). Kasket's (2012) study on the so-called 'In memory of ...' groups on Facebook concludes that some people experience the platform as "a particularly *effective* way of communicating with and feeling close to the deceased person, more so than graveyard visits, visits to the home, thinking thoughts, or writing letters" (p. 66). Like Camilla, several of the people in Kasket's study explicitly express a

7 Camilla underscores Facebook as a facilitator of intimacy and exclusivity between her and her sister while others in my study express a hyper awareness about the overhearing audience and describe online mourning as impression management; a difficult balancing act between sharing but not oversharing (see Raun, 2017).

belief that the dead are receiving the messages (op. cit., p. 65, Kasket, 2019, p. 56). Kasket therefore calls Facebook 'a medium' or a 'mediator deathworker': "just as they [the mourners] use it as a channel for information transmission in life, people use it to channel information to their dead friends, often believing that their communications are getting through to the person—no crystal balls or séance required" (Kasket, 2012, p. 68). However, what is particularly interesting in Camilla's case is the strong feeling of being co-present with her sister on Facebook. This makes closing her sister's profile unthinkable: "I feel that if I erase her from there, then she will be gone—completely gone." Deleting the account with all the digital traces of her existence, enabling Camilla to presence her, would be her death a second time around.

CHAPTER TWENTY

A Vigil for Some Bodies

XTINE BURROUGH

Each year since 2015, media artist xtine burrough hires Mechanical Turk workers to remember a lost loved one on All Hallow's Eve. Workers are paid twenty-five cents (US), the same price offered in cathedrals around the world to light a candle in prayer or remembrance of loved ones. In her interventions on Amazon.com's Mechanical Turk virtual job platform, she transforms the tool into a place to be human. The following is a 9-image excerpt from an ongoing portfolio of artworks entitled, "A Vigil for Some Bodies" (burrough, 2016)..

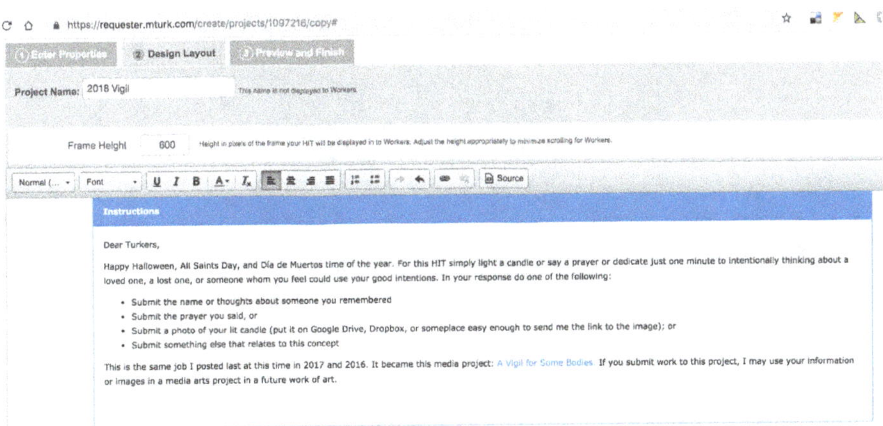

Figure 20.1: Workers are hired to remember someone they love in burrough's Human Intelligent Task (HIT) on Mturk.com. Source: xtine burrough

I want to say a prayer for my dad who has been gone for too long now. God bless him. I hope you are out of that wheelchair and walking around smiling and looking down on us. You never got to meet your granddaughter, but I hope you are watching over her. I miss you like crazy. You were taken way too young. I love you. Guide and protect me and my family. Love you so much Daddy. Amen.

I want to say "Brother I love you so much. When we were children you hated me so much and never wanted to talk to me again. But I wanted to reconcile with you at any cost. The time never came. Rather you died in accident. On that day, I was shattered. I don't think I am fine even now. I am still broken even after 4 years. I want to talk to you at least once. Please"

I've been to so many funerals. I've lost so many family members and friends. I'm blessed to be here. I don't think about it all the time. This hit made me take a second to think about some of those I've lost. I said a prayer for them. Thanks for this.

Figure 20.2: burrough hires one hundred workers each year, and collects their memories as part of her All Hallow's Eve ritual. Hiring the workers to share a memory of a loved one gestures towards the workers' humanity beyond the barrier of the virtual platform. Source: xtine burrough

Figure 20.3: Memories shared by the virtual workers are then transformed from digital data to objects of remembrance. burrough modifies LED candles, purchased on Amazon, to bring the workers' memories to public spaces. Since the platform protects participant identities, she includes each worker's alphanumeric handle. Source: xtine burrough.

Figure 20.4: To conduct a vigil for the lives important to Mechanical Turk workers in a physical Amazon location, burrough brought these candles to an Amazon Fulfillment Center (AFC) in Coppell, Texas during her application for a position as a seasonal employee in November, 2015. Source: xtine burrough

Figure 20.5: Candles sitting atop the Amazon Fulfillment Center (DFW6) sign, Coppell, Texas. Source: xtine burrough

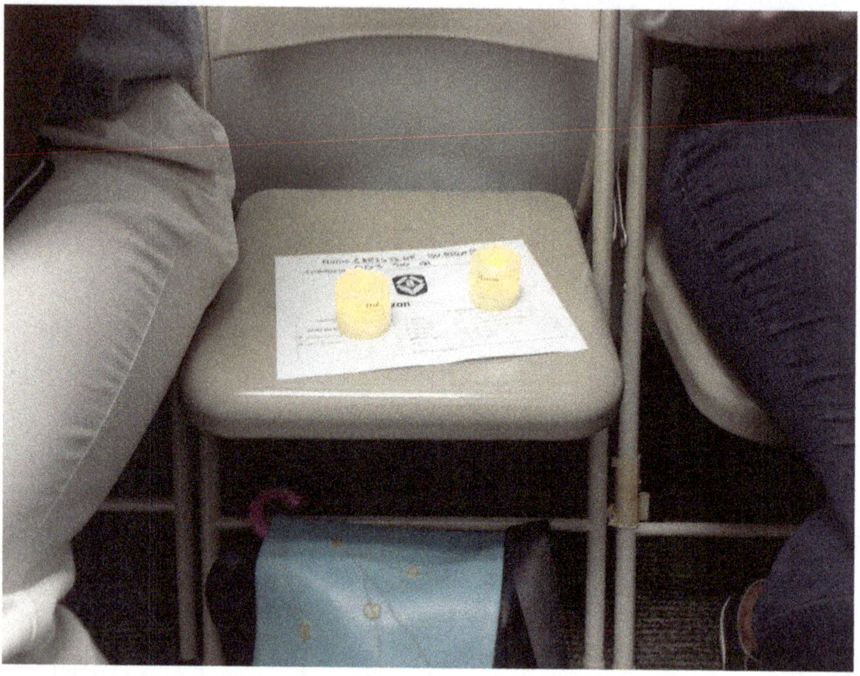

Figure 20.6: Waiting for the Drug Test, 2015, Amazon Fulfillment Center (DFW6), Coppell, Texas. Source: xtine burrough.

Figure 20.7: Taking the Drug Test, 2015, Amazon Fulfillment Center (DFW6), Coppell, Texas. Source: xtine burrough

Figure 20.8: One challenge to the intent of bringing this project to Amazon is extreme security measures in place at fulfillment center warehouses. Employees pass through a full body scanner on their way to work; bags are scanned and checked; and no phones or cameras are allowed inside. It was not possible to hold vigils in the AFCs as a warehouse worker. Instead, burrough commissioned UT Dallas Arts, Technology, and Emerging Communication MFA student Amanda Marder to construct a series of cardboard cubicles for an installation of the vigil first exhibited at the International Digital Media and Art (iDMAa) conference in October, 2016. Source: xtine burrough

Figure 20.9: A mid-shot of the installation, International Digital Media and Arts Association (iDMAa) Annual Conference Exhibit, Winona, MN, October 2016. Source: xtine burrough

CHAPTER TWENTY-ONE

Screenshooting Life Online: Two Artworks

SARAH SCHORR AND WINNIE SOON

Capture. Grab. Shoot. The terms associated with making a screenshot offer violent metaphorical associations. Markham's (1998, 2003) discussion of metaphors remind us how they function evocatively, highlighting certain aspects while limiting or obscuring our view of other aspects. In our own work, these violent terms fail to encapsulate the texture of working with screenshots as a practice in our everyday lives. Screen shooting can be gentler, slower, and a part of stitching together a pattern of parts, gesturing toward an idea. There is an inherent collaborative potential that goes along with the practice of remixing screen elements. There is also deep vulnerability associated with the knowledge that through deliberate or automated practices, one's life online is capturable. How does screen shooting as a sense making practice reflect life online and what is the distinct materiality of this mode of capture?

The internet could be thought of as a set of tools, but for reflective practitioners, tools are never simply instrumental, rather they are vessels for thought. In our artworks, we explore how a small tool associated with the internet era, the screenshot, becomes a generative sensemaking practice. Through making artworks with screenshots, one is able to follow the materials (Ingold, 2013) and reflect on the textured entanglement of humans and nonhumans. As Markham (2013) notes, certain "persistent characteristics of the internet" require or invite certain actions for doing things in the world, transforming "how we experience space, place and time, how we think about and enact the self, how we interact with others, and how we make sense of both local and global situations" (p. 283).

In the descriptions of our artworks below, we explore this idea. *Saving Screens: Temporary Tattoos and other Methods* (Schorr, 2019) considers the *screenshot* as a mode of thinking that expands the online reach of photographic arts practices. *Unerasable Images* (Soon, 2018) examines how the screenshot, operating within larger entanglements of techno-socio-political procedures, both generates and reflects varying worldviews emerging in the internet era. Through our artworks, we demonstrate how it may not make sense any longer to distinguish those tool and way of being aspects of the internet any longer, as they are inextricably linked for us.

SARAH SCHORR: *SAVING SCREENS: TEMPORARY TATTOOS AND OTHER METHODS*

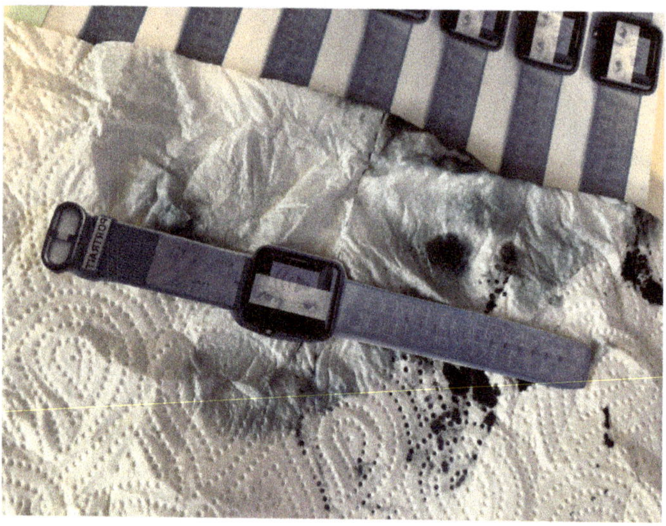

Figure 21.1: Collaging the digital remains of life online. Source: Sarah Schorr.

My father was a poet. His writing moved fluidly along an online and offline continuum. When he passed away, I was struck by how much his online life outlasted his physical presence. How does digital life continue after one's physical body dies? Markham (2003) writes that "technology does not hold a position as object outside the agency of the human. Rather, the categories are collapsed, to varying degrees (p. 10)." Through my artwork, *Saving Screens: Temporary Tattoos and other Methods,* I consider how this idea might manifest: If the categories of technology and agency of the human collapse, what remains when the physical body ceases to exist? How might the absence of a physical life highlight or uncover aspects of the nature of online life?

My father's online presence was an emanation, an extension of the way he thought entwined with how he existed in physical space. To explore and connect to his mutating online life, as well as the affective potential of my father's impressions and imprints, I collected these moments and pieced them together in temporary tattoos composed from photographic screenshot collages (cf. Figure 21.1).

Tobias Raun' (this volume) describes how a Facebook wall can channel the presence of the deceased. Similarly, through wearing the networked watch I inherited from my dad, I feel connected to his online presence. Creating and wearing these tattoos draws attention to the devices that we wear close to our skin and how the tactility is entwined with feeling connected (cf. Figure 21.2).

Figure 21.2: Sarah Schorr applies a tattoo to a visitor's skin during the exhibition opening at Galleri Image in Denmark. Source: Photograph by Mikkel Kaldal, Courtesy of Galleri Image 2019.

In this work, I examine the materiality of everyday life when the digital is interwoven, inextricable: Textures of physical devices leave residue, like stains on the cloth of one of my father's watch bands. The particular shapes and resolutions of the digital movements are captured in moments, juxtaposition of different screens (cf. Figure 21.3). The iterations in *Saving Screens: Temporary Tattoos and other Methods* build on and from Markham's descriptions of the Internet as a Way of Being and through composing still lives in these tattoos, explore how this metaphor extends to afterlife online.

Sherry Turkle (2007) has examined objects beyond their capacity for being instruments, describing them as emotional objects that assist the process of thinking. She navigates the "unfamiliar ground" of personal objects as provocation of thought (p. 5). Like her, I build on Claude Levi-Strauss' notion of bricolage to consider the affective benefit of thinking with objects. I move through the world with my father's digital material being, my way of being melding with his in sometimes surprising and other times unsurprising ways. These variations on his watch create our [mine and my father's] embodied expression of a thinking object. *Saving Screens: Temporary Tattoos and other Methods* is also my rumination on how digital devices carry fragments of thoughts and creative process in the way in which they are set up. Losing my father highlighted the kaleidoscopic nature of the online material that remained: published online poems continued to inspire comments while social media alerted me to links with his personal and professional network, for example a passage from his work that was referenced or personal message posted to him as an expression of grief. On one level, these occurrences emphasized the void of my father as the original source of the content or conversation. At the same time, without the physical person, I become more attuned to the colorful life flux of the content that remains.

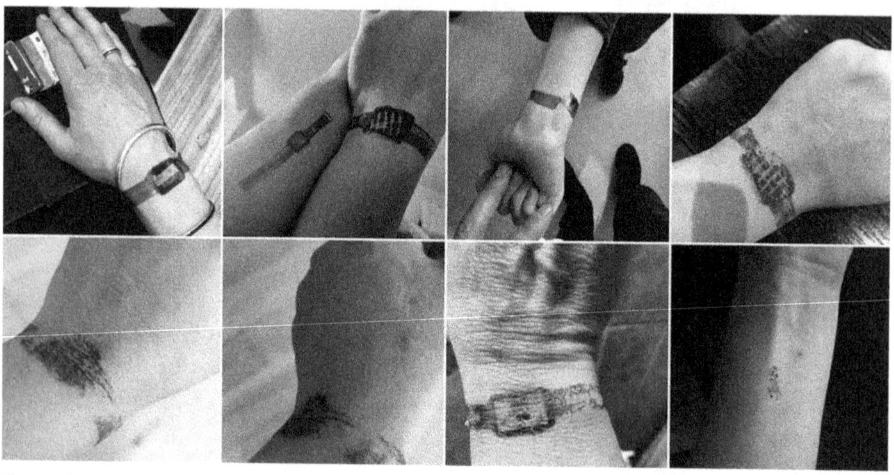

Figure 21.3: Sarah Schorr invites participants to send photographs of their tattoos as they fade. These collected images are adapted and incorporated into the installation. Source: Sarah Schorr

WINNIE SOON: UNERASABLE IMAGES

Unerasable Images[1] is a collection of screenshots (cf. Figure 21.4) in the format of a video art installation, exploring the cultural, technical, poetic and political dimensions of censorship and net neutrality. The internet network is often perceived of as a set of tools, where data, information and memories can be archived and retrieved.

1 See here for more details about the artwork: http://siusoon.net/unerasable-images/

More specifically, we can think of the internet as of a container metaphorically that holds or stores stuff of a predictable shape and size. In this case, the container has specific rules and priorities regarding what kinds of stuff easily fits, and what kinds of stuff cannot be contained. Even if storage space is seemingly unlimited on the internet, rules and priorities are still applied. Specific countries and political regimes impose rules depending on what the 'stuff' is and how it fits the local rules. In this sense, internet search engines operate and are regulated in a comparable manner to a container. The function with rules that decide what can be found, what order is the stuff exhibited in, what are the logics, priorities and biases of the search algorithms (Introna & Nissenbaum, 2000; Lovink, 2011; Noble, 2018) and the censorship of their results.

Figure 21.4: An example of the screenshot of Unerasable Images, which is taken on 2017-02-22 at 9.38.26 PM. Source: Winnie Soon

Within the context of Chinese Internet, censorship is regularly imposed in social media and search engines. Because some of the content is not immediately spotted by censoring machines, it takes some time for it to be erased and taken way. Therefore, censored content can leak out to other places within the golden window. I am particularly interested in a specific image of the Lego recreation of the famous scene with the "Tank Man," blocking the column of advancing tanks, that had been successfully uploaded in 2013 on a famous Chinese web portal as part of the event of Children's Day. Although it was swiftly censored and erased throughout China on all online platforms, this image is still searchable and, even after four years following its removal, occasionally appears on the first few rows of Google image search.

Figure 21.5: Nine selected images from Unerasable Images. Source: Winnie Soon.

The project *Unerasable Images* documents the screenshots taken during an almost daily Google image search over the course of the year 2017, using the Chinese characters "六四" as the image search keyword. The keyword is simply equivalent to the numerical values of 6 and 4, a reference to the date of the student-led Tiananmen Square Protest in Beijing. The word "六四" is also known as a sensitive and censored keyword in China, especially during the time around June Fourth every year. To me as a Hong Kongese, "六四" is not only a historical event, but also an encapsulation of fear, anxiety and hope that is brought forward to the present. "六四" is a reference point for citizens and critics to discuss, reflect and predict the future of Hong Kong.

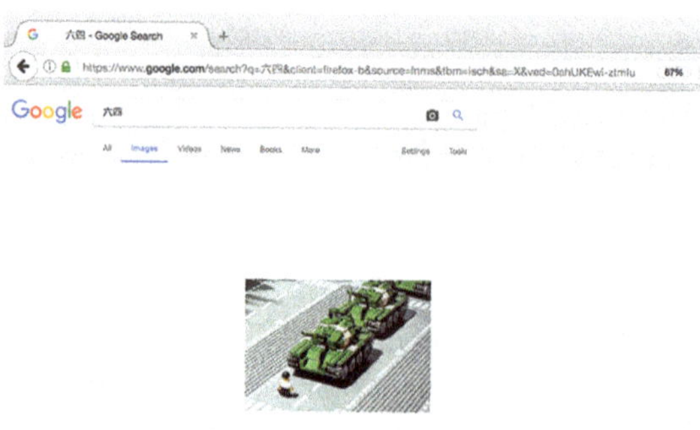

Figure 21.6: Unerasable Images, 2018 HD Video. Source: Winnie Soon

The screenshots, in this artwork, provide snapshots of an unstable archive, archiving complex relations of programmed and networked search. The screenshot is not only about the memory and subjectivities of archives; it also questions the technical infrastructure of the "archiving archive" (Derrida, 1998, p. 17). As the image moves around, off, and on the screen of the screenshot, we notice that it is a performance of a dynamic and unstable moment. Yet, it also demonstrates how networked images are persistent, durational and unerasable. Even as they are marked for removal by censoring machines, taken offline, and erased from the container that is the internet, they are still indexed, ranked, waiting to be crawled, and queried for retrieval. Screenshots capture and archive the intrinsic, inherent and political values built into or resulting from the cultural actions of Search. Screenshots in *Unerasable Images* address what the act of searching does to us. We perceive things through particular screens with their resolutions, aspect ratios and pixel dimensions. We see page titles. We see grids. In *Unerasable Images* the full screen mode of screenshots explicates the performative and geopolitical materiality of human and nonhuman searches. The collected screenshots are reappropriated to erase all the other image results from the search, depicted as negative white space (cf. Figures 21.5 and 21.6). The only image remaining is therefore the colored Lego Tank Man. Screenshots shows us the specific worldview that captures different life forms as unstable archives. It reminds the viewer that the Internet is not a utopian, free, or neutral space. The changing position of the Tank Man highlights how the Internet operates in compliance with various formats, standards, rules, priorities and parameters, contains geopolitical considerations and constraints that extend beyond their physical attributes.

This performative materiality of techno-cultural processes is what Markham may have meant when she talked about the internet as a way of being. Human and technological distinctions seem to collapse into a fluidity of experience. This is beyond the composition of images within screenshots, beyond images as content that is or is not allowed to stay in the container. At the time of pressing the key sequence to create a screenshot, the search results have returned filtered and sorted images that are situated in the techno-cultural domain. Search is a series of crawling and querying the entire web across geopolitical fibers, networked infrastructure and algorithmic logics of a giant database platform that is constantly updating. The entanglement of human and nonhuman search activities produces epistemic knowledge, apparently directing and affecting how we may perceive and understand things. Screen shooting is a method to reflect upon archive entangled interactions and configurations of ways of being.

CHAPTER TWENTY-TWO

Hurricane Season: Annual Assessments of Loss

DAISY PIGNETTI

10, September, 2017: *The Weather Channel*'s 24-hour coverage of Hurricane Irma repeatedly predicts the worst for South Florida. On CNN, Anderson Cooper appears in his signature black t shirt and rain slicker, reporting from Fort Myers, Florida.

Adrianna is there. She's my best friend since the third grade. She fled there from the nearby town of Cape Coral, from a house she's lived in for less than three months. She wanted to stay at work, a hospice care facility, to help both patients and staff, but when Irma turned west, emergency officials ordered mandatory evacuations in that zone. By this time, it was too late to drive north to join her parents and sister (who three days before drove 14 hours to the town of Montgomery, Alabama), so she's taking shelter in her mother-in-law's third floor apartment.

How do I know these details? Facebook.

I haven't actually heard Adrianna's voice in four months, when I last visited her over Memorial Day weekend. Like so many these days, we text rather than call, and message via Facebook rather than send emails. When she first moved to Florida from our hometown of New Orleans after our sophomore year of high school, we would write letters. After all, long distance phone calls were pricey in the early 1990s. When I moved to Tampa in 2003, we saw each other much more often.

Now, we see each other through our Facebook feeds. We understand each other's lives in ways both more and less powerful through social media. The immediacy and constancy is there, but the tenor of our voices chattering is not.

When Hurricane Katrina devastated the Gulf Coast and subsequent levee breaches flooded over 80% of New Orleans in late-August of 2005, Adrianna and I spoke every night on the phone, checking in on each other's friends and family members. She was the only person I knew who could understand the helplessness of watching the devastation of our hometown from afar. In a column for salon.com, Christopher Rice (a celebrated author in his own right, but perhaps more known for the fact that his New Orleans-born mother is vampire novelist, Anne Rice) would go on to express what both of us felt about what might remain of our city:

> Those of us who have migrated to the coasts of the country from its often maligned middle like to view our hometowns as *time capsules* [emphasis added]. We fault them for being too fixed and too rigid, but we also enjoy the ability to slip back into *familiar routines* [emphasis added] upon returning home. Both of those luxuries have been taken from me; New Orleans has spilled past the boundaries of my conflicted feelings for it. Those of us who are from there are being left with a storehouse of memories that have lost their *physical referents* [emphasis added]. (Rice, 2005)

While Irma ultimately did not damage Adrianna's home, both Cape Coral and Fort Myers, Florida, suffered enough flooding and wind damage to close schools—and thus disrupt families' lives—for over two weeks. As for what Katrina did to my childhood home in New Orleans in 2005, I wouldn't know for sure for months. Yes, Anderson Cooper was reporting from locations I was familiar with, but none were near my Gentilly neighborhood. With no eyewitness accounts, I could remain in denial about how many physical referents I may have lost. And I liked that.

TRUSTING STRANGERS

2, September, 2005: Sitting at my laptop after another failed attempt at contacting my parents who had evacuated New Orleans 6 days prior, I learned of the mapping resource below from the Association of Internet Researchers (AoIR) listserv:

> *One Web site,* www.scipionus.com, *is combating the confusion by encouraging users to annotate a Google Map of New Orleans with information about specific locations. Collectively, the community is creating a collaborative map Wikipedia. Anyone with something to add can enter a street address and leave a marker on the map at that location, providing a few lines of text about conditions at that spot.*
>
> *I clicked on my neighborhood and one post is just asking for information about Cameron Blvd. Another one reads, "lower half of UNO [University of New Orleans] including Ben Franklin High School is flooded." Those schools are only 3 blocks away and literally alongside a levee. So if we're down the street, shouldn't that mean our house isn't too bad? (Pignetti, 2005)*

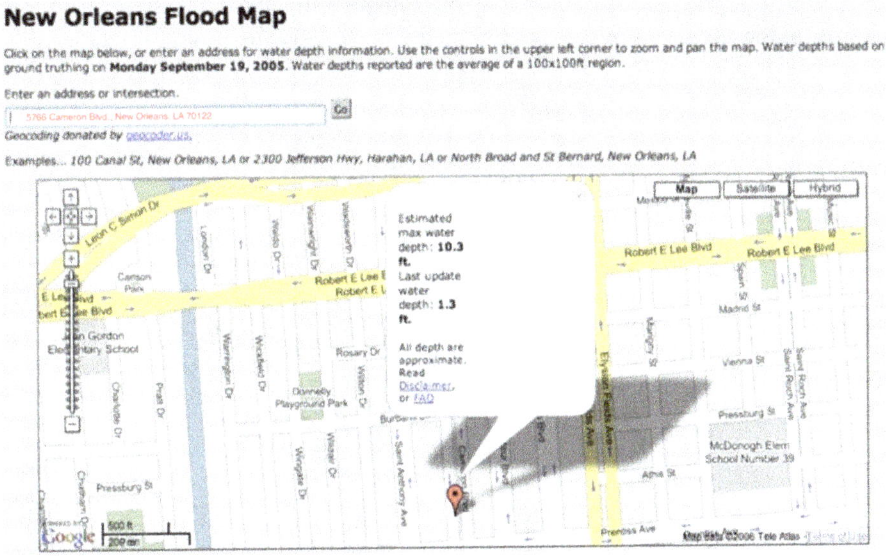

Figure 22.1: Text and Image from my personal blog (Pignetti, 2007). Source: Doctor Daisy.

I should have been thrilled that online resources like this (Figure 22.1) were available, especially since the television media remained focused on search and rescue efforts as well as the evacuations of people stranded at the Superdome and Convention Center. But even with these water depth estimates, supposedly obtained by "ground truthing," they were being estimated by everyday users on location, not named GIS specialists. There was the idea of many layers of information, immediately available, continually updated. But in the end, only my parents' seeing would lead to my believing.

After having evacuated 5766 Cameron Blvd. on August 28th, my parents were finally allowed back into the city in October, where they saw every house on our street had, in fact, been deluged by ten feet of water or more. Mold grew on every wall, our refrigerator was found upside down in the dining room, and all our furniture was so saturated with water that it crumbled at the slightest touch. Although I would not see this with my own eyes until February 2006 (photos are available at http://noladaisy.shutterfly.com/249), hearing these details from my parents left me numb.

Technically the house was there, but our home was gone forever.[1]

1 In fact, if the levees hadn't breached and flooded my Gentilly neighborhood, the only hurricane damage to our home would have been downed branches, cracks to the carport cover, and the loss of our back door awning.

After four years of insurance company and government agency paperwork, my parents made the decision *not* to rebuild. The house was gutted and then razed.

Figure 22.2: January 2010 photo of my brother in front of the empty lot at 5766 Cameron Blvd. With the physical referent of my house completely gone, so was the stability of a life lived in one place. Source: Daisy Pignetti

When I have dreams about my childhood home in New Orleans, which I frequently do, it takes me a few minutes after waking up to remember I'm a Wisconsin woman now and, even if I wanted to move back, that house no longer exists.

Until one day it did.

IN GOOGLE WE TRUST?

During a bout of web surfing procrastination in March of 2010, I saw my New Orleans house again via Google Street View (Figure 22.3). I can't remember what brought me to search for it, but there it was. Even though I knew it wasn't. This time it was I who felt gutted and razed as I stared at the screen. My beloved Cameron Blvd. home stood there with gleaming white siding, bright blue window awning, and, miraculously, no water line, although truthfully it is a blurry picture. The only evidence of it being taken post-Katrina, visible only to my eyes, were the lack of trees and bird fountain in the front yard.

Figure 22.3: Screenshot taken March 3, 2010. Source: Daisy Pignetti (Pignetti, 2010)

How could this be? The © 2009 Google stamp implies the picture was taken in 2009, although currently Street View images list both an "Image Capture" date *and* a copyright date, so I cannot be sure. Street View was launched in 2007 so perhaps it was taken earlier, although after conferring with my parents we can confirm the house was not demolished until late-2009. I have since Googled to try and learn how often they send their cars out to take pictures, and learned that "in residential areas, imagery gets updated every 2–3 years. It all depends on the available technology and the age of the imagery" (Llentirb, 2016).

It seems there is no plan for how disasters might incite or impact these updates. But as this type of mapping technology evolves, the chances of someone being surprised as I was in 2010 are rarer. And I'm not sure how I feel about that.

Seeing my house again made me hopeful that if I searched long enough, I could find anything I wanted on the Internet, even lost places. Because of the natural and man-made disaster that took my home, I am even more invested in both physical and virtual places that are rooted in memories of the past. Yet that leads me to ask myself some key questions: am I really "Be[ing] a New Orleanian" online? If so, what version of the city am I celebrating? More importantly, does it matter?

Figure 22.4: The Author in Santorini, Greece. "Be a New Orleanian. wherever you are."
Source: Daisy Pignetti

Originally a bumper sticker slogan created by Blake Haney a few months after Hurricane Katrina, his company *Dirty Coast* now prints it on t-shirts encouraging locals like myself who have been displaced by the storm to hold on to their identity and connect with others (Figure 22.4).

Despite having left Louisiana for graduate school, I retained my mobile phone's 504 area code until 2006 and never once changed my driver's license to reflect a current address until 2008. As Chris Rose, whose post-Katrina columns for *The Times-Picayune* earned him a Pulitzer Prize nomination, wrote:

> [S]he is a New Orleans girl and New Orleans girls never live anywhere else and even if they do, they always come back. That's just the way it is .... To hell with no house, no car, no job, no prospects. This is where she belongs. And her mama lives here. End of discussion. (2005)

Indeed, even with my "mama" having relocated to Mississippi (but only 50 miles away from New Orleans), in 2008 I was making plans to return to the Gulf Coast as soon as the academic year ended. Given my topic, it made sense to finish my dissertation on the burgeoning New Orleans blogosphere from there.

A job brought me to the Midwest, where I've lived ever since, so I never did end up going back. But it was here, in the Midwest, that I truly took to heart the idea that New Orleans is as much a mindset and way of being as a place (Haney, as cited in RX Fogarty, 2008). Rebecca Solnit seconds this sentiment in her innovative atlas project, *Unfathomable City*: "New Orleans has a kind of centripetal or magnetic or hypnotic force: when you are in it, you're absorbed, and other places cease to occupy much territory in your mind" (2013, p. 7).

Thanks to a life lived online, however, I don't have to be "in it" to be "absorbed." My research, my social networks (in all senses of the term), my way of being—everything connects back to being a New Orleans girl. I "… feel the spirit of New Orleans and … let her shine through in any situation, at any place and time, and in every way possible" (*Be a New Orleanian*, n.d.). Although I no longer live in New Orleans, a wifi connection allows me to connect with my friends who both live there and share those daily experiences online. Because "the self, information technology, everyday life, and other are vitally connected, co-existent" (Markham, 2003), *together* we can "be" New Orleanians.

I've examined my social media activity of late and can confirm it is only during Mardi Gras and the hurricane season[2] that I strive for up-to-date precision in its depictions of New Orleans. These seasons are my extremes: when I am most homesick and when I am most grateful not to live there. I, too, have a more captive audience on my social media sites during these times because of my status as a local. Just like Solnit's collaborator Rebecca Snedeker experienced when she left for college, "I ha[ve] one thing going for me. Everyone want[s] to know about my city, New Orleans" (Solnit & Snedeker, 2013, p. 11).

At all other times of the year, I'm content with passively liking touristy Instagram-filtered images of the city's signature food dishes and colorful architecture. I'm especially comforted by these posts from strangers because they obscure the headlines and status updates from friends who describe the harsh realities the city faces, e.g. increases in crime, gentrification, and unemployment. Other cities have similar problems, but adding the weather element and its impact on housing costs causes much anxiety, which returns us to hurricane season, "the season when the city's mortality is on everyone's mind" (Solnit & Snedeker, 2013, p. 12). As dire as that sounds, it is part of the city's "annual cycle" that locals endure (Solnit & Snedeker, 2013, p. 12).

2 The Atlantic hurricane season, which covers the areas of the North Atlantic, Caribbean, and Gulf of Mexico and spans from June 1 through November 30 every year (Ghose, 2017).

NOSTALGIA

I visit New Orleans at least once a year, but if I am being honest, I do not think those trips embody the view that, "No matter how deeply you come to know a place, you can keep coming to know it more" (Solnit & Snedeker, 2013, p. 11). Just like the select online activities I mentioned above, more often than not on each trip I enact Chris Rice's words and "slip back into familiar routines" (2005). I go to the same bars and restaurants, order the same menu items, and—thanks to social media—I know exactly where to find so many of my friends.

As I grow older, I realize that New Orleans has always been rooted in its own nostalgia, "resisting modernization with its national chains and referencing local institutions that, to quote the Benny Grunch song on the matter, 'Ain't Dere No More'" (Carmichael & Dajko, 2016, p. 248). If this is the city that shaped me, no wonder what I most enjoy about the internet are the nostalgic pleasures it provides.

CHAPTER TWENTY-THREE

Complicating the Internet as a Way of Being: The Case of Cloud Intimacy

THERESA M. SENFT

One of my favorite things to screen in class is a video that details how American editor Matt Stopera from Buzzfeed came to meet a random restaurant owner from South China over the Chinese internet (Stopera, 2015). In the video, Stopera explains that a few months earlier, his iPhone had been stolen at a bar—something he had forgotten about, until the day his iCloud began filling up with photos he didn't recognize, including a set of selfies featuring a Chinese man solemnly standing in an orange grove. After learning from a friend that "most stolen iPhones wind up in China," Stopera published his story (and the man's selfies) in a Buzzfeed article titled, "How did this man's photos wind up on my iPhone?" (2015).

The day after the story was published, Stopera's Twitter account began filling with notes from Chinese users, urging him to join them on the Chinese microblogging platform, Sina Weibo, where people were trying to locate the man they had nicknamed "Brother Orange." By the time Stopera had a Weibo account, his story was trending. In a matter of days, the mystery man had been identified as Li Hongjun, a small restaurant owner in the Guangdong Province of South China. Li had never used social media before, but with the help of his nephew, joined Weibo. There, he and Stopera began exchanging public greetings, (translated) messages, photos and videos, with users watching and cheering them on. Shortly thereafter, Stopera made a trip to China to meet his "brother" in the flesh. The video I screen in class documents the strangely emotional meeting between the men, as well as their newfound celebrity throughout China.

The Brother Orange video depicts what we might call 'cloud intimacy,' the feelings that arise when we become aware of the fact that the data that we have been encouraged to think of as ours routinely brushes, leans against, and becomes embedded with data amassed by other users, human or not. One way to conceptualize cloud intimacy is as a new way of being that presumes digital platforms to be the origin of our ideas about self and other, rather than mere transport mechanisms for them. For my students, *Brother Orange* features many aspects of intimacy, such as proximity, enmeshment, interdependency, risk. It develops a surprising plot trajectory from the all-too-common experience of phone theft, it involves likeable characters, it doesn't entirely ignore cultural differences, and it has a happy ending.

My students like how the story seems to rebut the argument that technological absorption has caused human intimacy to decline. Christopher Lauer makes a similar rebuttal, pointing out that contemporary anxiety over the wane of intimacy "arises not from any structural changes in the modern world, but from the contradictory demands that comprise the very structure of intimacy" (2016, p. 1). For Lauer, intimacy is best understood as a performance of dialectics, with its performers continuously oscillating between states like presence and absence; touch and space; giving and receiving; embedding and separating; fetishizing and conflict; and mourning and haunting (2016, p. 4).

To unfold cloud intimacy as a version of Markham's "way of being" we need to ask how it is enacted through contemporary platforms. How is a state like intimacy achieved in the first place? We can start by focusing on the idea that intimacy is performative: there is nothing intimacy "is" beyond a series of actions performed over time, adhering to culturally coded conventions. Judith Butler (1990) has argued that because gender emerges from inherently unstable discourses and norms, it is always in some way "troubled." Lauer sees intimacy in a similar way, arguing that its contradictory status as a "closeness beyond closeness" makes it impossible to fully achieve (2016, p. 155).

Building on this idea, we can say a story like *Brother Orange* also requires *platformativity*, which Thomas Lamarre describes as "a sort of performativity related to platforms." (2018, p. 206). In his work on video gaming, Lamarre tries to course-correct theorists (here he cites Butler, but also Freud and Marxist), who treat media platforms "as a mirror," one that winds up "scarcely problematized." (2018, p. 206) For Lamarre, attending to how platforms perform can help materialize and historicize power (2018, p. 206). As we consider what this implies in practice, we can think about how platforms are *themselves* performative, continually prescribing that which they purport to merely describe. In the increasing case of data and bodies performing, in addition to platforms performing, then in relation to intimacy, we might ask: who (or what) is running the show?

In *Brother Orange*, there is a moment where Stopera explains how after he published his story, his Twitter account was flooded with Chinese users urging him join the platform Weibo. The next sequence of the video features a shot of Weibo's "trending" list, written in Chinese, except for the name Matt Stopera, which is perched at the number one spot. The video continues to detail Weibo users' efforts to locate Brother Orange in South China, get him signed onto Weibo, and get the two men interacting with one another. Throughout, the affair is framed as a community effort.

Xiao Liu (2018), an academic who studies geopolitical flows through East Asia, provides a different take, noting that while Buzzfeed used the Brother story to generate clicks and advertising revenue for its platform, Sina (the Chinese company that owns Weibo) used it to give their platform a much-needed public relations boost. Once a dominant social media platform in China, Weibo has waned in popularity over the years, mostly due to the rapid ascendency of the "do everything" platform called WeChat, owned by rival Chinese media giant Tencent. In the Brother Orange story, Sina found an opportunity to present Weibo to a young Chinese consumer base as a platform where interesting, fun and "cool" socializing was still possible.

At a place like Buzzfeed, writing a story about your socialization experiences with strangers over the internet is all in a day's work. For someone like Li (aka Brother Orange), the experience was highly irregular. Like many men his age in China, Li has no formal education: a fact which may or may not affect his reading and writing abilities. Before this, he had never been online. A father of four, Li spent most of his time "struggling to support his family with various jobs as a migrant worker in the Pearl River Delta area before he went back to his hometown to open a restaurant on a boat" (Liu, 2018, p. 262). Given these facts, why did Li decide to get and use a Weibo account? Was he that hungry to chat with a stranger, in a language he did not speak, located in a part of the world he would most likely never be able to afford to visit?

To tackle these questions, it helps to recall that historically, the biggest investor in Chinese media companies has been the Chinese government. Whereas Sina spotted in the Brother Orange an opportunity to promote Weibo, the Chinese government perhaps saw in the Buzzfeed video a way to introduce international tourists Guangdong Province, where Li lives and works. Recalling that the last eight minutes of the Buzzfeed video are devoted to both men's celebrity treatment while traveling through the Guangdong Province, we can begin to more critically question whether their "natural connection" was so natural after all.

The performativity of platforms, combined with the platformativity of cloud intimacy provides us a set of concepts that can help clarify what happens once the internet disappears into a way of being (Markham, 1998, 2003). Against this backdrop, we know we need to act, but we aren't quite sure how. Of course, in current parlance, we are more likely to use the term "platform" as the enveloping framework for the capacities we once afforded to the internet. But what does this mean? As Tarleton Gillespie (2010) has noted, the desirability of the concept of the platform is its mutability. Borrowing from Gillespie, we can isolate at least four ways people speak about platforms across computing, industry, political and social environments. The first two are to conceptualize a platform as a technological entity or tool, or as a place or stage. These both align with Markham's framework for the internet, which would suggest we've simply replaced "internet" with "platform." However, platform is also conceptualized as an opportunity, which focuses on what a platform is or provides, (e.g. immediacy, variety, self-expression, friendship). A fourth conceptualization focuses on platforms as political, which emphasizes a platform's impact within and beyond its borders—on democracy, on self-determination, on free enterprise, on market control, and of course, on intimacy. These last two interest me because they emphasize the performativity rather than the shape or presence of the platform itself. If we focus on performance, performativity, and platformativity with these invisible partners, how might we explore the internet as a way of seeing?

I often follow up the Brother Orange story with what I call the Yemen story, one that ends differently. A few years ago, a link appeared on my Facebook page titled, "What are those kids doing with that enormous gun? The strange photos that showed up on the lost iPhone may not have been exactly what they seemed" (McGrath, 2015). The story focused on an American woman named Maura, who, like Stopera in the case of *Brother Orange*, also failed to change her iCloud settings after her phone was stolen. Maura woke one morning to find her photo stream full of images displaying the phone's trip from an electronics shop in Harlem, to the interior of an airplane, to a bedroom geotagged from Yemen, where Apple products are currently banned. A change in selfies loading to the stream indicated to Maura that the phone first belonged to middle-aged man, and then a younger man, possibly a nephew. The images posted in the story focused on the young man. They showed the universal stuff of teenaged boyhood: the shyness, the swagger, the song lyrics. It was all there.

At one point, Maura noticed a group of Arabic language contacts had been incorporated into her Skype account. She visited the Apple Genius Bar, where she was reassured that even if she was receiving data from Yemen, nobody there had her information. Then she discovered a photo she took on holiday, incorporated in the icon of one of her name Skype contacts. When Maura began receiving photos of young children standing next to automatic weapons, she called the FBI. Soon after that, the images stopped flowing into her iCloud. Perhaps a government entity had intervened. Perhaps the boy had finally changed his settings. Perhaps the phone had been destroyed in one of the American drone attacks reported nearby. Perhaps the boy himself had been destroyed.

For obvious reasons, the Yemen story hits students differently than *Brother Orange*, even though both originate on same platform: iCloud. My students are not naïve. They understand how *Brother Orange* charms by asking us to forget what we know about current U.S.-China relations, inviting us instead to imagine instead the possibility of digital platforms fostering brotherhood across borders. They also understand that the Yemen story fascinates in part because of what feels to many of them like an absence of platforms there: more than one student has confessed to knowing very little about life in that part of the world, save mention of wars.

But there are other reasons why one story of intimacy feels successful, while the other feels like failure. In its mission to generate clicks, Buzzfeed narrated *Brother Orange* through a tried and true frame: cloud intimacy as disconcerting and a bit creepy, but also funny when experienced with the right attitude—and sometimes, even life-changing. For Sina, *Brother Orange* represented not an opportunity for direct revenue through clicks, but a way to display to Weibo as a platform capable of thriving in the Age of WeChat. While the Yemen story appeared in an American online publication and was read widely, it offered little in the way of meme-worthy framing, nor did it allow opportunities for transnational corporate cross-pollination. Instead, it leaves us with an image of cloud intimacy that feels more than anything like a door on a broken hinge, sometimes swinging to reveal, other times unexpectedly closing shut.

CHAPTER TWENTY-FOUR

Echolocating the Digital Self

ANNETTE N. MARKHAM

Bats send out a stream of shrieks as they fly and use the returning echoes to build up a sonic map of their surroundings. The quality of the echo is used to determine the shape and location of objects in space. Bats can tell how far away something is by how long it takes for the sounds to return to them.

How is this related to lived experience of contemporary digital media?

In an era of constant connectivity and "always on" or more importantly, "always available" internet, mapping the Self occurs as we receive feedback from continual flows of information. The seemingly seamless and steady state of connectivity is, at the more granular level, a process of continual echolocation, in the way we might think of radar, sonar, or lidar, whereby the outline of an object in space is determined by sending a stream of signals and attending closely to the quality of the echo.

At the micro-interactional level, echolocation focuses our attention on what's happening in the constant flow of consciousness; at the level of the existential, between the I and the me, between the body and the world; to identify limits and boundaries between things, to assign meaning to various inputs and stimuli.

In the early days of the Internet, Richard MacKinnon (1995) remarked that it is no longer adequate to say "I think, therefore I am" (invoking Descartes) or even "I speak, therefore I am" (invoking the linguistic turn, generally). In the internet age, he said, the more appropriate phrase is "I am perceived, therefore I am." The symbolic interactionist in me took this one step further to write that if we take the dialogic process seriously, the phrase should actually be: "I am responded to, therefore I am" (Markham, 2005), a phrase that gives fuller attention to the continual dynamic of the relational self.

The social negotiation of self is made more visible by the traces of texts, tweets, and emojis that evidence this dynamic. Alongside the continual presencing, performing, posting, clicking, swiping, there are responses: pings of various sorts, including direct messages, indicators of attention like red notification dots on homescreens, numbers and hearts next to one's post; and double checkmarks in messaging apps like WhatsApp, Telegram, and iMessage.

What counts as a 'ping'? Automated responses were built into email in the 1970s. But the 'read receipt' didn't gain a foothold in messaging until the 2010s, when many social media messaging apps started adding automated pings, read responses, or attention indicators. These can be direct, like an email or the now outdated 'poke' on Facebook. Indirect pings include the 'like' or heart on an Instagram post. Platforms quantify responsiveness through red notification dots on screens. Messaging apps now include pings as defaults, like the checkmark in Whatsapp or iMessage, reassuring us the message was sent (✓), received (✓✓), and read (✓✓).

We can say the technical accomplishment of these pings adds layers of agency to the interaction, but more directly, these become active participants in the conversation. When Frosh (2017) writes about the ping as a wound, a puncture, a signal of termination, we can ask: what agent sends this termination notice, who or what punctures his senses with this checkmarked dagger? Highlighting this active role has long allowed scholars to explore the function of algorithms in constructing the self (e.g., Cheney-Lippold, 2017; Hayles, 1999).

Why does it matter that we identify the origin point of this ping? The symbolic interactions that form one's sense of Self are microscopic, invisible in some cases, as the interface functions on behalf of the person in ways that he or she cannot see or recognize. The gesture might be quite vague, like a raised eyebrow across a crowded room, that might be intended or just a twitch (as in Geertz's famous discussions of winks). Nonetheless it has impact, as Paul Frosh so poignantly notes, "The wrongly colored ticks are a wound, cutting into me as a blade. They are the puncture of the screenshot. The screenshot is a hard image. It bruises me, it immobilizes me, it reveals the termination of connection" (2017).

I suggest that vulnerability in this epoch is being disconnected.[1] Disconnecting from what is perceived as a steady stream of identity pings leaves us bereft of the continual marking of the boundaries that mark the edges of the Self.

Let me back up to summarize a bit of how I come to focus on disconnection as a way of getting closer to a key characteristic of digital existence. It is now well understood that because digital technologies have become somewhat ubiquitous

1 I use this declarative phrase for provocation purposes only. I am aware and troubled by my focus here on vulnerability in what is essentially a privileged cycle of connectivity.

and banal, they have become both less visible and more influential. And as we rely more and more on them, they become a *way of being*. But what does this mean? How does the technical or digital function in the continual construction and negotiation of identity and selfhood?

At the microscopic levels of interaction, this constant pinging is not always an effort to find others or get attention in social space, but might be an effort to identify and locate the self. I found this repeatedly in six years of ethnographic and phenomenological study of around 1,500 youth regarding their everyday digital media. It was not noticeable when I focused on their practices of being connected, but when they grappled with being *disconnected*. We know that disrupting the flow of affirmation and reaffirmation creates what in psychological terms we might label as anxiety and cognitive dissonance, especially for youth. The fear of disconnection is sometimes simplified as FOMO, or fear of missing out. But in the youths' poignant narratives, the vulnerability is more meaningful and disruptive:[2]

> *I keep reaching for my phone, even though I know it's not connected. I don't know why.*
>
> *I just want people to know I'm out there, that I exist.*
>
> *I'm so mad at myself. Why am I so obsessed with getting instant responses?*

Being disconnected doesn't just cut off communication from others, it puts the body in doubt. This is not like removing one of our senses or having a limb ripped off. Rather, the body suddenly appears as a discrete, separate, and isolated object. Disconnecting can bring on a state of extreme vulnerability, then, since there's no continual Other with whom you're bouncing off continual information pings. This matters, since even as we might intuit that the Self is relational, entangled, contextual, and complicated, at the end of the day, one's ontological security relies on creating coherency. The concept of echolocation returns analytical attention back to how micro elements of digitally-saturated social interactions are experienced and rendered sensible by individuals.

2 The quotes are representative of a common pattern, but hardly evocative in this limited space. After reviewing hundreds of stories from youth, I get a sense of intense cognitive dissonance and profound anxiety around disconnecting.

SECTION 6

Whose Internet? Whose Metaphors?

CHAPTER TWENTY-FIVE

Metaphoric Meltdowns: Debates over the Meaning of Blogging on Israblog

CARMEL VAISMAN

Blogs have long been a central feature of the Internet. They've been studied as tools for personal expression, variations on traditional self-expression media like journals or diaries, platforms, digital interfaces. These conceptualizations emerge through use and interface design choices, since digital objects have no boundaries without a built-in metaphorical power. As signs, digital entities can be articulated in arbitrary media or modalities (textual, auditory, pictorial, haptic), but once instantiated in a modality they become non-arbitrary, because of their indexical relation to code in software (Boomen, 2014).

While a traditional metaphor transfers meaning between different conceptual worlds, in a material metaphor, the transference occurs between symbols and physical artifacts (Hayles, 2002). In the case of digital artefacts, the transference is between the discourse metaphors of users or interface designs, and the architectures of software and hardware. As Lev Manovich (2001) pointed out, the same database could be accessed through and represented by two distinct interfaces, designed to generate different user experiences, which are based on different metaphors. In the case of blogs, just think of the difference between *LiveJournal* and *MySpace*. The transference between discursive metaphors and architecture can be one that elucidates how the technology operates or rather obscures it, as is the case with the metaphor of the cloud in cloud computing.

The notion of material metaphor elevates the operational reach of discursive metaphors beyond language and cognition towards material and social configurations, recognizing the way metaphors embody material affordances and specific connections to the digital back office (Boomen, 2014, p. 188). Therefore, we can use metaphors as heuristic tools to articulate what is being foregrounded, what is ignored, and what subject positions are made possible (Boomen, 2014). All of this is to say that whatever we take to be a digital object is the solidification of a metaphoric conception, fixed after the fact, retrospectively giving obdurate characteristics or universal meaning to what is and will always be a continuous process.

The blog/blogging phenomenon formally emerged in the Israeli web space in August 2001 with the creation of *Israblog*. Before 2001, most internet-savvy practitioners were already writing English-language blogs on international platforms or had opened scattered personal blogs in Hebrew on private domains. I initially assumed Israblog would be like most other platforms on which I blogged, an illusion that highlights how one's perception of any online space depends on one's own movements through these networks, something both Hine and Markham noted in their earliest works (Hine, 2000; Markham, 1998). Therefore, what a blog *is* or what a platform is *for* is all up for debate, sometimes fierce. This was made clear to me when *Israblog* publicly revealed its statistics for the first time. It turned out that the type of users I presumed were universal, since they were the ones I saw and interacted with, represented only 4 percent of the site's population—*Israblog* was in fact dominated by females (74%) and bloggers under the age of 21 (75%). I was considered a popular blogger on *Israblog*. Yet the vast majority of *Israblog* bloggers were teenage girls, a mere page away, but in experiential terms occupying a completely different dimension.

Lurking in this blogosphere within a blogosphere, I began to see blogs and blogging in a different light. For adult bloggers at the time (in the country and context I was studying), the blog was a text, and blogging meant writing. Sure, there was a lot to be said about how blogging wrought tensions between orality, literacy and performance, but it was teenage girls who truly explored the boundaries of blogging. For them, blogging was not about writing at all, but viewing (being viewed), as teenage blogger *Ariel*'s first post demonstrates:

> *My first blog was here [on Israblog—c.v] but it was designed so ugly and I didn't know how to use it so I opened another one on Tapuz [a newer Hebrew website—c.v]. But they don't have the functions that are available here so I decided to come back. I'm opening this new blog, in hopes that I'll figure out how to add background music, design it properly, make a cool designed cursor and well, just use it.*

Notice that the verb 'write' is absent from her post and replaced by 'design', 'add' 'make' and 'use'. Girls like *Ariel* used to comment on strangers' blogs in their search for new audiences with phrases like 'you've got a beautiful blog! You're invited to mine [link]', leaving other bloggers to wonder, post, and comment on how 'beauty' is even relevant to a blog. Blogs encourage not only textual, but visual expression as well, via user icons, memes, template selection, design and color scheme, titles, sidebars, selection of images, typeface, etc. (Hookway, 2008). Badger (2004) claimed that blogs are also 'something to look at' and 'if we think of weblogs as being homepages that we wear then it is the visual elements that tailor the garment to fit the individual'. Badger (2004) assumes we automatically adopt that visual literacy, but Hookway (2008, p. 102) shows that one needs to learn how to 'read' as well as 'view' blogs.

The girls on Israblog decorated their blogs in ways that seemed both like the material culture in their bedrooms and their subcultural dress styles. They engaged in collaborative games in which their blogs were factories of graphic design products, virtual shelves for digital collections, stages for performing blog contests, and venues in virtual cities where they were represented by digital dolly avatars.

When I tried to engage with them through my own blog, *Doctor Blog*, they completely ignored me. In their posts the girls were often begging for attention, soliciting readership and commentary, but they must have only targeted their peer group, since they ignored my comments entirely. I had to retreat to lurking in order to acquire the proper literacy, to figure out and perform the proper blogging 'rites' that would make me visible to them.

I had to change my conceptualization of what a blog was before I could break through. I finally stopped trying to engage girls through writing and started learning some basic graphic design through the tips and tutorials on their blogs. I began to treat *Doctor Blog* as my avatar and designed a new theme for it, including 'ordering' graphic design products from teenage bloggers who participated in the gift-economy style marketplace of designs—badges, graphic dividers, customized cursor, signature, etc. (Vaisman, 2014). Girls who had ignored my textual comments were suddenly exchanging designs with me, criticizing and complimenting on the look of my blog. Since blog design was perceived, inter alia, as dress style, I felt like a colonial-era ethnographer who sometimes needed to dress according to the norms in the researched community (Hammersley & Atkinson, 1995).

Finally, after recruiting my research subjects properly, I asked one of them to design a special blog badge that said (in Hebrew) 'I'm also being studied by Carmel' and most of the girls who volunteered for the research were happy to display it on their blog frame alongside other identity markers they designed and collected. Both the badge and the 'I'm also' text structure (a discursive convention of identity statement on girls' badges) were a way for me to speak their language and be with them—not in *the* field, but in *their* field (Figures 25.1 and 25.2).

Figure 25.1: "I'm also being studied by Carmel" Hebrew blog badge. Source: Screenshot by Carmel Vaisman

Figure 25.2: "Doctor Blog" design theme as designed by one of the teenage bloggers. Source: Screenshot by Carmel Vaisman

FROM 'METAPHORIC MELTDOWN' TO METAPHOR SOLIDIFICATION

Different competing metaphors might manifest as habits, conventions, norms, social settings and ways of meaning-making. Bloggers navigate between these in order to construct their subject positions; a continual construction and reconstruction of the meaning of blogging in context. Yet this controversy might not be evident, as the distinctions and diversity are collapsed into one set of practices referred to as 'blogging'. danah boyd (2005) referred to this as 'metaphoric meltdown', resulting in lawsuits, press misunderstandings and research challenges due to blogging being situated between a variety of different tensions—orality and textuality, corporeality and spatiality, practice and artifact. While those of us in the academy, like boyd, might be able to reflect on how these 'broken' metaphoric comparisons never give us the full picture, and we might be able to see blogging as a liminal practice, all of us were still, in some ways, continuously choosing between different interpretations of 'what a blog is'.

As I reflect back on my fieldwork and participation on Israblog during these years, it is clear that practically, we went back and forth between different decisions, preferring some constructions, narratives, and settings over others, whether this richness was visible or latent.

In clashes between actors of equal power this might result merely in textual drama and different blog genres, as was the case with adult bloggers wondering about teenage girls' blogging practices. However, when the platform itself was involved, its operators held the power of solidifying a particular metaphor—that is, encoding in software certain platform defaults, thus intervening in the mode of being of blogs and bloggers, which goes beyond simply imposing a standard.

In what follows, I tell a story that weaves together three key moments in the field: the struggle of the platform operators to make sense of their role while navigating discourse metaphors they cannot translate to code and solidify, the first failed attempt of the platform to solidify a metaphor that went against the grain of the blogging community, and the successful solidification of a discourse metaphor by the platform programmers in a way that favors one group of bloggers over another.

PLATFORM OWNERSHIP CHANGES AND "THE TOOLBAR" INCIDENT

A few days after opening my own blog, *Doctor Blog* on the *Israblog* platform, I contacted the founder and operator of the platform Yariv Habot, hoping for his help as an informant. Habot agreed, and thereafter supplied me with statistics when needed, helped with technical issues of capturing blog pages, and promoted my call for volunteers when my research proposal was approved. But his own position in the field was an interesting case study of metaphoric meltdown. Habot had seen himself as a computer programmer who designed code for a certain type of webpage that afforded freedom of expression to all, and maintained a formal blog for announcements and technical support. *Israblog* was merely his hobby.

As the platform grew beyond a few thousand blogs, Habot found himself busy with less code and more conflicts. Teen bloggers saw him as 'the man behind the curtain' and worshipped him to the point of embarrassment. Since many bloggers saw themselves as a community, or even a family, they referred to Habot as *Israblog*'s God, king, magician, or father, and approached him with personal conflicts beyond the scope of tech support. He found himself performing the roles of parent, sheriff, and judge, mediating between girls who accused each other of copying graphic designs, as well as identifying and scolding bloggers who tweaked their blog counter to appear more popular.

Habot was an introvert programmer who was not cut out to fill this role. Though he often referred to *Israblog* as 'his baby' project, he never dreamed he would actually have to 'babysit' thousands of bloggers; yet, he was not always able to ignore bloggers' drama since it often had ramifications on the code. For instance, bloggers who tweaked the counter exploited a bug that damaged the counters of all blogs. It had to be fixed on the level of code and all blog counters were off for a few days. This 'counter blackout' became a community crisis he had to deal with on additional levels: the counter was the representation of the audience and the pulse of the blog, so bloggers were practically freaking out without it, blogging frantically about being 'left alone in the dark' and begging audiences to 'show themselves' through comments now that their presence left no digital trace.

Habot felt he had not signed up for this and could no longer handle the multiple facets of this operation. As *Israblog* kept expanding and new challenges emerging, Habot got weary and sold *Israblog* to a media-content company, *Nana*.

Nana assumed they purchased a publishing platform, a golden goose producing free content. They assigned it a content manager, media professional Ilana Tamir, and their first action was to brand it by adding its logo header and toolbar automatically to every blog page. They could not fathom the scandal that broke out among thousands of bloggers who were extremely invested in their blog design, reflecting their virtual bedroom, inner moods, and cultural styles. The blogs were perceived as personal spaces and digital bodies. Imagine their reaction when they woke up one morning to see an unremovable header and toolbar on their screens. It was described by bloggers as forcing them to hang a huge picture they hated in their bedroom, or enforcing a unified dress code. Even adult bloggers who viewed blogs more as diaries written for public audiences, complained over the commercialized aesthetic that discouraged them from writing personal narratives.

The bloggers were quick to organize through platform tools: they opened a protest blog to coordinate a strike, setting a date in which all of them will abstain from writing as a show of power. In addition, they designed and distributed graphic blog badges demanding the omission of the toolbar. *Nana* brought in Habot, the founder, as a mediator, and after a week of organized protest that made traditional media coverage, finally gave in. *Nana* took down their toolbar, leaving only a small logo aside the original *Israblog* logo.

From content management to community management

Now that 'the man behind the curtain' was gone, the metaphors of God and magician died with him, but Ilana Tamir was expected to 'put on her red shoes' and follow his footsteps. She was most often referred to as 'the mother of *Israblog*', and after a while her title at *Nana* was changed from *content* manager to *community* manager, a reflection of the shift in *Nana's* perspective after the toolbar incident.

For each problem she faced daily, Tamir had to decide: was the blog primarily a text? A place? An avatar of the blogger? Or a way of being? For example, when the phenomenon of *Pro-Ana*[1] blogs drew attention, some bloggers demanded these blogs be closed down to prevent the veneration of anorexia, but Tamir could not treat them solely as propaganda texts: the parents of some girls emailed her requests to let the blogs be, since following these representation of the girls' body was a vital way to monitor them. She decided to contact a professional expert and asked him to comment on the girls' blogs to start a dialogue. The Pro-Ana bloggers ignored all of the expert's communication until he was persuaded by Tamir to open his own blog on *Israblog*. Once he 'moved into their neighborhood' and engaged them as a fellow Israblogger, a dialogue indeed opened, thus the spatial metaphor provided the solution in this case.

Tamir faced a similar dilemma when an anonymous young pedophile blogged about his problems promoting awareness of his impossible situation and offering his point of view. His blog was filled with thousands of hate comments alongside intriguing conversations with worried mothers. Again, Tamir had to decide if this was a matter of text and she had to afford him the freedom of speech he claimed, or a matter of space and she could ban him from the territory of the community she is responsible for. Finally, it was agreed that he would continue to blog on an independent *Wordpress* platform and those who wanted to could follow him there. The text was still accessible, a page away, but bloggers were relieved he was no longer 'among' them as a resident of their community.

1 Pro-ana (stands for pro-anorexia) blogs proclaim that anorexia is a lifestyle choice and not a disease. The blogs, often written by female adolescents, provide places for "anas" to receive support, share experiences, and offer encouragement, including specific instruction for initiating and maintaining anorexia nervosa. For an example of scholarship on this topic, see Gay, Kristen Nicole, "Unbearable Weight, Unbearable Witness: The (Im)possibility of Witnessing Eating Disorders in Cyberspace" (2013). *Graduate Theses and Dissertations*. http://scholarcommons.usf.edu/etd/4676 for a discussion of the consequences of deleting such content from the web.

There was even one instance in which Tamir had to decide if she was responsible for what bloggers were doing offline: *Israblog*gers started organizing meetups on national holidays, held in a public place that was easily accessible from all over the country—the rooftop of the prestigious Azrieli Towers Mall in Tel Aviv. I attended two of these meetings as part of my ethnography, and it was as overwhelming as a carnival. Thousands of bloggers flocked to the mall unannounced. Some wore costumes and accessories, some carried cardboard signs with messages from their blogs, some wrote catchphrases on each other's skin, as if they were using their bodies as the avatars of their blogs.

After a few noisy events that ended with loitering and minor vandalism, the management of the mall called *Nana* and asked Tamir to do something about it or they would sue for damage. Tamir explained she was only responsible for bloggers' online texts and had no authority over their physical bodies, even if they were performing their identity as bloggers in the geographical space.

From community back to platform: The decline of the virtual cities

Most conflicts of interest between various groups of bloggers as described above defied transcoding, in the sense of being able to translate the dominant interpretation into the interface software. However, there was one clear incident which brought to surface a tiny and seemingly insignificant programming constraint that carried profound implications for *Israblog*. It also demonstrated that while *Nana* refrained from modifying platform aesthetics ever since the toolbar scandal, it used its power to shape the platform through back office programming.

As the platform grew, so did the tension between adult bloggers who produced personal narratives and teen bloggers, mostly girls, who used the blogs as storage spaces for graphic designs. At the time, many girls were operating collaborative blogs that functioned as virtual cities. The practice seemed like something between building Lego, building within SIMS, and playing with a dollhouse, except that the materials were digital images.[2] One morning, the most successful virtual city blog posted a sudden farewell post:

2 Virtual city blogs use blog posts as spaces and invite bloggers to 'move in': each blogger that is accepted into the city gets their own 'townhouse' which consists of at least 3 rooms. Each blog post represents a room in which the content of the post consists of pictures of furniture and sometimes room inhabitants. Activity on such blogs consists of constantly posting more spaces as the city expands as well as to represent movement and events in the city. For instance, if there is a party, dozens of posts may be created to represent the club and additional residents joining the party. The posts content would feature resident pictures, their choice of party cloths, drinks etc. One can think of it as a draft animation for 'hanging out' in a virtual world without the actual technology for it.

> *We are retiring due to the new blog posting limit, which means we're not working anymore, which means the city closes. Since we reached a respectable amount of posts, 588, we now have a limit of 5 posts per day; that number makes it impossible to maintain a city. Setting up a house for one person takes 3 posts. So because Israblog introduced this limitation and our editing interface stops working after 5 posts a day, we are forced to retire. Sorry, we hope you enjoyed the city while it lasted.*

I noticed this post published on April 17th 2006 since teen bloggers lamented the closing of the successful city, however, it had little meaning for me at the time. Looking back and considering the concept of digital material metaphor, I realize this was a turning point for *Israblog*, which had struggled with the tension between the blog as a text, a space, and a way of being since its inception. Adult bloggers often complained over teen girls' blogging practices, describing them as a "contamination of the blogosphere" and some took issue specifically with the genre of virtual cities, demanding *Nana* delegitimize it, as this was not considered 'blogging' to them.

Limiting one's updates to five a day might make sense for asynchronous communication and may even be an arbitrary theoretical programming decision. In fact, most adult users would never become aware of the existence of such a limitation. However, for girls who used the blog as a representation of a geographical space that held their digital avatars, each blog posting represented a single move 'into' and 'around' this space. After only five moves, they would figuratively 'hit a wall', forcing them to stop 'building' and expanding.

Through this programming limitation, *Nana* communicated a clear message that *Israblog* was primarily a text and could only be a space within the boundaries of that text. Adult bloggers saw it as a win and other active virtual cities were discouraged since they now knew they could only grow so far. But keep in mind this was 2006, before the explosion of social networks. *Israblog* was the only option for teens who needed a malleable platform with a Hebrew interface. This small programming limitation had silenced the voices and limited the subcultural practices of many girls at their tween years.

The retrospective framing and afterlife of Israblog

When Ilana Tamir left her job at *Nana* in 2012, she was not replaced by another media professional, but by a veteran blogger from the community, Mariette Cohen. When she took over the official *Israblog* management blog, she changed its name to *Miss Israblog*, accompanied by a header of an animated image of a young girl that bore some similarities to Cohen's external features (Figure 25.3)

Figure 25.3: "Miss Israblog" header on the official management blog. Source: Screenshot by Carmal Vaisman.

In 2013 *Israblog* celebrated 12 years since its founding and Cohen's blog post congratulated *Israblog* on its 'bat mitzvah', a Jewish rite of passage for twelve-year-old girls. One blogger commented: 'I never thought of *Israblog* as a she before'. The community manager gets to shape the policy of the platform according to her perceptions, and it would seem that Cohen favored the metaphor of the blog as a way of being, representing the dominant demography of *Israblog* which was always, and continues to be, girls in their tweens, or perhaps viewing the entire community as her avatar, an entity shaped in her own image, as one of its first bloggers.

A year later *Nana* experienced financial difficulties and formally withdrew from *Israblog*. Bloggers who cared about the platform and wanted it to exist amidst the rich contemporary social media landscape, took it upon themselves to maintain it without any official support. Cohen chose to continue as a volunteer manager. *Israblog* was abandoned by its media company as a content website, and abandoned by most of its users as they migrated from its territory to other social networks. It now stands alone as a textual archive, or a memorial website. It was picked up by Israeli National Library who views it as a text and preserves it as part of its cultural legacy archives, however, it is better characterized as a material artifact of the internet as a way of being, an integral part of the past selves of many bloggers who came of age and became social media influencers, journalists, activists, artists, and even academics, like yours truly, *Doctor Blog*.

DISCUSSION AND CONCLUSIONS: WHAT DOES A PLATFORM THINK IT IS?

The case of *Israblog* demonstrates that 'what the internet is' for particular groups, at particular times is an ongoing process of choices—and perhaps clashes—between metaphors that actively construct and negotiate this position. This chapter highlights the practices of various platform stakeholders to cope with the multiplicity of positions that subjects and spaces occupy simultaneously, as a mutual interactive process of learning and negotiating. The 'metaphoric meltdown' was resolved eventually, through a process whereby one metaphor became the dominant heuristic for making sense of what the platform was and consequently, the basis for policy. Its solidification in code formalized the digital materiality of this metaphor.

In the *Israblog* story, text is still the primary point of departure, and it is put into question only when it clashes with a different meaning of blogging. The concept of community slowly took root during those years, but as soon as its boundaries were challenged by attempting to extend it offline, *Israblog* withdrew to the textual frame to explain that it was only responsible for bloggers as a discourse community rather than a spatial one. Adult bloggers were actively defending the blog as a text, accepting its community aspect as an imagined community, while marginalizing and harassing girl bloggers over practices that took the blog for a representation of actual spaces (storage, geography, etc.) and bodies. This treatment drove a few girls out of the platform or towards a different blog genre, however, when the platform programmers solidified the textual metaphor through a posting limitation, the girls' defeat was rapid and finite.

While discourse metaphors might entertain multiple meanings, material metaphors represent a choice of a single or a dominant meaning, ignoring and erasing other layers of meaning. Therefore, the type of power that a platform has can perhaps be viewed in terms of the means to solidify discourse metaphors in software code, turning them into digital material metaphors. It is by such dynamics that digital artefacts are forced into familiar categories rather than cultivated into more transformative cultural potentials.

What do the platform operators or owners assume they're operating? How do their assumptions get reflected through default options, interface updates, terms of services, and general use policies? How committed are platforms to accommodate and materialize in code the multiplicity of meanings held by their users? To what extent can users become aware of and subvert the many digital material metaphors that might be working within the platform, the interface, or the norms for use that limit their freedom of expression? According to Andrew Feenberg (1999), users have an 'interpretive flexibility' about technology, which comes with the ability to creatively appropriate technology in ways that alters its modes or subverts the original intentions of its creators. Feenberg operates under the assumption the internet is an unfinished project, still open for negotiations between different actors, but does this assumption hold in the age of algorithm-governed platforms? His key example is French Minitel. In the 1980s, Minitel designed a database that users 'subverted,' using this capacity for their own personal communication, thus forcing Minitel to change its design and designation accordingly. One can find a more recent example in Twitter, which was designed with a specific mode of communication in mind—microblogging via SMS. Users, borrowing from IRC, instituted many symbolic systems for dialogic and topic-based communication such as user mentions and hashtags (see boyd et al., 2010). Twitter, Inc. later chose to materialize these in code, thus accepting the repurposing of the platform.

Users' legal interpretive flexibility seems significantly limited in the era of algorithms, thus the key path of subversion left is through communication norms, but it can only be done within the limits of the dominant digital material metaphor. For example, there could never have been a code or an algorithm capable of forcing the teen bloggers or Pro-Ana bloggers I studied in the early 2000s to respond to communication they deemed irrelevant, since unwanted communication would stand outside their community or literacy practices.

If the girls wanted to continue virtual cities blogging, pushing their spaces against the limits of text, they could have taken advantage of the replicability of digital platforms: open another blog, link the two and declare the first 'a neighborhood in full capacity'. Tween girl bloggers knew how to get their way, they mustered impressive forces to ignore hate speech, bullying, and irrelevant communication; they fought fiercely for the their rights by appealing often to the management, so I wonder why they simply gave up on virtual cities blogging over a coding limitation, without putting up the tiniest fight.

A decade later, after witnessing my share of conflicts of interests between participants and platform algorithms, I can only speculate that the answer lies in a technological determinist perception. Knowing tween *Israblog* bloggers, I am certain that if *Nana* would have announced a platform upgrade that hindered virtual cities, a scandal would have erupted that would remove this 'upgrade' in less than a day. However, the more a system becomes complex and bureaucratic, the more we tend to naturalize and morally neutralize its technical constraints, accepting them as a given even if they are newly introduced. Once they are assimilated, materialized in code, it is as if the verdict cannot be overturned.

CHAPTER TWENTY-SIX

Political Ideologies of Online Spaces: Anarchist Models for Boundary Making

JESSA LINGEL

Almost as soon as people began coming together on the web, they began debating the rules of participation. When someone spams a listserv, what's an appropriate response (see Brunton, 2013)? If someone harasses someone else in a community, how can that person get kicked out (see Dibbell, 1998)? Political ideologies have long shaped discourses about what the web is for and how it should be regulated.

Whether at the micro-level of managing individual online communities or the macro level of legislating an entire industry, arguments about the guiding political ethos of digital technologies have taken on new urgency following a slew of victories among right wing and national extremists. In combination with concerns of harassment and discrimination in the industry, concerns over political implications of digital media have led many observers to call into question the long-held assumption that digital technologies are inherently democratic (Cadwalladr, 2016; Edsall, 2017). Amid so much controversy, perhaps it's helpful to consider more radical alternatives to the political logics of online spaces and publics. Drawing on my research with online countercultures as well as some of my activist work, I will suggest *anarchist* models of boundary making as a generative set of practices for managing online community space.

The word "space" is somewhat charged when it comes to talking about online phenomena. Many early studies of the web noted the tendency among internet users to talk about the time they spent online using *spatial metaphors*. For example, in her influential text *Life Online*, Markham noted the tendency of her participants to describe digital interactions as having created meaningful spaces that produce a sense of community or identity work (1998, p. 150). Spatial metaphors seeped into everyday conversations about the web early on, whether talking about web *sites* or page *visits*. Eventually, scholars in digital studies began critiquing spatial metaphors (e.g. Druick, 1995; Harrison & Dourish, 1996; Lyman, 1998; Stefik, 1997), arguing that relying on language of space to describe the web ignores geographic differences that manifest online. Space shapes the infrastructure of internet connectivity and differences in geography have a way of asserting themselves into online communications (Burrell, 2012; Nakamura, 2001). In other words, talking about the internet as a space can render the significance of physical geography irrelevant in ways that are deeply problematic.

With these criticisms about spatial metaphors in mind, I return to Markham's (1998) comparisons between online and offline spaces as a way of structuring inquiry into political ideologies and online communities. I will argue that anarchism offers a set of interventions in conversations about political dynamics of online communities. I begin with a brief review of political dimensions of online communities before turning to my own fieldwork and activist experiences to consider anarchist models for managing space. While democratic values have dominated Western ideologies of digital culture, anarchist ethics have important lessons for thinking about managing small-p politics of online spaces.

CONTEXT: POLITICAL LIFE ONLINE

Early internet discourse positioned the web as a tool of democracy (see Dahlberg & Siapera, 2007; Ferdinand, 2000; Trippi, 2008), emphasizing democratic capacities of self-reliance (in terms of gaining knowledge about how to use digital technology), universal access to knowledge (or at least, universal to those with a modem), and tolerance (through exposure to diverse viewpoints). Summing up these tropes, Markham (2005) noted that:

> Although this period was not without empirically based and theoretically grounded research, there was a feeling of utopianism in descriptions of how technology might (or should) free us from the constraints of worldwide shackles like hierarchy, traditional social stereotypes, embodiment, and even death. (p. 797)

When we think about how the web was initially characterized as a tool of neoliberal progress, a key emphasis was on providing access or the idea that simply giving someone a computer or internet connection could resolve disparities of wealth or education (e.g. in projects like One Laptop per Child, see Warschauer and Ames, 2010). This viewpoint leverages determinist connotations with the internet as a DIY mechanism for self-improvement and autodidactic learning that moreover fosters tolerance by connecting users to people across the globe who are fundamentally different.

This utopian hype can be (and indeed has been) critiqued for advancing hyper-individualist narratives that ignored experiences of race, gender and privilege (e.g. Chun, 2006; Nakamura, 2001), and for failing to recognize the ways that differences in geography and privilege can be sharpened rather than reduced by online connectivity (Burrell, 2012). While some of the early promises about the democratic force of the web have endured, particularly in a neoliberal ethos that emphasizes individualism and meritocracy (Marwick, 2013), recent political turmoil such as the 2016 US presidential election has led technophiles as well as technophobes to ask whether the web has delivered on promise of tolerance, DIY education and diversity (e.g. Kreiss, 2016).

In conceptualizing the political implications of the internet in a contemporary online landscape, the (often panicked) rhetoric that emerges highlights the extremism of content, the hyper-segmentation of publics and the uneven virality of amplifying some voices over others (e.g. Cadwalladr, 2016; Edsall, 2017; Polonski, 2016). As Gerbaudo (2015) has argued in his analysis of social movements' relationship to technology, "traditional features of populism (appeal to unity, anti-establishment and anti-institutional rhetoric, strive for direct democracy, suspicion of intermediaries) come to be matched with a set of tropes that make up what we could call the 'ideology of social media' (interactivity, openness, directness)" (p. 68). For Gerbaudo, it may in fact be the case that a populist reality has emerged instead of the democratic promises hyped by techno-determinists. Rather than claiming that the early web was truly democratic and has now been corrupted, I'm attempting to trace dominant narratives about the internet as a tool of democracy, and to suggest that we are seeing a pessimistic shift in thinking about what the internet is for and what kinds of politics it supports.

Much of what I've just described relies on characterizations and hype, which risks eliding important nuances of life online. Bad actors have always existed on the internet and life online can still be and often is wonderfully democratic. By sketching these ideological views, my goal is not to polarize internet discourse further, but rather to clarify some of the underlying logics used to generate optimism about online communities. In the next section, I turn to a discussion of anarchist ethics as a framework for managing online spaces.

AN ANARCHIST ETHIC FOR THE TREATMENT OF TROLLS

All too often, anarchism is dismissed as a chaotic, nihilist and violent anti-politics. However, we can also reference anarchism as a political praxis that privileges consensus, bottom-up decision making, equality and radical transparency.[1] Anarchism "can be understood as the *generic* social and political idea that expresses the negation of *all* power, sovereignty, domination, and hierarchical division, and a will to their dissolution" (Wieck, 1978). Consideration of anarchist ethics have a long history in dialogues about online publics. A number of researchers have worked on how anarchist groups use digital technologies for political praxis (Collister, 2014; Maddox et al., 2016; Owens & Palmer, 2003), while others have focused more on anarchism as a set of principles for managing online communities (Freelon, 2010; Jensen, 2003; Papacharissi, 2004; Townley & Parsell, 2006). The latter is most in keeping with my interest in sketching anarchist ethics for community building. Below, I offer a brief reflection on activist activities and my fieldwork with countercultural communities to reflect on how anarchist practices can be mobilized in regulating online spaces, particularly as an ethic to guide decisions around community boundary-making. I first consider an encounter with an anarchist event dealing with a problematic community member. I then shift to how an online countercultural community dealt with similar problems on its platform as a way of reflecting on anarchist ethics can manifest in online spaces.

In 2013, I attended the Anarchist Book Fair (ABF) as a member of Radical Reference (Rad Ref), a group of activist librarians and archivists. The ABF is an annual event that brings together different activist groups and presses aligned with anarchism to connect and share resources. The event also includes workshops, discussion groups and trainings geared towards anarchist politics. RadRef has active chapters in many cities and the New York City collective often has a table at the ABF to promote their work and attract new members. As the bookfair neared, I learned that a number of organizations were threatening to pull out because a provocative figure (I'll call him Horace) in the local anarchist community had signed up to attend. Contrary to common assumptions that anarchist interactions are pure chaos, the episode illustrates an emphasis on documentation, process and transparency.

Ultimately, Horace wasn't granted a table or allowed in the ABF space. But in learning about the process of an anarchist community deciding whether to allow a self-professed anarchist to attend a community event, I was struck by just how procedural the response to Horace was. The process involved a series of conversations, documentations and investigations. Email exchanges about IRL meetings emphasized a need for evidence, for process and for allowing Horace to respond to accusers. Concerned anarchists produced prior documentation from earlier

1 I credit Antliff (2012) as a text that helped me recognize my own failure to acknowledge the legitimacy of anarchist politics, while noting that the knee-jerk dismissal of anarchism (like the dismissals of feminism as silly, shrill or misandrist) as a viable set of practices is one of the most effective tools of maintaining hegemonic, capitalist norms.

confrontations. Horace had in fact been subject to a number of adjudication and accountability processes, as a result of accounts of violence, abuse, disruption and snitching. In this case, anarchist ethics for managing disruptive behaviors were fundamentally centered on collective processes and accountability, holding people to a particular set of group-centered ideals.

What does this kind of practice look like online? In my work on countercultural communities and digital technologies (Lingel, 2017), I've observed similar processes of documentation when it comes to removing someone from a community. For example, in my study of an online community for body modification enthusiasts, a key part of removing members (meaning deleting their accounts from the platform) involved a Terms of Service (TOS) forum, where complaints were vetted as to whether someone had violated the site's clearly articulated ethics of tolerance and diversity. The message board, which was viewable by all members of the platform, also provided documentation of users' removal from the site, such that if you logged into the site one day and realized that a user no longer "existed" you could check the TOS forum and see if and why that person had been removed.

Contrast these two instances to the "removal-through-flagging" approach of sites like Facebook, YouTube and Twitter. Crawford and Gillespie (2016) have argued that flags are a remarkably thin mode of documenting intra-platform dissent. Often the process of objecting to content ends with the flag itself, with no possibility of following the process of adjudication or even necessarily being alerted to the outcome. While anarchists are frequently misconstrued as lawless and chaotic, they rely on clear mechanisms for managing violations of standards and ethics, much like the countercultural community described above. In contrast, sites like Facebook and YouTube are in fact far more inchoate and chaotic in terms of their protocols, which are almost entirely invisible to everyday users.

CONCLUDING THOUGHTS

Whether online or off, spaces have to be managed when it comes to accommodating new members or ensuring that people treat each other according to community guidelines. This chapter has presented a brief thought experiment to consider how offline approaches to handling trolls within anarchist communities could play out on mainstream social media platforms. In thinking about what we might learn from how the ABF and online countercultural communities manage spaces, we see the need for collective and localized approaches to managing people in online spaces. There isn't just one Internet, there are many, and a single policy cannot hold water in all of them. A one-size fits all approach to managing a diverse and growing internet will always fail some group or subject position, usually those on the margins. ABF's protocols for Horace worked because it reflected local norms and values, and relied on consensus and documentation. A transparent process of documentation is vital for the integrity of a community, in contrast to the

invisible process of flagging, a disappearance of users and context that leaves no trace, no explanation and affords no possibility of protest.

A user-versus system process of adjudication makes no sense if the system lacks community level ideology; although Facebook phrases its policies as "community standards," it is ludicrous to think of Facebook as having an identifiable sense of community ethics. Moreover, the notion of community dissolves as soon as it becomes solely incumbent on the individual user to report behavior. Anarchist ethics for managing disruptions of community norms underscore the extent to which these processes need to be collective not only in terms of grassroots procedures for adjudication, but also a conceptualization of disruption that accounts for collective rather than individual violations.

Social media will continue to shift and fork, and different forces—from industry as well as government and non-state actors—will continue seeking ways to constrain the power of online connectivity. Within debates around how the coextensive relationships between digital technologies and political values, how can we make room for alternative ideologies, practices and concepts? How can we incorporate radical politics into the everyday work of managing online spaces?

CHAPTER TWENTY-SEVEN

No Country for IT-Men: Post-Soviet Internet Metaphors of Who and How Interacts with the Internet

POLINA KOLOZARIDI, ANNA SHCHETVINA, AND KATRIN TIIDENBERG

The internet is not understood in the same way by all people, everywhere. This statement is fair enough, but it is an inadequate challenge to the erasure of varied histories and experiences of the Internet outside the West.

This chapter introduces an alternative understanding of what the internet might mean if we take into account its world-wide history. In the fieldwork presented in this piece, the Russian authors interviewed a group of early internet pioneers. These people (men) were the first to encounter and use the internet in Russian cities. And their description of the relationships with the internet don't match what Markham (1998, 2003) describes as 'tool, place, or way of being'. Why?

In this piece we first turn to a historical and cultural context to describe some of the fundamental principles of 'human+technology' relationships in USSR (Soviet Union) and post-Soviet culture. In this historical Soviet context, the roots of the modern attitude toward the internet are built. This narrative emphasizes what elements of the relationships between people and technologies in the Soviet culture might be useful to explain the peculiarities we've faced in the field. Second, we identify some key features of the narratives about the internet used by internet pioneers in Russia drawing from our empirical materials. We focus on three features of an attitude towards the internet that our participants hold: externality of the internet to the user, collectivity of usage, and a possibility of the internet to be technically "spoiled." Based on what they say (metaphorical expressions), how they say it (linguistic constructions), and in what situation they say it (local Russian contexts), we propose that despite similarities between Western and Russian metaphors (through, say for instance, Markham's 1998 conceptual framework of tool, place, and way of being), different histories and cultures of technologies create significant distinctions in what meaning is conveyed.

Our materials are based on a series of interviews in 2017–2019 with internet pioneers from Tyumen, Tomsk, Kazan, Pereslavl-Zalessky and Voronezh. In what follows, we describe how Russian internet history can be understood through the idea of conveyance metaphors (because these reflect cultural features), and we decenter both users and usage as the central parameters of the metaphors of the internet.

HISTORICAL BACKGROUND OF OUR FIELDWORK

The artist Vladimir Arkhipov initiated an online-offline project called *The Other Things Museum* (Arkhipov, n.d.) in the 1990s. He travelled "around Russia and its borders," collected different things, created by ordinary people for their own use (e.g., a berry piercer made from a bottle cork or a lamp from pipes), and conducted interviews with their makers. Their stories often demonstrate that this everyday engineering is treated as a rather ordinary practice for those who were brought up in the Soviet context. But labeling this as being representative of a DIY-culture would be misleading because of the Western ideology and technological determinism embedded in that terminology. (Braybrooke & Jordan, 2017). Rather, Gerasimova and Chujkina (2004) call it MDM: "make do and mend." People in the USSR had to mend things, when those things broke, as it was impossible to buy substitutes. They had to make things, as they couldn't buy things with the functionality they needed.

In the late 1980s, Woolgar gave the world an understanding of a machine as a text, which is written and read, and the user, who is configured (1990). His ethnographic research at a microcomputing company demonstrated how technology designers or computer engineers imagine technology in its inevitable connection with the person. In accordance with this idea, since the person is a user separated from technology, technology should be configured with the user in mind (or perhaps even in collaboration with the user) so it is attractive for potential buyers. But in the Soviet Union (i.e. USSR, 1922–1991) there were no "users" in this sense. For a long time there was no consumer capitalism. And perhaps more importantly, the overall history of human interactions and relations with technology in the Soviet Union is different from the history that became in large part universalized by Woolgar.

THE THREE TENETS OF HUMAN/MACHINE INTERACTION

Some of the people-thing relations need to be traced back to the period after the Russian Revolution (1920s). These were times of both an economic and political transformation as well as cultural change. Many Russian artists, engineers, filmmakers, writers, and architects imagined and developed the world of today and tomorrow. Along with other inventions and ideas, this meant developing and inventing various machines and imagining their relationships with people (both in literature and in practice). Three key features of that time have been described by researchers and theorists:

People shouldn't use things, but work together with things

Russian researcher of Soviet photography and cinema Tatiana Dashkova (2002) described a common genre of journal photos of the 1920–1930s as a Human+Machine Centaur. People in these photos were shown at work, there were no names of models or photographers, and the caption usually said: "A woman/man on a machine". As Dashkova describes it:

> "A machine" ("a rostrum"/"a cow"/"a test-tube") on such photos is an extension of the body—it is not about a human working on a machine, it is a "human machine." The body is inseparable from the machinery, it is uncompleted and unimportant without the machine. This object is a centaur, a single body. (p. 119).

People in such relations with technologies are workers. But they are not struggling workers like those depicted by Charlie Chaplin in his film "Modern Times." Rather, they are co-workers, working together with those pieces of technology they used.

People should explore and construct things, not consume them

In 1924 Marietta Shaginyan made *things* the actors in her novel "Mess-mend or Yankee in Petrograd" (Shaginyan, 1960). Things acted on their own and helped Soviet people to defeat capitalism by closing and opening (doors) or by taking pictures (camera). Later Ekaterina Degot' (2000) cited Shaginyan's idea as a key articulation of that period's understanding of human-thing relations: "The master of the things is the one who makes them, the one who uses them is a slave." Degot' situated this thesis in the context of Socialist-Capitalist opposition regarding the Fordist labor approach or workforce organization.

Degot also analyzed the early critique of what will be later called consumerism: the temptation by capitalist things exhibited in shops. She analyzed artist Alexander Rodchenko's letters to his wife, which were not so much a critique of consumerism as an emerging opposition. An alternative to consumerism is suggested in those letters: things are introduced as "comrades" eager to help and collaborate. This was not a utopian vision, but rather a practical perception in a country after the Civil War and Russian Revolution. This perception was later reproduced in Soviet and socialist culture, as seen in movies of Muratova, Forman, Khutsman and others as well as the early movies of Polansky .

People should have long relations with things

This tenet had practical, everyday origins. Things acquired were sometimes not immediately suitable for use. Buying a car, a Soviet man/woman had to be prepared for repairing it, sometimes even before use (Gerasimova & Chujkina, 2004). The same was true for other technical objects. For example, people combined TV-sets and computers to make a soviet PC and there was a popular radio-set sold as a built-it-yourself kit. Old buses were used as houses in the countryside, clothes and shoes were routinely repurposed. This might be similar to what is called a zero-waste lifestyle today. However the similarity is shallow, for the ideology and context were different (Tatarchenko, 2019).

What happened to these ideas?

By the beginning of the 1930s, the Soviet state had begun to control industrial development and cultural initiatives. Independent engineers and inventors were oppressed (Graham, 1993), but the intellectual basis and rhetoric of exploration and invention did not disappear at once. Moreover, the post-Stalinist period was fruitful for the new initiatives like the Scientific Cities (*akademgorodki*, see Tatarchenko, 2013). In fact, between its victory in World War II and its defeat in the Cold War, the Soviet Union developed an array of technologies, some of which were never used.

A variety of technological industries flourished between the 1930s and 1980s, advancing radio, military services, transportation, space exploration, and the like. The disruption of the Cold War meant the Soviet Union's engineers were obliged to use prototypes from the U.S. and Europe but, at the same time, had almost no contact with the original developers (Abramov, 2017b, p. 67).

The ETW, or Engineering-Technical Worker, is generally held as the key figure of the Soviet technological transformation. This term was introduced in the 1920s and meant a person engaged in technology production, whether as an engineer or as a worker. They were more multi-functional than their Western colleagues, as ETWs were engineers, inventors, designers, assemblers, and managers, not just the developers of a given technology (Kukulin, 2017). The ETWs social reflection was specifically cultivated in opposition to what was taught in Soviet humanities programs, and can be understood in the popular phrase "physics vslyrics." This anti-humanities thinking merged with ideas from sci-fi, and the ETWs own intellectual findings like TRIZ or think-act approach.[1]

This specific stratum is still important for Russia. Recent research on Russian techno-entrepreneurs has emphasized their distinction from Finnish and Korean counterparts. For example, Kharkhordin et al. (2019) found that people from Russia are more oriented towards inspiration, a willingness to change the world. They treat invention as something that is opposite to industrial routine and money-making.

Despite the fact that Soviet technological development was similar to the American in its postwar genealogy, there was a different ideological vector. Benjamin Peters reconstructs two cybernetic projects as being connected both to the development of WWII computer systems on the one hand, and the needs of the Cold War on the other. However, the institutional conditions differed (Peters, 2016). The Soviet computer project was a localized economically-oriented project; thus was less globally influential than and not as idealistic as the American ARPANET. However, the Soviet computer project presumed that Russia would join the future as a collective of people, not appropriating it, but sharing and teaching each other. This focus on the collective identity of the user must be seen as a strong part of our participant's background in the 1980s.

THE INTERNET PIONEERS OF THIS STUDY—FROM ZASTOI TO PERESTROIKA

During the 1980s, being 15–16 years old, our participants were members of special clubs for youth[2] and dreamed of becoming engineers. Then, the Soviet Union disintegrated. For our participants it was a surprise. While sometimes skeptical about the Soviet Union, they were not very engaged in it on a political level and had not expected it to disappear. Yet, this was the time when these people, carrying with them the background we've described above, became internet pioneers. As

1 TRIZ is a soviet term, an acronym for a theory of the resolution of invention-related tasks. It was introduced in the 1950s by the Soviet inventor and science-fiction author Genrich Altshuller. TRIZ as a theory had a practical methodology for generating innovative solutions for problem solving. It was developed as a useful approach for problem formulation, system and failure analysis. Think-act approach is a theoretical and practical doctrine interrelating the acts and thoughts in an organization in order to establish effectiveness. The latter is now quite popular in Russia and used in governance organization.

2 They were clubs for pupils and youth to develop their hobbies in math, programming and computing. There were also plenty of groups engaged in early digital computing and programming (Tatarchenko, 2019)

Abramov (2017a) writes, "They had to find a symbolic bridge from being a 'Soviet engineer' to a 'successful businessman' or an 'entrepreneur" (p. 73).

The first USSR computers were constructed during the 1960s–1980s, but even in the early 1990s people mostly used computers only at work. It was too expensive to have one at home. However, even from work computers, these early users started joining BBS, Usenet and FIDO (Konradova et al. 2006). After the dissolution of the USSR in 1991, they then joined the Internet, and the use of networks and computers in post-Soviet Russia took off.

CONVEYANCE METAPHORS OF THE INTERNET AMONG THE POST-SOVIET EARLY ADOPTERS

MacCormac's (1985) work on the role of metaphors in the process of cognition distinguishes between basic metaphors and conveyance metaphors. Basic metaphors reflect some initial essential conjecture, or intuition, which forms the foundation of the whole imaginary or theory. We can say that metaphors of "tool," "place" and "way of being" are basic when they are used to constitute an image, usage and policy of the internet (Markham, 1998, 2003). Surrounding these metaphors, there are plenty of additional linguistic constructions that may not always correspond to the basic metaphor but still convey it. These constructions—used to express a specific feeling or to evoke an idea of an individual opportunity—are also important for our understanding of the relationships between people and the internet.

Basic Western metaphors don't adequately encapsulate the Russian framework around what the internet is and does. Based on the interviews we gathered in Russian regions in 2017 and 2018, we identified three imaginaries around the internet and its usage that we suggest function as conveyance metaphors. Our participants—all men, mostly educated in physics or engineering, mostly of the "lost soviet generation" (Yurchak, 2005)—were among the first in the post-Soviet Russia to use the internet. They said "we" instead of "me;" perceived the Internet as something that had come to them from the outside; and were mostly disappointed about the current state of the internet, feeling nostalgic towards the 1980s.

Not I but we

The most obvious feature of our participants' speech is their reference to themselves as users within a plural pronoun. We have only two interviews in which the biographical story starts with the narrative of "me + Internet." And only once did the participant speak about himself as a hero and an actor from the first to the last phrase. All the other participants, at least partly, referred to themselves as "we" as a part of a collectivity. They stated clearly that the Internet was the thing which came to "us." Nevertheless, the nature of this collectivity remains quite abstract. "We" meant a wide description of a collective entity which enacted technology. However, just as the Internet was connected with "us," it was also "ours." Konradova et al. (2006) suggest that this sensibility is more than just a language barrier; it represents a key distinction between Western and Russian internet users, even among the early adopters.

This abstract 'we' and the idea that the internet is 'ours' may have also been fostered by the memory that the internet emerged spontaneously, or just happened, without any particular individual or group's effort:

> *I think these stories [about the early development of the internet in Russian regions] simply materialized at some point as everybody happened to be in the right place at the right time, with the appropriate approach. Everybody was feeling like … how should I put it … it [=entity] wasn't there, but we all seemed to bring something to somehow build it. Someone brought more, someone less, it doesn't matter, but here we are, somehow [doing something] together.*
>
> *(A. Tomsk)*

It is difficult to translate into English the Russian phrase "*tak proizoshlo*" because the Russian language contains impersonal verbs which do not have analogues in English. They mean that something happens without any intentional will and there is no subject of an action. Probably the closest analogue in English would be "it happened to be" or "so it was."

However, this does not mean our participants were passive in the process of the internet happening to them. They "adopted" the technologies to the local conditions, mending and customizing to the weather or social conditions. For example, they created new types of boxes for internet wires. These improvements were often not patented and did not become a business. Just as in the MDM (make do and mend) tradition, the customization was treated as a natural part of the people-technology co-living and local business.

The Internet just happened

One of our participants was very critical of present-day programmers, IT production and services. He was sure that the market logics force people to work faster and more inaccurately. He said that some parts of modern computers are "rudimentary," out of date, and this was ridiculous to him. He couldn't understand why computer workers nowadays are less interested in innovations and more in sales. The word "rudimentary" (a Darwinian term) in his complaint about the modern times echos the excitement and hope people felt when they saw the first IBM PC in the 1980s. He speaks about computer technologies as if they were subject to a natural process of development and obsolescence.

> *All that hardware simply died one day because of the Intel processors with their capacity and multi-processing units. It is just a natural way of life.*
>
> *(A. Tomsk)*

Many of our informants referred to the Internet as something that develops because of the forces of nature somewhere beyond the horizon of their personal influence. Our informants never created anything like the IBM processor, or any other technology they admire. They adapted it and co-constructed it in their cities or probably regions (country-level ambitions were infrequently mentioned). The internet became an additional feature of a new way of being, but it was not something that our informants developed. It was adapted, implemented and applied, not invented.

Therefore, unlike in the Western narratives about the good old days of the Web we created (cf. Chapter Three) or even the popular story of RuNet described as a space for programmers, journalists, artists, and, of course, countless homepages (Kuznetsov, 2004) our participants did not feel they were creators or founding fathers. The big RuNet, with its mission and mythology, was almost never mentioned by any of our participants. For them, the internet had been neither global nor even national. It was a natural, but external growth of the various technologies they had helped to build locally.

Internet was spoiled

In 1990s Russia, special spaces for using the Internet appeared: Internet cafes and clubs, engineering circles based on interests, university labs, and offline meetings of chat members. This period of computer clubs, students' online initiatives and small businesses ended in the 2000s. In the era of smartphones and startups, our engineers finally became old people from a different epoch. Our participants' narratives were often nostalgic, and spoke of an Internet that had somehow been spoiled. When they started using the internet it could only be experienced in, and thus only existed in, specific material places and social conditions.

The good, understandable, useful, easily controlled *technology* of the early internet became technically spoiled for our participants. It became overpopulated with users and overgrown cultural practices, which made it dangerous and unpredictable, blurring its instrumentality. Users on this new internet can steal, lie and insult. Our informants are at a loss as to how to deal with a situation where technology is not a privilege of a small group, a thing to be used by professionals, but something with lots of different users. Today's internet, thus, is seen as something hopelessly entangled with diverse, often stupid, cultural practices (cat memes, sms, forums, social media). The early internet, in contrast, was a tool for human connection. As Natalia Konradova (2006) writes in "Our Runet:"

> The idea about technological determinism seems to be much more popular among Russian academics, scholars and artists of my generation ("the generation of the 1990s"—a group formed in the years of perestroika, with its own specific socio-psychological features). There could be an ideological point: to be under the rule of technology means to be free of the human (cultural) factor. (p. 19)

The metaphor of "spoiling" corresponds to the change of the material, social and organizational context and blends nostalgia with utopia. We presume that the metaphor of the internet "being spoiled" or "being broken" is not unique to the Russian context, but the particular Soviet historical perspectives gives the term "spoiled"different connotations.

BROADENING TOOL/PLACE/WAY OF BEING FRAMEWORK

Our analysis shows a variety of continuations between those people-technologies relations we know from the history of the USSR and our participants' attitudes towards the internet. Our informants might broadly use metaphors of "tool," "place" or "way of being," but paying attention to the Russian socio-historical context allows us to better understand what these metaphors actually mean for them.

Not only users

Approached from the Russian, post-Soviet perspective, the tool/place/way of being metaphoric framework seems to objectify technology, and separate it from the person. The technology *is used* as a Tool/Place/Way of Being. However, for our participants the people-technology relation is not that of usage, but of a Centauric techno-collective entity growing with the help of the people we have interviewed. We found a variety of narratives and metaphors about *relationships with technologies* or the power and inner dynamics of technology, but not about the technologies themselves, as passive objects. To understand how these people make sense of the internet, we need to see beyond the concept of "user" or "individual" or "human," and pay attention to a variety of human+technology superpositions. This may only be achieved by examining not only basic metaphors, but also more local linguistic constructions that can transfer metaphorical meaning.

Relationships with the Internet are dynamic

Our participants attitudes toward the internet shifted as the internet changed during their lifetime. This was evident as our participants talked about how the internet developed, how it was an external force of nature and how it became spoiled. Our participants used bio-metaphors to describe the process—they described the "life," "death" and "ethnogenesis" of websites, platforms or applications. This natural growth could be understood optimistically as an evolution that developers are not controlling, but taking part in it, or in a more pessimistic way as a cruel force that leads to the impossibility of controlling the dynamic changes of the internet. Beyond how the internet develops, our participants also used dynamic metaphors to describe how people's engagement with the internet changes. Here the language of quickly passing trends was used. People become bored of playing with one thing and go to play with another. This is unpredictable and has no final aim. As our informants say: "*The Internet is a toy,*" "*people have already played enough on the Tatnet (Tatar-language segment of the Internet).*"

Internet exists in a specific material and organizational context

Describing the experience of using the internet as something isolated and separated from the context obscures many things. Our participants' experiences and articulations of those experiences were highly contextual. This is where attention to conveyance metaphors becomes particularly helpful. To understand what it means to Russian internet pioneers to refer to the Internet as a way of being, we need to take into account the historical context and their preferred metaphor of "spoiling." Internet as a way of being thus becomes a complex structure of being: within special places (internet clubs, offices), social interactions (both offline and online) and specific schedules of the day.

CONCLUSION

French philosopher Gilbert Simondon's book *On the Mode of Existence of Technical Objects* (2011) provides a framework for describing the co-existence and co-production of technology, nature and person that contradicts the way in which usage is treated in consumer capitalism. He states that in order to establish relations without exploitation between humans, we need to establish the same type of relations between humans and technology. We can be friends with technologies.

The way popular discourse articulates technologies is not suitable for such a future, therefore we are looking for alternatives. The shift towards metaphors of relations we've described in this chapter may offer such an alternative. As researchers, we (the Russian authors of this article) are a part of a Western academic culture and personally belong (at least partly) to the global Internet culture. That is why we consider it important to understand where boundaries of "Western" and "global" lie, when these determinations will not work, and most importantly, whether alternatives exist. At the same time, we are also post-Soviet people and our everydayness embodies the remnants of the Soviet socio-technological background. It is reflected both in our discourse and in the way our everyday life is organized. The roots of this organization are in the Soviet past, with all its promises, transformations and cruelty. We have observed the reflections of the 1920s to think of things as comrades and centaurs. We have described how the necessity of invention was part of people's everyday life. Things were something that people had to co-construct and adapt to their own needs. Finally, technologies were a part of big projects on both sides of the Cold War. This provides a mix of understanding of technology as something, which "comes to us" and needs to be mended and domesticated a bit. Our internet pioneers think of themselves as a group that tinkers with technology, but does not think about the user experience as the ultimate aim.

The peculiarities of post-Soviet narratives influence our understanding of metaphors and suggest their limitations. We suggest that in attempts to understand how the internet is made sense of, we should also focus on how technology participates in relations (and is not just used), what the dynamics of internet change are, and whether there is a possibility for collective identity and relations with the internet. By extending the metaphorical framework of the internet as a tool, place, and a way of being in such a way, we can think about the past and the future beyond borders.

CHAPTER TWENTY-EIGHT

Remixed into Existence: Life Online as the Internet Comes of Age

RYAN M. MILNER

COMING OF AGE ON THE MADCAP MASH UP INTERNET

I began my life online in the early aughts, at a time when the robust, playful, and personal dimensions of online interaction Annette Markham charted in 1998 were already growing more prevalent and prominent. More people, more platforms, and more modes of communication were corroborating Markham's arguments about the social and cultural "themes of life in cyberspace." Access was opening a little wider with increased broadband connection. "Web 2.0" interfaces allowed users to create, circulate, and transform content a little easier. Conversations became more multimodal; images, videos, and GIFs came to share prominence with the word play, ascii art, and emoticons long woven through chatrooms, MUDs, and forums. With new participants, new sites, and new tools came new ways of being stitched together by shared social practices.

For my part during this proliferation, I was one of the legion of pop-culture obsessed geeky gamer kids who set the barbed, absurdist, ironic tone on sites like Something Awful, 4chan, and eventually Reddit, a constellation of then backwaters that we, their inhabitants, reckoned an empire. Or at least that's how I assumed we reckoned them, and at least that's who I assumed we were. After all, I had no way of really knowing the identities and motivations of the people I was talking with. And yet, I never even questioned whether the buzzing collectives on my screen were comprised of people like me. Why wouldn't they be? I was a suburban American white dude, and so until I heard otherwise I got to assume *every*body was like me. As far as I knew or cared, I was spending my days (well mostly late nights) with countless other suburban American white dudes who had a reliable internet connection and sufficient time on their hands. When I thought of "internet people" that's who I thought of, because I never really had to think of anyone else.

This assumption wasn't exactly challenged by my interactions. The majority of my conversations took on that same standard pop-culture-obsessed-geeky-gamer-white-dude-with-a-reliable-internet-connection tone. A tone detrimental to a lot of other tones and a lot of other voices; the jokey, casual, "ironic" (but still explicit) sexism and racism all too common in the online backwaters I frequented got a pass in part because no one seemed to seriously assume women or people of color were even there; if they were, they weren't the ones who got to be seen. We had a lot of collective fun, but we were also a safe harbor for perspectives none of us should have suffered so gladly. We said we were legion, but we were legion only because we molded our discourse to the same familiar and partial tropes, motifs, and themes.

Like the denizens of cyberspace Markham spent her time with in the 90s, this social imaginary[1] used technological tools to carve a metaphorical place with its own *lingua franca*, its own customs, practices, and expectations premised on the swirling cacophony of what we were seeing others do. We shitposted screeds, memes, and copypasta, all the while developing a complex rat's nest of jargon and esoteric lore to amuse ourselves and befuddle outsiders ("lurk more").[2] We scored an ambivalent cultural symphony by sharing and resharing injokes and catchphrases, slang and stories, along with a hefty dose of slurs and stereotypes. Only we didn't call this cultural symphony "cyberspace" much anymore, and we didn't talk in terms of an "information superhighway." We (pretty arrogantly) just called ourselves The Internet.

And proper noun it was, an oft-used metonymic shorthand for the nebulous constellation of collective practices occurring within and across the niche platforms we populated. It was an imagined community that was less about the guts of the machine (the wires, routers, and undersea cables) and more about shared social practices and social texts (the shitposts, screeds, and memes). And myopic though this appropriation be ("The Internet" = "*My* Internet"), it resonates to this day, for instance as a still oft-employed shorthand for "internet culture," which itself labels a nebulous constellation of collective sites and collective conversations about

1 A "social imaginary" is Arjun Appadurai's (1996) term for a group that professes collective connection even if it doesn't exhibit the local interdependence of traditional communities.

2 In the jargon of these esoteric collectives, a *shitpost* was a contribution to a conversation that instead denigrated the conversation, a *meme* was an oft-adapted joke, trope, or reference, *copypasta* was humorous stories copied and pasted between different contexts, and *lurk more* is what insiders told outsiders who didn't yet know any of this.

whatever happens go viral on any given day. That's the *The Internet* that I came of age with, that still discursively dominates so much online participation, and consequently shapes so many ways of being in the digital age. I present that Internet here in title case, befitting its collectively-imagined monolithic grandeur.

This Internet had a defining feature. More than anything, The Internet that I came of age with was a remix machine. It was spoken into existence by the reappropriation, recombination, and repurposing of what had come before in the name of new conversation, creativity, and commentary. Remix manifested in the multimodal photoshops, auto-tunes, mash ups, hashtag games, and reaction GIFs that dominated our interactions. Indeed, proficiency with remix was what allowed us to converse within the *lingua franca* at all; it was how we showed we belonged and policed the belonging of others. And it felt like we had the whole world at our disposal. The constant flow between "internet culture" and "popular culture" eroded whatever boundaries there had been between life online and life offline; now, an endless deluge of cut ups, references, and translations ensured that digital media and mass media clanged and sang together. Even our collective identity was a remix; it was a social imaginary that mashed up and homogenized as it rehashed and reused, filtered and distilled perspectives, commentaries, and professed standpoints.

Fittingly, for all its gleeful, self-aware self-importance, The Internet's remix machine wasn't doing anything all that new. It's no secret that remix is essential to individual and collective expression, online or off. Entire social worlds, from norms and ideologies to arts and entertainment, are mixes of mixes of mixes; people sample from what's come before as they drop new tracks of their own. Arguments about the centrality of remix to digital media, like those forwarded by David J. Gunkel (2016) and Lawrence Lessig (2008), have been prevalent for at least a decade. And long before that, Mikael Bakhtin (1935) and Roland Barthes (1977) were, without ever using the term, talking about how remix guides even apparently singular literary texts, which stitch together original expression from established contexts. Claude Lévi-Strauss (1962) calls this work "bricolage," the gritty, everyday repurposing of whatever's at hand for new artifacts and new ideas. Michel De Certeau (1984) talks about cultural adaptation in terms of "poaching," a concept Henry Jenkins (1992) applies to media participation explicitly. And whether Richard Dawkins (1976) knew it or not, he was talking about remix when he framed human social organization in terms of the memes we spread. For all the problems with Dawkins' biological read on human culture, he does get one thing right: people make the world around them through the imitation and transformation of what others have made before. If, like Kirby Ferguson (2015) says, "everything is a remix," it's because everything is memetic. Samples all the way down.

Remix happens during banal conversations, which Deborah Tannen (1989) says depend on the integration of fixed social tropes into novel situations. Remix happens when people make jokes or, more often than not, when they adapt an old joke they've heard for a new audience (Dundes, 1987). Remix happens as people circulate and transform folk stories, like fairy tales (Zipes, 2013) and urban legends (Brunvand, 1981). As Markham (2013) herself puts it, "remix is not something we do in addition to our everyday lives; it is the way we make sense of our world" (p. 70). Like all good scholars, I'm remixing right now, mashing decades of thought down into two paragraphs, which also happen to be distillations of arguments I've made before (Milner, 2016; Phillips & Milner, 2017).

But for all these continuities, digital media amplify the ubiquity, speed, and consequence of remix. Two decades after Markham penned her themes of life in cyberspace, and fifteen years after I first stumbled onto The Internet, its nonstop polyphonic remix pervades online participation across multiple sites, platforms, and apps; digital media remix has crawled out of the backwaters in a big way. New tools afford the easy imitation, manipulation, and transformation of what others have produced, themselves imitators, manipulators, and transformers. The interaction, opinion, content, and commentary that greets us on sites big and small—on Facebook, Twitter, TikTok, YouTube, Pinterest, Snapchat, Instagram, on private Discord channels and Slack groups and GroupMe threads—is premised on remix. Reaction GIFs ripped from the film *Mean Girls*, jokes scandalizing PBS's *Arthur*, #foodporn hashtags applied to posts with varying degrees of irony, all are simultaneously vernacular life online and creative media remix. According to Markham (2013), this deluge of remixed content, and our part in the process, creates "momentary meaning structures, mini-remixes that get remixed again and again" (p. 71) as new participants sample new notes on their own pages, feeds, and forums.

Now that the remix practices paramount to The Internet are more accessible, there are more pockets where the class comfortable white male hivemind that invisibly defined the social imaginary over a decade ago isn't the discursive default. It's harder now for even geeky gamer white dudes to assume that the invisible *every*one on their Internet is a geeky gamer white dude (some have taken the news better than others). And this is only speaking of the largely-English, mostly-Western sites I spend my time on; memetic remix is also essential to the global internet cultures studied by the likes of An Xiao Mina (2014), Adeyemi Adegoju and Oluwabunmi Oyebode (2015), and Najma Al Zidjaly (2017). As technologies have democratized, so too have the social practices they afford.

But despite the present vibrancy of this remix machine, old ghosts linger within it. The exclusion and dehumanization that too many participants, myself included, gave a pass in 2003 and too many scholars, myself included, glossed over in 2011 has thrived, growing steadfast inside The Internet that has sustained it. It's a cancer robbing a body of its vibrancy; it's a sour note in a song. Facebook hoaxes spread from photoshop to photoshop, Daily Stormer memes rehash stereotype after stereotype, and State propaganda is distributed by Twitter bots who influence susceptible partisans by replicating the social media self-presentation of those same susceptible partisans. The madcap mash up Internet brought to life during the last two decades still sets much of the public tone online today, and the worst of it will continue to corrupt that tone unless we better understand its clattering song.

The themes of life in cyberspace Markham charted in 1998 can help that understanding. In her study she says that some participants see the internet as a tool they use to get things done, some see it as a place where they convene, and some see it as a way of being intertwined with their very selves. Twenty years later and The Internet I came of age with, the one forged by collective remix, is tool and place and way of being all at once, and fosters good and bad and everything in between. Given this ubiquity, it's essential to ask how we can remix more empowering social worlds into existence.

REMIX AS TOOL, PLACE, AND WAY OF BEING; REMIX AS UNSWEET SONG

Even if remix is now a dominant explanatory framework for life online, conceptualizations of The Internet as a tool, a place, or a way of being—or all three intertwined—are as relevant as ever, and remix is congruent with all three. Remix is a quintessential digital tool, remix helps The Internet feel like a place, and remix is so pervasive that it constitutes a way of being, an ambivalent *modus operandi* for participation in online collectives.

Underscoring this *modus operandi*, of course, are the digital technologies at its heart, a point Whitney Phillips and I (2017) make when explaining how online affordances—like modularity, modifiability, archivability, and accessibility—provide participants the means to collectively store, recall, manipulate, and share content in service of vernacular expression. But not only do digital tools afford remix, remix is itself a sort of second order tool employed to accomplish myriad social purposes. Remix is a relational tool, as evidenced by the ever-growing cacophony of static images, animated GIFs, and YouTube clips that constitute the endless MFW/TFW ("my face when"/"the feeling when") corpus so essential to conversations online. These reactions, pinned to Twitter replies, uploaded adjacent to 4chan posts, and embedded in Imgur comments, poach from whole worlds of pop-cultural or found-footage source material in order to convey a sentiment, emotion, or reaction. As they're employed, participants use remix to filter nonverbal social cues into mediated interactions, and thus convey themselves a bit more emphatically.

These reaction images are part of the broader memetic *lingua franca*, one crafted through the multimodal remix of accepted tropes, injokes, catchphrases, and motifs. Being able to participate socially in the conversations occurring on many sites requires the ability to riff on how others participate, to artfully balance imitation and transformation, and to walk the fine line between familiar creativity and worn-out pastiche. From the most niche corners to the most massive platforms, remix is a tool for connecting to some, disconnecting from others, crafting a mediated social imaginary all the while.

Remix is also a powerful civic and political tool, and the ambivalence of that power has become all too clear over the last decade. It's a dominant framework that can sway conversations toward justice or oppression. In 2011, the Occupy Wall Street protest movement launched with photoshopped posters and resonant sloganeering shared on a slew of social platforms; the movement's aesthetics were so resonant in fact that they were quickly refashioned and mocked on those same platforms by those who sought to discredit protesters' aims. In 2014, after a misogynistic mass murder in Isla Vista, CA, women reappropriated the men's rights activist call that "not all men" are violent misogynists by responding that, be that as it may, "yes, all women" have to live in a culture of violent misogyny. Thus the #YesAllWomen hashtag was born as women spoke to this grim reality. However, misogynistic combatants could use the same hashtag, and the tool wrought conflict. A similarly ambivalent cycle has occurred with the Black Lives Matter movement, whose titular slogan has been thoroughly misappropriated by the common "All Lives Matter" rejoinder. Now, online and off, a mention of the first is all too often countered with the second, and supporters must time and again explain that advocating for the lives of black folks is in no way tantamount to disparaging or dismissing the lives of white folks.

U.S. Presidential candidate Hillary Clinton learned in 2016 how hard it is to control a meme spiraling through the remix machine when she called the explicitly bigoted branch of Trump supporters "deplorables"; Trump supporters of all stripes proudly adopted the term as a rallying cry, in the process casting their lot with the worst among them. They fixed the moniker to their Twitter handles, printed it on t-shirts, and threw "Deploraballs" on election night. Cartoonist Matt Furie also learned a hard lesson that same year when white nationalist millennials reappropriated Pepe, the comic book frog he created in 2005, declaring it the mascot of their movement. Prominent hatemonger Richard Spencer has even publicly worn a Pepe lapel pin; in January 2017, he famously told reporters "it's kind of a symbol" before a protestor ran up and punched him in the face (Spencer subsequently met the same fate as the cartoon he appropriated; footage of him being hit became a remix sensation). In reappropriating "deplorables" and Pepe, participants used remix practices long tantamount to The Internet itself to spin the source texts they poached straight off a cliff. If The Internet sounds like an unsettling cacophony, it's because so many people are using its primary tool to do so many things, so many of them ambivalent at best, to such dizzying effect.

Despite this dizzying cacophony, however, remix also brings some order to the chaos; it crafts a sense of place in the midst of the churning interactions that constitute contemporary life online. To be sure, The Internet is now so consequential to life beyond the screen that metaphors casting it as some virtual elsewhere look passé. And of course, and as was my experience coming of age online, when people talk about The Internet as a place, they mostly just mean "the people that I assume *we* follow" or "the sites where I assume *we* spend our time" (Beyoncé "broke The Internet," the journalistic coverage hails, with her Instagram post/baby bump/new video/feminist proclamation). But even if it's incomplete to codify a nebulous constellation of participants, practices, and sites as a singular Internet, the social imaginary resonates as much and as broadly now as it did when I began my life online.

The place metaphor persists for those who speak of inhabiting sites like 4chan, Reddit, Tumblr, along with more collective pockets of Twitter and YouTube. In these collectives, The Internet is still called "The Internet"; it's a technological and cultural amalgam still seen as an environment, an ecology, and that still-resonant sense of place matters for how it's brought into existence and how it shapes the interactions of those adherent to it.

Underscoring that place metaphor, it turns out, is remix. The Internet is a place to its participants—or at least a landscape of neighborhoods, villages, towns, and metropolises marked by URLs, user demographics, communicative norms, and meta understandings—because remix tools give way to remix practices that allow those participating to affiliate with insiders and set themselves apart from outsiders. Participants placemake by riffing, ripping, referencing, cutting, connecting, and combining. This placemaking happens discursively, as familiar memes are employed in new conversations, manifesting the *lingua franca* that marks those who inhabit The Internet (however it happens to be conceptualized by a given person in a given moment) and those who don't.

Placemaking happens through explicit meta reference to specific sites as specific localities and to The Internet in general as a terrain to be navigated. "Welcome to The Internet; I'll be your guide" has long been a common memetic refrain on many sites, signaling a sense of exotic place. In its visual form, the phrase often captions remixed images of striking individuals: an old woman with a cane floating in outer space on a surfboard, a cat firing a handgun in the air while riding a shark, Nicholas Cage with an elongated upper head that's being enveloped by a bird, that kind of thing. Each new version of the joke reiterates an accepted premise, that The Internet is an island of misfit toys (usually, of course, with no admission of the race, class, and gender dominance of its professed core constituency).

This placemaking implies that The Internet is somewhere outside the confines and expectations of everyday polite society. The sense that The Internet is somehow different than "real life" just won't die no matter how many Nazis march wearing Pepe pins. Through this persistent juxtaposition, The Internet is defined by what it's not and where it's not for those who spend their free time uploading, scrolling, captioning, commenting, sharing, and transforming, often with the implication that this is where they most belong. An embrace of eccentricity makes The Internet a refuge for *avant garde* creativity, expression, and humor; it also gives us a lot of Nazi forums. And therefore The Internet, or any *cul-de-sac* within its borders, is a place only as healthy as the resonant discourses that build it. If The Internet to you is your Tumblr friends sharing GIFs from *Supernatural* while you talk about fan art, then you might have a pretty nice home. If *The Internet* to you is the echo chamber legion of quasi-ironic (read *deadly-serious*) white nationalists that populate the sites you frequent, then you've got a home too, and your home has an anthem, one mashed up by clamoring hate.

As this social and cultural placemaking occurs, as participants reappropriate and spread what resonates again and again and again, remix proves so ubiquitous that it becomes a way of being. The constant ceaseless echo chamber maelstrom noise is complete enough that when we're not calling The Internet a place, we're calling it a hivemind ("The Internet went wild" when Senator Ted Cruz liked a porno on Twitter). So complete and total is this *modus operandi* for online interaction, from the most minute and situated to the most grand and consequential, that media remix is now firmly embedded within our relationships, professions, and politics. Participants evidence a remixed way of being every time they use a SpongeBob picture on Tinder to suggest someone take a hike, every time they screenshot that Tinder interaction and post it to Reddit, and every time that Reddit thread is picked up by BuzzFeed and shared on Pinterest.

This ubiquitous sampling has defined my online experience. Like many, I've thought in memes, worked in memes, responded in memes. Pervasive memetic remix is an aesthetic, a mode of discourse, a lens for reading the room and relating to others. It's a way of inhabiting a particular social world, one premised on all the bricolage we've long known about, but amplified by the affordances of digital media. When I've rickrolled someone yet again or found myself rickrolled for the sixth time in a month, when I've Instagrammed a study session and captioned it with an ironic "lit," when I've creatively embellished for a Twitter hashtag, when I've used my rudimentary photoshop skills to insert a Guy Fawkes mask and a tiny hovering shoulder-parrot dragon into my bio photo ("expect us"), I've remixed myself into existence. My way of being is one of self-curation through Reddit posts, Twitter threads, Pinterest boards, YouTube comments, and Tumblr reblogs. That's *The Internet* I came of age with, and it has come to define digitally mediated participation today.

Remix, of course and as we've seen, has always been a way of being for humans, but digital media accelerate and amplify its ubiquity, along with our awareness of it. In a hypermediated environment, there's no end to the samples we can weave into a song; there's no end to the soundbites we can dredge up for whole new purposes. Composite work dominates the digital age, and *The Internet* that made it a way of being is now a full blown zeitgeist. And if the waters seem choppy that's because this rising tide of remix so thoroughly unmoors text from context, making it hard to know the veracity of what's being signaled by whom to what ends, which is all good fun when people are maybe ironically, maybe sincerely covering a song on YouTube, but less so when people's faces are being convincingly mapped onto pornographic footage of someone else's body.

It's a disorienting way of being. I've written extensively about how Poe's Law, the internet axiom declaring that online it's hard to discern the motives of the people you're talking to, casts a long, ambivalent shadow over mediated interaction (Milner, 2016; Phillips & Milner, 2017). It's a constant specter that shades life online, and at its heart, it's a remix problem. It's the appropriation of the familiar for ambivalent reasons to ambivalent ends, and its stakes have never been higher. On the madcap mash up Internet, Twitter agitators could be Russian bots meant to be mock ups of South Carolina conservatives or California Bernie Bros (then again, they could *not* be); flat earthers could be creating really bad photoshops because they earnestly want to help the cause or because they mischievously want to discredit it; people alleging again and again that Hillary Clinton ran a child trafficking ring out of the basement of a pizza shop that doesn't have a basement might be doing so for a laugh—until one of them shows up at that shop with a gun.

Poe's Law is born of recognizable tropes untethered from motive, from memetic samples applied over and over until it's hard for us, like the masquerading Sneetches in Dr. Seuss's (1961) morality tale, to tell "whether this one was that one … or that one was this one, Or which one was what one … or what one was who" (p. 21). When the most hateful cultural tropes get sent round and around again through The Internet's remix machine, we're left only with their distilled essence; they grow more potent—not weaker—as the nature and intent of their source is stripped away. No matter the motive of that source, each new iterative voice makes the hateful song a little louder.

Life online can be a dizzying hurricane of noise, debris flinging past us in the gale. There's vibrancy and energy in this way of being, but also anxious, disconcerted agitation. It's a blaring and fractured cacophony, but it's also an echo chamber where the loudest ideas, the most resonant memes, and the most used samples drown out the smaller sounds. The powerful voices that got to decide what was funny and what was no big deal and what was normal and what was "just the Internet" in 2003, that got to decide who was *us* and who was *other*, feel louder now than ever. You can hear them like deafening bass rattling every window; *boom boom* every time a woman is harassed because she spoke up about her assault, *boom boom* every time white nationalists get to say they're being ironic when they sling racial slurs, *boom boom* every time the new *Star Wars* has not enough white dudes in it, and the comments are here to let you know. The same old never ending song.

Despite all the creativity and hilarity and camaraderie so many of us have hailed for so many years, The Internet that came of age with me, the result of countless tiny tones that rose into a crashing deluge, doesn't sound so pretty these days. Lots of notes have been mixed all wrong: tools applied to dehumanize, places premised on antagonistic exclusion, and a way of being marked by sonic discord. The ever-present hope, however, is that we can compose a new score, a new way of being mashed up from different components than we have now, but remixed into existence all the same.

MAKING THE BEST OF LIFE IN CYBERSPACE (OR WHATEVER YOU END UP CALLING IT)

Even—and especially—at a time when it looks to so many that so much of life online is going so wrong, there are lessons to be learned. Most fundamentally, the predominance of remix carries with it an important reminder: the resonant metaphors we use to frame the worlds we inhabit are temporal, themselves a bricolage of technological affordance, lived experience, cultural zeitgeist, and the socially-driven intertwine of the three. The "cyberspace" that stalwart early users look back on nostalgically was every bit the social imaginary that The Internet is for me. And the new metaphors and new framings dreamed up by the 17-year-olds passing around absurdist memes in their Discord channels or Instagram accounts will be too.

But, social constructs though they are, there's of course value in unpacking the affordances and experiences that spawn our dominant framings. Those framings have consequences; whole worlds are made by what is spoken into existence, by the perspectives and behaviors that come to dominate collective conversations. The remix machine embraced by those (discursively speaking, at least) geeky gamer white dudes on sites like 4chan and Reddit has in some ways more thoroughly distributed creativity, giving voice to those who shrug at capital *A* Authorship and who poach what they want from where they want and use it how they want to use it. The contemporary *modus operandi* has made great strides, to borrow Markham's (2013) point, in "de-privileging expert knowledge, decentralizing culture production, and unhooking cultural units of information from their origins" (p. 64). On the other hand, the notes so thoroughly sampled as part of this *modus operandi*, rehashed racism and misogynistic "joke" after misogynistic "joke," are also remixes, and ones that get louder as more people sing to their tune. De-privileging, decentralizing, and unhooking are great for mashing up *Dragon Ball Z* and *Harry Potter*. But they're also great for using a photo of Black Lives Matter protesters blockading a highway in Boston to falsely accuse the movement of impeding aid to hurricane ravaged Houston.

Given how thoroughly remix untethers text and context, how it simultaneously enables individual voice and the dehumanizing memes that collectively suppress voice, the dominant struggle of contemporary life online is a struggle over how to use remix tools and their accompanying frameworks justly and humanely. And the dominant question is whether they can indeed at all be used justly and humanely. How do we most empathetically and supportively apply tools, build places, and manifest ways of being? How do we, best we can, get the most voices in the choir? How do we best live in a cacophony that's both more polyphonic than ever and not nearly polyphonic enough?

The most basic advice is that we mind our memes and consider what notes we're adding to the collective song. Hatred is easier to remix because it's less nuanced, more reductionist, and therefore more readily sampled. Denigrating stereotypes, pre and post Internet, are memetically healthy for just this reason. So are the worst bits of contemporary public discourse. It's easy for supporters of President Donald J. Trump on Twitter to talk like President Donald J. Trump on Twitter ("bigly!" "sad!" "fake news!" "#MAGA!") because he gives them easy talking points. A little nickname. A comforting lie. A slogan instead of an argument. It's also easy for critics to talk like Trump because he gives them easy satirical ammunition. A little nickname. A comforting lie. A slogan instead of an argument. But if we're not careful, critique and commendation can sound the same. When people talk like Trump no matter why they're talking like Trump, when they sample his notes to make songs of their own, Trump's message spreads. And if you, like me, are of the opinion that Trump's message is one of corrupt, white supremacist, authoritarianism, then there are better notes to play. Now more than ever, it's time to stop taking the easy bait. It's time to set a new tone.

It was all fun and games in 2003 when misanthropy felt like an inconsequential part of the symphony. When too many were able to uncomfortably tolerate, if not downright endorse, rehashed resurgences of explicit racism and aggravated misogyny because it was "just a joke," and one of the worst sins you could commit was mistaking The Internet for "serious business." In reality The Internet *was always* serious business, and all the fun and games is what got us here. Now The Internet—*That* Internet—has come of age, the chickens have come home to roost, and the song feels like a battle hymn. If remix is a way of being, reflecting on what we're remixing is the first step to existing in the most empowering way possible. If "just a joke" ever requires, even "ironically," trotting out the same dehumanizing stereotypes and characterizations that have been sampled time and again to write songs of oppression, then maybe the joke's not funny. Maybe there's a better song to sing than the same tired memes. And maybe if we're thoughtful, we can stem the tide and use our tools to create a place premised on voice; maybe we can remix a sweeter song into existence.

References

Abidin, C. (2013). Cyber-BFFs: Assessing women's 'perceived interconnectedness' in Singapore's commercial lifestyle blog industry. *Global Media Journal Australian Edition*, *7*(1). Retrieved from http://www.hca.westernsydney.edu.au/gmjau/?p=217

Abidin, C. (2016). *Sorry not sorry: Influencers, shamelebrity, and para-apologetic transgressions*. Selected papers of Internet research 17: The 17th Annual Meeting of the Association of Internet Researchers. Retrieved from https://spir.aoir.org/index.php/spir/article/view/1301/pdf

Abramov, R. N. (2017a). Sovetskie tehnokraticheskie mifologii kak forma «teorii upushhennogo shansa»: na primere istorii kibernetiki v SSSR [Soviet technocratic mythologies as a form of the lost-chance theory: The example of the history of cybernetics in the USSR]. *Sociologija Nauki I Tehnologij*, *2*, 61–78.

Abramov, R. N. (2017b). Sovetskaja inzhenerno-tehnicheskaja intelligencija 1960–80-h gg.: v poiske granic kollektivnogo soznanija [The Soviet engineering and technical intelligentsia of the 1960–80s: In a search of the boundaries of collective consciousness]. *Vestnik Instituta Sociologii*, *20*, 114–130.

Adegoju, A., & Oyebode, O. (2015). Humour as discursive practice in Nigeria's 2015 presidential election online campaign discourse. *Discourse Studies*, *17*(6), 643–662.

Al Zidjaly, N. (2017). Memes as reasonably hostile laments: A discourse analysis of political dissent in Oman. *Discourse & Society*. https://doi.org/10.1177/0957926517721083

Alcoff, L. (2006). *Visible identities: Race, gender, and the self.* New York, NY: Oxford University Press.

Amatriain, X. (2013). Mining large streams of user data for personalized recommendations. *ACM SIGKDD Explorations Newsletter*, *14*(2), 37–48. doi:10.1145/2481244.2481250

Anderson, B. (1991). *Imagined communities: Reflections on the origin and spread of nationalism*. London, UK: Verso.

Antliff, A. (2012). *Anarchist pedagogies: Collective actions, theories, and critical reflections on education.* PM Press.

Appadurai, A. (1996). *Modernity at large: Cultural dimensions of globalization.* Minneapolis: University of Minnesota Press.

Arkhipov, V. (n.d.). The Other Things Museum [Online project and a series of exhibitions]. Retrieved from URL http://otherthingsmuseum.com

Arnold, D., & Bongiovi, J. R. (2011). Literature Review, Draft. Precarious, informalizing and casualizing labor: Concepts and definitions [PDF file]. A paper prepared for the workshop *Precarious Work in Asia*, Chung-Ang University, Seoul, South Korea, July 19–20, 2011 University of North Carolina at Chapel Hill. Retrieved from http://sawyerseminar.web.unc.edu/files/2011/02/Precarious-labor_Literature-Review_Arnold-and-Bongiovi.pdf

Avdikos, V., & Kalogeresis, A. (2016). Socio-economic profile and working conditions of freelancers in co-working spaces and work collectives: Evidence from the design sector in Greece. *Area.* https://doi.org/10.1111/area.12279

Badger, M. (2004). Visual blogs. In L. Gurak, S. Antonijevic, L. Johnson, C. Ratliff, & J. Reyman (Eds.), *into the blogosphere: Rhetoric, community, and culture of weblogs.* University of Minnesota. Retrieved from: http://blog.lib.umn.edu/blogosphere/visual_blogs.html

Baker, A. J. (2014). *You get what you need: Stories of fans of the rolling stones.* McLean, VA: Miniver Press.

Bakhtin, M. M. (1935 [1981]). Discourse in the novel. In M. Holquist (Ed.), *The dialogic imagination: Four essays* (pp. 259–422). Austin: University of Texas Press.

Bakhtin, M. M. (1970). *Speech genres and other late essays* (M. Holquist & C. Emerson, Eds.). Austin: University of Texas Press.

Bakhtin, M. M. (1981). *Dialogic imagination: Four essays.* Austin: University of Texas Press.

Banks, I. (1994). *Freesum endjinn.* London, UK: Orbit Publications

Barlow, J. P. (1996, February 8). *A declaration of the Independence of cyberspace.* Retrieved from https://projects.eff.org/~barlow/Declaration-Final.html

Barthes, R. (1977). *Image, music, text.* New York, NY: Hill and Wang.

Barthes, R. (1981). *Camera Lucida.* New York, NY: Hill and Wang.

Bateson, G. (1972). *Steps to an ecology of mind: Collected essays in anthropology, psychiatry, evolution, and epistemology.* Chicago, IL: University of Chicago Press.

Baym, N. K. (2000). *Tune in, log on: Soaps, fandom and online community.* Thousand Oaks, CA: Sage.

Baym, N. K. (2015). *Personal connections in the digital age* (2nd ed.). Cambridge: Polity Press.

Be a New Orleanian. Wherever you are. *Dirty Coast Press.* (n.d.). Retrieved from https://dirtycoast.com/products/be-a-new-orleanian-wherever-you-are-navy-1090

Bechmann, A., & Lomborg, S. (2014). *The ubiquitous Internet, user and industry perspectives.* Routledge: New York.

Bell, J., Bailey, L., & Kennedy, D. (2015). 'We do it to keep him alive': Bereaved individuals' experiences of online suicide memorials and continuing bonds. *Mortality (Abingdon, UK), 20*(4), 375–389. doi:10.1080/13576275.2015.1083693

Berger, J., 1972. *Ways of seeing.* London, UK: BBC and Penguin Books.

Bezemer, J. (2012). What is multimodality? [webpage]. UCL Institute of Education. Retrieved from https://mode.ioe.ac.uk/2012/02/16/what-is-multimodality/

Blanco, M. D. P., & Peeren, E. (2013). The ghost in the machine: Spectral media. In M. D. P. Blanco & E. Peeren (Eds.), *The spectralities reader: Ghosts and haunting in contemporary cultural theory* (pp. 199–206). Bloomsbury.

Boellstorff, T. (2008). *Coming of age in second life: An anthropologist explores the virtually human*. Princeton, NJ: Princeton University Press.

Boler, M. (2007). Hypes, hopes and actualities: New digital Cartesianism and bodies in cyberspace. *New Media & Society*, *9*(1), 139–168. https://doi.org/10.1177/1461444807067586

Boomen, M. van den (2014). *Transcoding the digital: How metaphors matter in new Media*. Amsterdam: Institute of Network Cultures.

Bourdieu, Pierre. 1990 [1965]. Photography: A *m*iddle-*b*row *a*rt. Cambridge: Polity Press.

boyd, d. (2005, June 22–26). *Broken metaphors: Blogging as liminal practice*. Paper presented at Media Ecology Association conference (MEA 2005), New York, NY.

boyd, d. (2011). Social network sites as networked publics: Affordances, dynamics, and implications. In Z. Papacharissi (Ed.), *Networked self: Identity, community, and culture on social network sites* (pp. 39–58).

boyd, d. (2014). *It's complicated: The social lives of networked teens*. New Haven, CT: Yale University Press.

boyd, d., Golder, S., & Lotan, G. (2010). Tweet, tweet, retweet: Conversational aspects of retweeting on Twitter. In *Proceedings of HICSS-42, persistent conversation track*. Kauai, HI: IEEE Computer Society. Retrieved from http://www.danah.org/papers/TweetTweetRetweet.pdf

Braybrooke, K., & Jordan, T. (2017). Genealogy, culture and technomyth. *Digital Culture & Society*, *3*(1), 25–46. doi:10.14361/dcs-2017-0103

Browne, K. (2006). 'A right geezer-bird' (man-woman): The sites and sights of 'female' embodiment. *ACME: An International E-Journal for Critical Geographies*, *5*(2), 121–143.

Browne, K., Lim, J., & Brown, G. (Eds.). (2007). *Geographies of sexualities: Theory, practices and politics*. Aldershot, Hampshire: Ashgate Publishing.

Bruns, A.(2019). *Are filter bubbles real?*Polity.

Brunvand, J. H. (1981). *The vanishing hitchhiker: Urban legends and their meanings*. New York, NY: W.W. Norton.

Bucher, T., & Helmond, A. (2017). The affordances of social media platforms. In J. Burgess, A. Marwick, & T. Poell (Eds.), *The Sage handbook of social media* (pp. 223–253). London, UK: Sage.

Burgess, J. (2006). Hearing ordinary voices: Cultural studies, vernacular creativity and digital storytelling. *Continuum: Journal of Media & Cultural Studies, 20*(2), 201–214.

Burrell, J. (2012). *Invisible users: Youth in the Internet cafés of urban Ghana*. Cambridge, MA: MIT Press.

burrough, X. (2016). *A vigil for some bodies*. http://missconceptions.net/vigil/

Butler, J. P. (1990). *Gender trouble: Feminism and the subversion of identity*. London, UK: Routledge.

Cadwalladr, C. (2016, December 4). Google, democracy and the truth about internet search. *The Guardian*. Retrieved from https://www.theguardian.com/technology/2016/dec/04/google-democracy-truth-internet-search-facebook

Carmichael, K., & Dajko, N. (2016). Ain't Dere no more: New Orleans language and local nostalgia in Vic & Nat'ly comics. *Journal of Linguistic Anthropology*, *26*, 234–258.

Carroll, N. (2001). Modernity and the plasticity of perception. *Journal of Aesthetics and Art Criticism*, *59*(1), 11–17

Chalfen, R. (1987). *Snapshot versions of life*. Bowling Green, OH: Bowling Green State University Popular Press.

Charmez, K. (2006). *Constructing grounded theory*. London, UK: Sage.

Chayko, M. (2017). *Superconnected: The Internet, digital Media, and techno-social life*. Thousand Oaks, CA: Sage.

Cheney-Lippold, J. (2017). *We are data: Algorithms and the making of our digital selves.* New York: New York University.

Christensen, D. R., & Sandvik, K. (2015). Death ends a life not a relationship: timework and ritualizations at Mindet.dk. *New Review of Hypermedia and Multimedia, 21*(1–2), 57–71. doi:10.1080/13614568.2014.983561

Chun, W. H. K. (2006). *Control and freedom: Power and paranoia in the age of fiber optics.* Cambridge, MA: MIT Press.

Collister, S. (2014). Abstract hacktivism as a model for postanarchist organizing. *Ephemera, 14*(4), 765–779.

Courtois, A., & O'Keefe, T. (2015). Precarity in the ivory cage: Neoliberalism and causalisation of work in the Irish higher education sector. *Journal for Critical Education Policy Studies, 13*(1), 43–66.

Crawford, K., & Gillespie, T. (2016). What is a flag for? Social media reporting tools and the vocabulary of complaint. New Media & Society, 18(3), 410–428. 10.1177/1461444814543163

Cresswell, T. (2006). *On the move.* London, UK: Routledge.

Cresswell, T. (2014). Friction. In P. Adey, D. Bissell, K. Hannam, P. Merriman, & M. Sheller (Eds.), *The Routledge handbook of mobilities* (pp. 107–115). Oxon: Routledge.

Dahlberg, L., & Siapera, E. (Eds.). (2007). *Radical democracy and the Internet: Interrogating theory and practice.* Springer.

Dash, A. (2012a, December 13). The web we lost. Retrieved October 7, 2017, from http://anildash.com/2012/12/the-web-we-lost.html

Dash, A. (2012b, December 18). Rebuilding the web we lost. Retrieved October 8, 2017, from http://anildash.com/2012/12/rebuilding-the-web-we-lost.html

Dash, A. (2013, April 24). How we lost the web. Retrieved October 7, 2017, from http://anildash.com/2013/04/harvard.html

Dashkova, T. (2002). "Ideologija v licah. Formirovanie vizual'nogo kanona v sovetskih zhurnalah 1920-h–1930-h godov" [Ideology in faces. Formation of the visual canon in Soviet journals of the 1920s–1930s]. *Kul'tura i vlast' v uslovijah kommunikacionnoj revoljucii XX veka.* Pod red. K. Ajmermajhera, G. Bordjugova i I. Grabovskogo. Moskva: AIRO-XX.

Dawkins, R. (1976). *The selfish gene.* Oxford: Oxford University Press.

De Certeau, M. (1984). *The practice of everyday life.* Berkeley: University of California Press.

Degot' E. (2000). Ot tovara k tovarischu. Logos (5–6). Retrieved from http://www.ruthenia.ru/logos/number/2000_5_6/2000_5-6_04.htm

Derrida, J. (1998). *Archive fever: A Freudian impression.* Chicago, IL: University of Chicago Press.

Derrida, J., & Stiegler, B. (2002). *Echographies of television. Filmed interviews.* Cambridge: Polity Press.

Deuze, M. (2011). Medial life. *Media, Culture & Society, 33*(1), 137–148.

Deuze, M., Blank, P., & Speers, L. (2012). A life lived in media. *Digital Humanities Quarterly, 6*(1).

Dibbell, J. (1998). *My tiny life: Crime and passion in a virtual world.* New York, NY: Holt.

Doan, P. L. (2010). The tyranny of gendered spaces—Reflections from beyond the gender dichotomy. *Gender, Place & Culture, 17*(5), 635–654. doi:10.1080/0966369x.2010.503121

Dodge, M., & Kitchin, R. (2000). *Atlas of cyberspace.* London, UK: Routledge.

Douglas, M. (1966). *Purity and danger: An analysis of the concepts of pollution and taboo.* London, UK and New York, NY: Routledge.

Dr. Seuss (1961). *The sneetches and other stories.* New York, NY: Random House.

Druick, Z. (1995). The information superhighway, or the politics of a metaphor. *Bad Subjects, 18.* Retrieved from http://bad.eserver.org/issues/1995/18/druck.html

Duguay, S. (2017). Identity modulation in networked publics: Queer women's participation and representation on Tinder, Instagram and Vine (PhD dissertation). Queensland University of Technology. Available online: https://eprints.qut.edu.au/111892/

Dundes, A. (1987). *Cracking jokes: Studies in sick humor cycles and stereotypes*. Berkeley, CA: Ten Speed Press.

Dzieza, J. (2014, August 20). A history of metaphors for the Internet. *The Verge*. Retrieved from https://www.theverge.com/2014/8/20/6046003/a-history-of-metaphors-for-the-internet

Edsall, T. (2017, March 2). Democracy, disrupted. *The New York Times*. Retrieved from https://www.nytimes.com/2017/03/02/opinion/how-the-internet-threatens-democracy.html

Ellis, C., Bochner, A. P. (2000): Autoethnography, personal narrative, and reflexivity: Researcher as subject. In N. K. Denzin & Y. S. Lincoln (Eds.), *Handbook of qualitative research* (pp. 733–768). Thousand Oaks, CA: Sage.

Evans, S. K., Pearce, K. E., Vitak, J., & Treem, J. W. (2017). Explicating affordances: A conceptual framework for understanding affordances in communication research. *Journal of Computer-Mediated Communication, 22*, 35–52.

Farman, J. (2012). *Mobile interface theory: Embodied space and locative media*. New York, NY: Routledge.

Faucher, K. X. (2014). Alienation and precarious contract academic staff in the age of neoliberalism. *Confero, 2*(1), 35–71.

Feenberg, A. (1999). *Questioning technology*. London, UK and New York, NY: Sage.

Felstead, A., Jewson, N., & Walters, S. (2005). *Changing places of work*. New York, NY: Palgrave Macmillan.

Ferdinand, P. (2000). The Internet, democracy and democratization. *Democratization, 7*(1), 1–17.

Ferguson, K. (2015). Everything is a Remix. Retrieved from https://vimeo.com/139094998

Flecker, J., & Schönhauer, A. (2016). The production of 'placelessness': Digital service work in global value chains. In J. Flecker (Ed.), *Space, place and global digital work*. London, UK: Palgrave Macmillan. Retrieved from https://doi.org/10.1057/978-1-137-48087-3

Folbre, N. (2013). The unregulated work of mechanical Turk. *New York Times*, March 18, 2003. Retrieved September 10, from https://economix.blogs.nytimes.com/2013/03/18/the-unregulated-work-of-mechanical-turk

Foucault, M. (1984). Des espaces autres (conférence au Cercle d'études architecturales,14 mars 1967). *Architecture, Mouvement, Continuité, 5*, 46–49.

Founders Fund. (2011, August 9). Retrieved August 12, 2019, from http://web.archive.org/web/20110809183001/http://www.foundersfund.com/

Freelon, D. G. (2010). Analyzing online political discussion using three models of democratic communication. *New Media & Society, 12*(7), 1172–1190.

Frishcmann, B. (2018). The misleading power of Internet metaphors. *Scientific American*. Retrieved from https://blogs.scientificamerican.com/observations/the-misleading-power-of-internet-metaphors/

Frosh, P. (2017, October 30). *Vital signs: Screenshots, social media and existential delegation. Presentation at Precarious Media Life: Digital Existence II*. Sigtuna Foundation.

Fuller, M. (2005). *Media ecologies: Materialist energies in Art and technoculture*. Cambridge, MA: MIT Press.

Gandini, A. (2016). *The reputation economy* [e-book]. Cambridge: Palgrave Macmillan.

Garrett, L. E.,Spreitzer, G. M., & Bacevice, P. A. (2017). Co-constructing a sense of community at work: The emergence of community in coworking spaces. *Organization Studies*. https://doi.org/10.1177/0170840616685354

Gaver, W. (1996). Situating action II: Affordances for interaction: The social is material for design. *Ecological Psychology, 8*, 2.

Gerasimova, E., & Chujkina, S. (2004). Obshhestvo remonta [Society of repair]. *Neprikosnovennyj Zapas, 34*(2).

Gerbaudo, P. (2015). Populism 2.0: Social media activism, the generic Internet user and interactive direct democracy. In D. Trottier & C. Fuchs (Eds.), *Social media, politics and the state: Protests, revolutions, riots, crime and policing in the age of Facebook, Twitter and YouTube* (pp. 67–87). New York, NY and London, UK: Routledge.

Gergen, K. J. (2009). *Relational being: Beyond self and community*. Oxford, UK: Oxford University Press.

Gershon, I. (2010). Breaking up is hard to do: Media switching and media ideologies. *Linguistic Anthropology, 20*(2), 389–405. http://doi.org/10.1111/j.1548-1395.2010.01076.x.H

Ghose, T. (2017, January 30). Hurricane season: Here's what to expect. *LiveScience*. Retrieved from http://www.livescience.com/57671-hurricane-season.html

Gibney, B. (2011). *What happened to the future?* Retrieved from http://web.archive.org/web/20170413234322/http://foundersfund.com/the-future/#

Gibson, J. J. (1979). *The ecological approach to visual perception* (1st ed.). Mahwah, NJ: Erlbaum, Lawrence Associates.

Gibson, W. (1984). *Neuromancer*. New York, NY: Ace.

Gillespie, T. (2010). The politics of "platforms." New Media & Society, 12(3), 347–364. https://doi.org/10.1177/1461444809342738

Gillespie, T. (2014). The relevance of algorithms. In T. Gillespie, P. J. Boczkowski, K. A. Foot, L. A. Lievrouw, & I. Siles (Eds.), *Media technologies: Essays on communication, materiality, and society*. Cambridge, MA: MIT Press.

Gillespie, T. (2017). The platform metaphor, revisited. *Digital Society Blog*. Retrieved August 30, from https://www.hiig.de/en/the-platform-metaphor-revisited/

Goffman, E. (1956). *The presentation of self in everyday life*. Edinburgh: University of Edinburgh Social Sciences Research Centre.

Goffman, E. (1963). *Behavior in public places: Notes on the social organization of gatherings*. New York, NY: Free Press of Glencoe.

Goffman, E. (1974). *Frame analysis*. New York, NY: Harper Colophon Books.

Graham, L. R. (1993). *The ghost of the executed engineer: Technology and the fall of the Soviet Union* (No. 87). Harvard University Press.

Gregg, M., & Seigworth, G. J. (2010). The affect theory reader. Durham, NC: Duke University Press.

Grier, A. (2005). *When computers were human*. Princeton, NJ: Princeton Press

Grønning, A. (2018). *Digitale samtaler*. Frederiksberg: Samfundslitteratur.

Grosz, E. (1995). *Space, time and perversion: Essays on the politics of bodies*. New York, NY: Taylor & Francis.

Gunkel, D. J. (2016). *Of remixology*. Cambridge, MA: MIT Press.

Haddon, L. (2006). The contribution of domestication research. *The Information Society, 22*, 195–204. Retrieved from https://www.hiig.de/en/sharing-from-ploughshares-to-file-sharing-and-beyond/

Hakim-Fernández, N. (2017). An experimental autoethnography of mobile freelancing. *Digital Culture and Society, 3*(2). https://doi.org/10.14361/dcs-2017-0215

Hamilton, C. (2019). Popular music, digital technologies and data analysis: New methods and questions. *Convergence, 25*(2), 225–240. doi:10.1177/1354856519831127

Hammersley, M., & Atkinson, P. (1995). *Ethnography: Principles in practice* (2nd ed.). New York, NY: Routledge.

Haraway, D. (1991). *Simians, cyborgs and women: The reinvention of nature*. New York, NY: Routledge.

Hardt, M., & Negri, A. (2000). *Empire*. London, UK: Harvard University Press.

Harrison, S., & Dourish, P. (1996). Re-place-ing space: The roles of place and space in collaborative systems. In *Proceedings of CSCW '96*. Retrieved from http://www.dourish.com/publications/1996/cscw96-place.pdf

Hathaway, J. (2017, February 21). The rare Pepe economy is real, and there's serious money behind it. *The Daily Dot*. Retrieved from https://www.dailydot.com/unclick/rare-pepe-frog-meme-economy/.

Hayles, K. (1999). *How we became posthuman: Virtual bodies in cybernetics, literature, and informatics*. Chicago, IL: University of Chicago Press.

Hayles, K. (2002). *Writing machines*. Cambridge, MA: MIT Press.

Helmond, A. (2015). The platformization of the web: Making web data platform ready. *Social Media + Society, 1*(2). https://doi.org/10.1177/2056305115603080

Hennion, A. (2001). Music lovers: Taste as performance. *Theory, Culture & Society, 18*(5), 1–22. doi:10.1177/02632760122051940

Hepp, A., Hjarvard, S., & Lundby, K. (2015). Mediatization: Theorizing the interplay between media, culture and society. *Media, Culture & Society, 37*(2), 314–324. doi:10.1177/0163443715573835

Hine, C. (2000). *Virtual ethnography*. London, UK: Sage.

Hine, C. (2015). *Ethnography for the internet: Embedded, embodied and everyday*. New York, NY: Bloomsbury Publishing.

Hines, S. (2007). *TransForming gender: Transgender practices of identity, intimacy and care*. Bristol, UK: Policy Press.

Hirsch, T., & Lee, J. S. (2018). Understanding the complexities of transnational family language policy. *Journal of Multilingual and Multicultural Development*, 1–13.

Hodkinson, P., & Lincoln, S. (2008). Online journals as virtual bedrooms: Young people, identity and personal space. *YOUNG, 16*(1), 27–46.

Hogan, B. (2010). The presentation of self in the age of social media: Distinguishing performances and exhibitions online. *Bulletin of Science, Technology & Society, 30*(6), 377–386. https://doi.org/10.1177/0270467610385893

Hookway, N. (2008). Entering the blogosphere: Some strategies for using blogs in social research. *Qualitative Research, 8*(1), 91–113.

Horowitz, A. (2013, April 29). In tech we trust? A debate with Peter Thiel and Marc Andreessen. Retrieved October 10, 2017, from http://a16z.com/2013/04/29/in-tech-we-trust-a-debate-with-peter-thiel-and-marc-andreessen/

Horst, H. A., & Miller, D. (2013). *Digital anthropology*. London, UK: Bloomsbury Publishing.

Hutchby, I. (2001a). Technologies, texts and affordances. *Sociology, 35*(2), 441–456.

Hutchby, I. (2001b). *Conversation and technology: From the telephone to the Internet*. Cambridge: Polity Press.

Ingold, T. (2013). *Making: Anthropology, archaeology, Art and architecture*. London: Routledge.

International Digital Economy and Society Index. (2018, November 29). Retrieved July 22, 2019, from https://ec.europa.eu/knowledge4policy/publication/international-digital-economy-society-index-2018_en

Introna, L. D., & Nissenbaum, H. (2000). Shaping the web: Why the politics of search engines matters. *The Information Society, 16*, 69–185.

Jamet, D. (2010). What do Internet metaphors reveal about the Internet? *Metaphork, 18*, 7. Retrieved from https://www.metaphorik.de/fr/book/export/html/272

Jenkins, H. (1992). *Textual poachers: Television fans and participatory culture.* New York, NY: Routledge.

Jensen, J. L. (2003). Public spheres on the Internet: Anarchic or government-sponsored–A comparison. *Scandinavian Political Studies, 26*(4), 349–374.

John, N. (2017). Sharing—From ploughshares to file sharing and beyond. *Digital Society Blog.* Retrieved August 30, from https://www.hiig.de/en/sharing-from-ploughshares-to-file-sharing-and-beyond/

Johnston, L. (2015). Gender and sexuality 1: Genderqueer geographies? *Progress in Human Geography, 1*, 1–11.

Johnston, R. (2009). Salvation or destruction: Metaphors of the Internet. *First Monday, 14*(4). doi:10.5210/fm.v14i4.2370

Jurgenson, N. (2012). When atoms meet bits: Social media, the mobile web and augmented revolution. *Future Internet, 4*(1), 83–91.

Kasket, E. (2012). Continuing bonds in the age of social networking: Facebook as a modern-day medium. *Bereavement Care, 31*(2), 62–69. doi:10.1080/02682621.2012.710493

Kasket, E. (2019). *All the ghosts in the machine. Illusions of immortality in the digital age.* London, UK: Robinson.

Katzenbach, C., & Larsson, S. (2017). Imagining the digital society—Metaphors from the past and present. *Digital Society Blog.* Retrieved August 30, from https://www.hiig.de/en/imagining-the-digital-society-metaphors-from-the-past-and-present/

Kaye, J. J. (2006). I just clicked to say I love you: Rich evaluations of minima communication [PDF File]. Extended Abstracts Proceedings of the 2006 Conference on Human Factors in Computing Systems, CHI 2006, Montréal, QC, April 22–27, 2006. Retrieved from http://alumni.media.mit.edu/~jofish/writing/kaye-less-is-more8.pdf

Khan, I. (2015, April 12). 4chan's Pepe the Frog is bigger than ever—And his creator feels good, man. *The Daily Dot.* Retrieved from https://www.dailydot.com/unclick/4chan-pepe-the-frog-renaissance/

Kharkhordin, O., Bychkova, O., Gladarev, B., Cinman, Zh. (2019). *Fantasticheskie Miry Rossijskogo Haj-Teka [shi-fi worlds of Russian high-tech].* Moskva: EUSP Press

Kiberd, R. (2015, April 9). 4chan's frog went mainstream, so they tried to kill it. *Vice's Motherboard.* Retrieved from https://motherboard.vice.com/en_us/article/vvbjbx/4chans-frog-meme-went-mainstream-so-they-tried-to-kill-it.

Kiel, P. (2016). Dead online: Practices of post-mortem digital interaction. *Selected Papers of Internet Research 16: The 16th Annual Meeting of the Association of Internet Researchers.* Retrieved from https://journals.uic.edu/ojs/index.php/spir/article/download/8528/6795

Kittler, K. (1988). Fiktion und Simulation. In Arts Elecronica (Ed.), *Philosophien der neuen Technologie* (pp. 57–80). Berlin.

Konradova, N., Schmidt, H., & Teubener, K. (Eds.). (2006). *Control+ shift: Public and private usages of the Russian internet.* BoD–Books on Demand.

Kreiss, D. (2016). Social media did not give us Trump and it is not weakening democracy. *Culture Digitally.* Retrieved from http://culturedigitally.org/2016/11/social_media_trump/

Kukulin, I. (2017). Periodika dlja ITR: sovetskie nauchno-populjarnye zhurnaly i modelirovanie interesov pozdnesovetskoj nauchno-tehnicheskoj intelligencii [Periodicals for engineers and technicians: Soviet popular science journals and modeling interests of the late Soviet scientific and technical intelligentsia]. *Novoe Literaturnoe Obozrenie, 3*, 61–85.

Kumar, P., & Schoenebeck, S. (2015). The Modern Day Baby Book: Enacting Good Mothering and Stewarding Privacy on Facebook. Proceedings of the 18th ACM Conference on Computer Supported Cooperative Work & Social Computing, pp. 1302–1312. https://doi.org/10.1145/2675133.2675149

Kuznetsov, S. (2004). *Oshhupyvaja slona. Zametki po istorii russkogo interneta [Feeling the elephant. Notes on the history of the Russian Internet].* Moskva: Novoe literaturnoe obozrenie.

Laing, R. D. (1969). *Self and others.* London, UK: Tavistock.

Lakoff, G., & Johnson, M. (1980). *Metaphors we live by.* Chicago, IL: University of Chicago Press.

Lamarre, T. (2018). *The anime ecology: A genealogy of television, animation, and game Media.* Minneapolis: University of Minnesota Press.

Larsen, J., & Sandbye, M. (Eds.). (2014). *Digital snaps. The new face of photography.* New York, NY: Palgrave Macmillan.

Latour, B. (1991). Technology is society made durable. *The Sociological Review, 38*(1), 103–131.

Lauer, C. (2016). *Intimacy: A dialectical study.* London, UK and New York, NY: Bloomsbury Academic.

Lefebvre, H. (1991). *The production of space.* Oxford: Blackwell.

Lehdonvirta, V. (2016). Algorithms that divide and unite: Delocalisation, identity and collective action in 'microwork'. In J. Flecker (Ed.), *Space, place and global digital work* (pp. 53–80). London, UK: Palgrave Macmillan.

Lessig, L. (2008). *Remix: Making Art commerce thrive in the hybrid economy.* New York, NY: Penguin.

Lévi-Strauss, C. (1962). *The savage mind.* London, UK: Weidenfeld and Nicolson.

Lewis, J. (1991). *The ideological octopus.* London, UK: Routledge Press.

Liegl, M. (2014). Nomadicity and the care of place—On the aesthetic and affective organization of space in freelance creative work. *Computer Supported Cooperative Work: CSCW: An International Journal, 23*(2), 163–183. https://doi.org/10.1007/s10606-014-9198-x

Lipman, S. (2012). Teens waiting to get drivers' licenses, prefer public transport. *CSMonitor.com.* Retrieved from https://www.csmonitor.com/The-Culture/Family/Modern-Parenthood/2012/0712/Teens-waiting-to-get-drivers-licenses-prefer-public-transport

Liu, A. (2016). *Drafts for against the cultural singularity* (book in progress) [Online]. Retrieved July 26, 2019, from http://liu.english.ucsb.edu/drafts-for-against-the-cultural-singularity, doi:10.21972/G2B663

Liu, X. (2018). The travel of an iPhone: Ineluctable connectivity, networked precarity, and postsocialist politics. *Social Identities, 24*(2), 255–270.

Lingel, J. (2017). Networked field studies: Comparative inquiry and online communities. Social Media + Society, 3, 7, https://doi.org/10.1177/2056305117743139

Livingstone, S. (2008). Taking risky opportunities in youthful content creation: teenagers' use of social networking sites for intimacy, privacy and self-expression. New Media & Society, 10(3), 393–411. https://doi.org/10.1177/1461444808089415

Llentirb, N. (2016, July 27). How often does the picture of a home get updated? *Google Maps & Earth Help Forum* [online forum post]. Retrieved from https://productforums.google.com/forum/#!topic/maps/_OyoDTfCAZU;context-place=forum/maps

Lovink, G. (2011). *Networks without A cause: A critique of social Media.* Cambridge: Polity Press.

Lynch, M. P. (2016). *The Internet of us: Knowing more and understanding less in the age of big data.* New York, NY: WW Norton.

MacCormac, E. R. (1985). *A cognitive theory of metaphor.* Cambridge, MA: MIT Press.

MacKinnon, R. C. (1995). Searching for the Leviathan in usenet. In S. G. Jones (Ed.), *Cybersociety: Computer-mediated communication and community* (pp. 112–137). Thousand Oaks, CA: Sage.

Maddox, A., Barratt, M. J., Allen, M., & Lenton, S. (2016). Constructive activism in the dark web: Cryptomarkets and illicit drugs in the digital 'demimonde'. *Information, Communication & Society*, *19*(1), 111–126.

Madianou, M., & Miller, D. (2012). Polymedia: Towards a new theory of digital media in interpersonal communication. *International Journal of Cultural Studies*, *16*(2), 169–187.

Magaudda, P. (2011). When materiality 'bites back': Digital music consumption practices in the age of dematerialization. *Journal of Consumer Culture*, *11*(1), 15–36. doi:10.1177/1469540510390499

Malinowski, B. (1923). The problem of meaning in primitive languages. In C. K. Ogden & I. A. Richards (Eds.) (1965) *The meaning of meaning. A study of the influence of language upon thought and of the science of symbolism* (pp. 296–336). London, UK: Routledge and Kegan Paul.

Mannheim, K. (1955 [1936]). *Ideology and Utopia: An introduction to the sociology of knowledge*. San Diego, CA and New York, NY: Harcourt.

Mannheim, K. (1982). *Structures of thinking*. London, UK: Routledge & Kegan Paul.

Manovich, L. (2001). *The language of new Media*. Cambridge, MA: MIT Press.

Markham, A. N. (1998). *Life online: Researching real experience in virtual space*. Walnut Creek, CA: Alta Mira.

Markham, A. N. (2003). Metaphorically shaping our understanding of the Internet: Tool, place, way of being. Retrieved from http://annettemarkham.com/writing/MarkhamTPWwebversion.html

Markham, A. N. (2004). Internet as research context. In C. Seale, J. Gubrium, D. Silverman, & G. Gobo (Eds.), *Qualitative research practice* (pp. 358–374). London, UK: Sage.

Markham, A. N. (2005). The methods, politics, and ethics of representation in online ethnography. In N. Denzin & Y. Lincoln (Eds.), *The Sage handbook of qualitative research* (pp. 793–820)Thousand Oaks, CA: Sage.

Markham, A. N. (2013a). Remix cultures, remix methods: Reframing qualitative inquiry for social media contexts. In N. Denzin & M. Giardina (Eds.), *Global dimensions of qualitative inquiry* (pp. 63–81). Walnut Creek, CA: Left Coast Press.

Markham, A. N. (2013b). The dramaturgy of digital experience. In C. Edgley (Ed.), *The drama of social life: A dramaturgical handbook* (pp. 279–294). Farnham: Ashgate.

Markham, A. N., & Stavrova, S. (2016). Internet/digital research. In D. Silverman (Ed.), *Qualitative research* (pp. 229–244). London, UK: Sage.

Marwick, A. E. (2013). *Status update: Celebrity, publicity, and branding in the social media age*. New Haven, CT: Yale University Press.

Marwick, A. E., & boyd, d. (2010). I tweet honestly, I tweet passionately: Twitter users, context collapse, and the imagined audience. New Media & Society, 13(1), 114–133. https://doi.org/10.1177/1461444810365313

McGrath, W. (2015, September 22). What are those kids doing with that enormous gun? *The Atlantic*. Retrieved October 23, 2019, from https://www.theatlantic.com/technology/archive/2015/09/what-are-those-kids-doing-with-that-enormous-gun/405769/

McLuhan, M., & Quentin, F. (1967/2007). *The medium is the message*. New York, NY: Random House.

McVeigh-Schultz, J., & Baym, N. K. (2015). Thinking of you: Vernacular affordance in the context of the microsocial relationship app, couple. *Social Media + Society*, *1*(2), 1–13. http://doi.org/10.1177/2056305115604649

Meyrowitz, J. (1985). *No sense of place: The impact of electronic media on social behavior*. New York, NY: Oxford University Press.

Meyrowitz, J. (1998). Multiple media literacies. *Journal of Communication*, *48*(1), 96–108. https://dx.doi.org/10.1111/j.1460-2466.1998.tb02740.x

Miller, D. (2011). Designing ourselves. In A. J. Clarke (Ed.), *Design anthropology: Object culture in the 21st century*. Wien: Springer.

Miller, D., & Sinanan, J. (2014). *Webcam*. Cambridge: Polity Press.

Milner, R. M. (2016). *The world made meme: Public conversations and participatory media*. Cambridge, MA: MIT Press.

Mina, A. X. (2014). Batman, Pandaman, and the Blind Man: A case study in social change memes and Internet censorship in China. *Journal of Visual Culture*, *13*(3), 359–375.

Molotch, H. (2011). Objects in sociology. In A. J. Clarke (Ed.), *Design anthropology: Object culture in the 21st Century*. Wien: Springer. https://doi.org/10.1017/CBO9781107415324.004

Nakamura, L. (2001). Race in/for cyberspace: Identity tourism and racial passing on the Internet. *Reading Digital Culture*, 226–235.

Nardi, B. (2009). *My life as a night owl priest: An anthropological account of world of warcraft*. Ann Arbor: University of Michigan Press.

Nash, C. J. (2010). Trans geographies, embodiment and experience. *Gender, Place & Culture*, *17*(5), 579–595. doi:10.1080/0966369x.2010.503112

Nash, C. J., & Bain, A. (2007). 'Reclaiming raunch'? Spatializing queer identities at Toronto women's bathhouse events. *Social & Cultural Geography*, *8*(1), 47–62. doi:10.1080/14649360701251809

Negroponte, N. (1995). *Being digital*. New York, NY: Vintage Books.

Negus, K. (1997). *Popular music in theory: An introduction*. Middletown, CT: Wesleyan University Press.

Noble, S. U. (2018). *Algorithms of oppression: How search engines reinforce racism*. New York: NYU Press.

Norman, D. (1988). *The psychology of everyday things*. New York, NY: Basic Books.

Osborne, S. (2017, May 8). Pepe is dead: Meme creator kills off controversial frog after it was hijacked by white supremacists. *The Independent*. Retrieved from http://www.independent.co.uk/news/world/americas/us-politics/pepe-frog-dead-meme-matt-furie-kills-alt-right-image-white-supremacists-hijacked-a7723586.html

Oslon, M. (2011). Post-Internet. *Foam Magazine*.

Owens, L., & Palmer, L. K. (2003). Making the news: Anarchist counter-public relations on the World Wide Web. *Critical Studies in Media Communication*, *20*(4), 335–361.

Papacharissi, Z. (2004). Democracy online: Civility, politeness, and the democratic potential of online political discussion groups. *New Media & Society*, *6*(2), 259–283.

Papacharissi, Z. (2011). *A networked self: identity, community and culture on social network sites*. New York, NY: Routledge.

Pearce, K. E., Carr, C. T., Vitak, J., & Hayes, R. A. (2018, May). *Conceptualizing socially mediated visibility*. Paper presented at the 68th International Communication Association Conference, Prague, Czech Republic.

Pensoneau-Conway, S. L., & Toyosaki, S. (2011). Automethodology: Tracing a home for praxis-oriented ethnography. *International Journal of Qualitative Methods*, *10*(4), 378–400.

Peters, B. (2016). *How not to network a nation: The uneasy history of the Soviet internet*. Cambridge, MA: MIT Press.

Phillips, W., & Milner, R. M. (2017). *The ambivalent Internet: Mischief, oddity, and antagonism online*. Oxford: Polity Press.

Pigg, S. (2014). Emplacing mobile composing habits: A study of academic writing in networked social spaces. *College Composition and Communication*, *66*(2), 250–270.

Pignetti, D. (2005, September 2). Map Resource [Web log post]. Retrieved from http://www.daisypignetti.com/2005/09/02/map-resource/

Pignetti, D. (2007). The "I" of the storm: How hurricane Katrina changed my life and my methodology. *Computers and Composition Online*. Retrieved from http://cconlinejournal.org/Pignetti/title.html

Pignetti, D. (2010, March 3). Google Map Time Machine [Web log post]. Retrieved from http://www.daisypignetti.com/2010/03/03/google-map-time-machine/

Pink, S., Ardevol, E., & Lanzeni, D. (2016). *Digital Materialities*. London, UK: Bloomsbury Press.

Polonski, V. (2016, August 5). Is social media destroying democracy? *Newsweek*. Retrieved from http://www.newsweek.com/social-media-destroying-democracy-487483

Postill, J., & Pink, S. (2012). Social media ethnography: The digital researcher in a messy web. *Media International Australia*, *145*(1), 123–134.

Postman, N. (1992). *Technopoly: The surrender of culture to technology*. New York, NY: Knopf.

Potter, J., & Wetherell, M. (1987). *Discourse and social psychology: Beyond attitudes and behaviour*. New York, NY: Sage.

Prey, R. (2015). Henri Lefebvre and the production of music streaming spaces. *Sociologica*, *9*(3), 1–22. doi:10.2383/82481

Prieto-Blanco, P. (2010). Family photography as a phatic construction. *Networking Knowledge: Journal of the MeCCSA PG Network*, *3*(2). Retrieved September 14, 2017, from http://ojs.meccsa.org.uk/index.php/netknow/article/download/48/48

Prieto-Blanco, P. (2015). Visuelles Tele-Cocooning im Ausland. Eine Autoethnographie. *Ultrashort Reframed*, *5*, 50–54.

Prieto-Blanco, P. (2016a). (Digital) photography, experience and space in transnational families. A case study of Spanish-Irish families living in Ireland. In A. Lehmuskallio & E. Gómez Cruz (Eds.), *Digital Photography and Everyday Life* (pp. 122–140). London, UK: Routledge.

Prieto-Blanco, P. (2016b). *Transnational (dis)affect in the Digital Age. Photographic practices of Irish-Spanish families living in Ireland* (Unpublished doctoral dissertation). National University of Ireland, Galway, Republic of Ireland.

Radner, J., & Lanser, S. (1993). Strategies of coding in women's cultures. In J. Radner (Ed.), *Feminist messages: Coding in women's folk culture* (pp. 1–30). Champaign: University of Illinois Press.

Rainie, L. (2017, February 9). Digital divides—Feeding America. Retrieved March 1, 2017, from Pew Research Center: Internet, Science & Tech website: http://www.pewinternet.org/2017/02/09/digital-divides-feeding-america/

Raptis, D., Kjeldskov, J., Skov, M. B., & Paay, J. (2014). What is a digital ecology? Theoretical foundations and a unified definition. *Australian Journal of Intelligent Information Processing Systems*, *12*(4).

Raun, T. (2017). 'Talking about his dead child, again!': Emotional self-management in relation to online mourning. *First Monday*, *22*(1). doi:10.5210/fm.v22i11.7810

Raun, T. (2018). Connecting with the dead: Vernacular practices of mourning through photo-sharing on Facebook. In R. Andreassen, M. N. Petersen, K. Harrison, & T. Raun (Eds.), *Mediated intimacies, connectivities, relationalities and proximities* (pp. 193–207). London, UK: Routledge.

Redström, J., & Wiltse, H. (2019). *Changing things: The future of objects in a Digital World*. London, UK: Bloomsbury.

Rettberg, S., Lehmuskallio, A., Karhio, A., Cheng-Syun Tang, A., Zacher Sørensen, M.-M., & Solberg, R. (2019). *We were always right all along, or, how we learned to stop worrying and love the machine, 2068*. Unpublished manuscript.

Rice, C. (2005, September 4). My New Orleans. *Salon*. Retrieved from http://www.salon.com/2005/09/04/rice_20/

Rieder, B. (2016). Big data and the paradox of diversity. *Digital Culture & Society*, *2*(2), 39–54. doi:10.14361/dcs-2016-0204

Roberts, S. (2019). *Behind the screen: Content moderation in the shadows of social media*. New Haven, CT: Yale University Press.

Rose, C. (2005, December 6). The storm that keep killing. *The Times-Picayune | NOLA.Com*. Retrieved from http://www.nola.com/rose/index.ssf/2005/12/the_storm_that_keeps_killing.html

Ruud, E. (1997). Music and identity. *Nordic Journal of Music Therapy*, *6*(1), 3–13. doi:10.1080/08098139709477889

RX Fogarty [Robert]. (2008, October 13). Be a New Orleanian. wherever you are [Web log post]. Retrieved from http://post-katrinaneworleans.blogspot.com/2008/10/be-new-orleanian-wherever-you-are.html

Samarajiva, R. (2012). Facebook = Internet? LIRNEasia [blogpost]. Retrieved August 1, 2019, from https://lirneasia.net/2012/05/facebook-internet/

Schorr, S. (2019). *Saving screens: Temporary tattoos and other methods* [Artwork]. United States. Retrieved from http://www.sarahschorr.com/Artist.asp?ArtistID=5380&Akey=Y2PRX-C5P&ajx=1#!Group1_Pf184212

Schreiber, M. (2016). Amplification and heterogeneity: Seniors and digital photographic practices. In A. Lehmuskallio & E. Gomez Cruz (Eds.), *Digital photography and everyday life. Empirical studies on material visual practices* (pp. 52–69). London, UK: Routledge.

Schreiber, M. (2017). *Digitale Bildpraktiken. Handlungsdimensionen visueller vernetzter Kommunikation* (Unpublished PhD dissertation). University of Vienna, Austria.

Schulte, S. R. (2013). *Cached: Decoding the Internet in global popular culture*. New York: NYU Press.

Sconce, J. (2000). *Haunted media: Electronic presence from telegraphy to television*. Durham, NC: Duke University Press.

Shaginyan, M. (1960). *Mess-mend or Yankee in Petrograd*. Novel-tale. M: Detgiz. Cited by Degot' (2000).

Simondon, G. (2011). On the mode of existence of technical objects. *Deleuze Studies*, *5*(3), 407–424.

Solnit, R., & Snedeker, R. (2013). *Unfathomable city: A New Orleans Atlas*. Berkeley: University of California Press.

Soon, W. (2018). *Unerasable Images* [Artwork]. Hong Kong. Retrieved from http://siusoon.net/unerasable-images/

Spinuzzi, C. (2012). Working alone, together: Coworking as emergent collaborative activity. *Journal of Business and Technical Communication*, *26*(4), 399–441. https://doi.org/10.1177/1050651912444070

Stefik, M. (1997). *Internet dreams: Archetypes, myths, and metaphors*. Cambridge, MA: MIT Press.

Stephens, M. (1998). *The rise of the image, the fall of the word*. Cambridge: Oxford University Press.

Stephenson, N. (1992). *Snow crash*. New York, NY: Bantam Books

Stevens, R. (1996). *Understanding the self*. Thousand Oaks, CA: Sage.

Stoller, S. (2000). Reflections on feminist Merleau-Ponty skepticism. *Hypatia: A Journal of Feminist Philosophy*, *15*(1), 175–182. doi:10.2979/hyp.2000.15.1.175

Stopera, M. (2015). How I became a minor celebrity in China (After my stolen phone ended up there). *Buzzfeed*. Retrieved October15, 2019, from https://www.buzzfeed.com/mjs538/how-i-became-a-minor-celebrity-in-china-after-my

Streeter, T. (2017). The Internet as a structure of feeling: 1992–1996. *Internet Histories*, *1*(1–2), 79–89. https://doi.org/10.1080/24701475.2017.1306963

Sundén, J. (2003). Material virtualities. New York: Peter Lang.

Tannen, D. (1989 [2007]). *Talking voice: Repetition, dialogue, and imagery in conversational discourse* (2nd ed.). Cambridge: Cambridge University Press.

Tassy, A. (2018, November 30). It-anvendelse i befolkningen—2018. *Statistics Denmark*. Retrieved July 22, 2019, from https://www.dst.dk/da/Statistik/Publikationer/VisPub?cid=29448#

Tatarchenko, K. (2013). *"A house with the window to the west": The Academgorodok computer center (1958–1993)* (PhD thesis).

Tatarchenko, K. (2019). "The man with a micro-calculator": Digital modernity and late Soviet computing practices. In *Exploring the Early Digital* (pp. 179–200). Cham: Springer.

Thompson, D. (2014). The Shazam effect. *The Atlantic*. Retrieved July 26, 2010, from https://www.theatlantic.com/magazine/archive/2014/12/the-shazam-effect/382237/

Tiidenberg, K. (2015). Odes to heteronormativity—Presentations of femininity in Russian-speaking women's Instagram accounts. *International Journal of Communication, 9*.

Tiidenberg, K. (2018a). Visibly ageing femininities: Women's visual discourses of being over-40 and over-50 on Instagram. *Feminist Media Studies, 18*, 61–76.

Tiidenberg, K. (2018b). *Selfies, why we love (and hate) them*. Bingley, UK: Emerald.

Tiidenberg, K., & Baym, N. K. (2017, January–March). Learn it, buy it, work it: Intensive pregnancy on Instagram. *Social Media + Society*.

Tiidenberg, K., & Whelan, A. (2019). "Not like that, not for that, not by them" social media affordances for critique. *Communication and Critical/Cultural Studies, 16*(2), 83–102.

Tiidenberg, K., Markham, A. N., Pereira, G., Rehder, M., Sommer, J., Dremljuga, R., & Dougherty, M. (2017). *"I'm an addict" and other sensemaking devices: A discourse analysis of self-reflections of lived experience on social media*. Proceedings of the 8th International Conference on Social Media & Society. Article No. 21. Available: http://dl.acm.org/citation.cfm?doid=3097286.3097307

Townley, C., & Parsell, M. (2006). Cyber disobedience: Gandhian cyberpunks. *Scan, 3*(3).

Treem, J., & Leonardi, P. M. (2012). Social media use in organizations. *Communication Yearbook, 36*, 143–189. Retrieved from papers3://publication/uuid/C0737AFA-CEEA-4D9A-B85F-355E795F2593

Trippi, J. (2008). *The revolution will not be televised: Democracy, the Internet, and the overthrow of everything*. New York, NY: Harper.

Tuan, Y.-F. (1979). Space and place: Humanistic perspective. In S. Gale & G. Olsson(Eds.), *Philosophy in geography* (pp. 387–427). Dordrecht, Holland: D. Reidel.

Tuan, Y.-F. (2001). *Space and place: The perspective of experience*. Minneapolis: University of Minnesota Press.

Tufekci, Z. (2015). Algorithmic harms beyond Facebook and Google: Emergent challenges of computational agency. *Colorado Technology Law Journal, 13*, 203–218.

Turkle, S. (2007). *Evocative objects: Things we think with*. Cambridge, MA: MIT Press.

Twitchell, J. B. (1997). *For shame: The loss of common decency in American culture*. London, UK: St. Martin's Griffin.

University and College Union (UCU). (2016). *Precarious work in higher education. A snapshot of insecure contracts and institutional attitudes* [PDF file]. Retrieved from https://www.ucu.org.uk/media/7995/Precarious-work-in-higher-education-a-snapshot-of-insecure-contracts-and-institutional-attitudes-Apr-16/pdf/ucu_precariouscontract_hereport_apr16.pdf

Vaisman, C. (2014). 'The designs industry': Israeli tween girls play with production and power on blogs. In A. Bennett & B. Robards (Eds.), *Mediated youth cultures: The Internet, belonging and new cultural configurations* (pp. 95–113). Palgrave Macmillan.

van den Berg, B. (2008). Self, script, and situation: Identity in a world of ICTs. In S. Fischer-Hübner, P. Duquenoy, A. Zuccato, & L. Martucci (Eds.), *The Future of Identity in the Information Society* (Vol. 262, pp. 63–76). Boston, MA: Springer.

Van Dijck, J. (2013). 'You have one identity': Performing the self on Facebook and LinkedIn. *Media, Culture & Society*, *35*(2), 199–215. doi:10.1177/0163443712468605

Van Dijck, J. (2014). Datafication, dataism and dataveillance: Big Data between scientific paradigm and ideology. *Surveillance & Society*, *12*(2), 197–208. doi:10.24908/ss.v12i2.477

van Eijck, K. (2001). Social differentiation in musical taste patterns. Social Forces, *79*(3), 1163–1185. https://doi.org/10.1353/sof.2001.0017

van Zoonen, L. (2013). From identity to identification: Fixating the fragmented self. *Media, Culture & Society*, *35*(1), 44–51. https://doi.org/10.1177/0163443712464557

Villi, M. (2015). Photographs of place in phonespace: Camera phones as a location-aware mobile technology. In A. Lehmuskallio & E. Gomez Cruz (Eds.), *Digital photography and everyday life. Empirical studies on material visual practices* (pp. 107–121). London, UK: Routledge.

Vivienne, S. (2018). Between fire-fighting and flaming: Collective and personal trans* and gender-diverse social media. In A. S. Dobson, B. Robards, & C. Nicholas (Eds.), *Digital intimate publics and social media* (pp. 193–209). London, UK: Palgrave Mcmillan.

Vivienne, S., & Barnett, T. (2017). Curating technologies of memory and affect. *Media International Australia*, *165*(1), 14–24. https://doi.org/10.1177/1329878X17727626

Warfield, K., & Hassan-Zarabadi, S. (2018). *Feminist New Materialism in Education*. Milton Park, UK: Taylor & Francis.

Warschauer, M., & Ames, M. (2010). Can one laptop per child save the world's poor? *Journal of International Affairs*, 33–51.

Webster, J., Gibbins, N., Halford, S., & Hracs, B. J. (2016). Towards a theoretical approach for analysing music recommender systems as sociotechnical cultural intermediaries. In *Proceedings of the 8th ACM Conference on Web Science* (pp. 137–145). New York, NY: ACM. doi:10.1145/2908131.2908148

Weinberg, M. (2017). If you're happy and you know it: Music engagement and subjective well-being. *Psychology of Music*, *4*(2), 257–276.

Weiser, M. (1991). The computer for the 21st century. *Scientific American*, *265*, 94–104. http://dx.doi.org/10.1038/scientificamerican0991-94

White, P. B., & White, N. R. (2005). Keeping connected: Travelling with the telephone. *Convergence: The International Journal of Research into New Media Technologies*, *11*(2).

Wieck, D. (1978). Anarchist justice. In Anarchism, ed. J. R. Pennock and J. W. Chapman. New York: New York University Press, pp. 227–28.

Wikipedia. (2019). Internet metaphors. https://en.wikipedia.org/wiki/Internet_metaphors

Wilchins, R. (2017, June 13). Is Trans Over? [LGBTQI+ News & Commentary]. Retrieved January 31, 2018, from http://www.advocate.com/transgender/2017/6/13/trans-over

Wittkower, D. E. (2016). Principles of anti-discriminatory design. Philosophy Faculty Publications, *28*. https://digitalcommons.odu.edu/philosophy_fac_pubs/28

Woolgar, S. (1990). Configuring the user: The case of usability trials. *The Sociological Review*, *38*(S1), 58–99.

Wright, S., & Parchoma, G. (2011). Technologies for learning? An actor-network theory critique of 'affordances' in research on mobile learning. *Research in Learning Technology*, *19*(3), 247–258.

Wulff, H. J. (1993). Phatische Gemeinschaft/Phatische Funktion. Letikonzepte einer pragmatischen Theorie des Fernsehens [Phatic community/phatic function. Key concepts of a pragmatical theory of television]. *Montage A/V*, *2*(1), 143–163.

Wyatt, S. (2004). Danger! Metaphors at work in economics, geophysiology, and the Internet. *Science, Technology, & Human Values, 29*(2), 242–261. https://doi.org/10.1177/0162243903261947

Yurchak, A. (2005). *Everything was forever until it was no more: The last Soviet generation.* Princeton, NJ: Princeton University Press.

Zillien, N. (2008). Die (Wieder-)Entdeckung der Medien das Affordanzkonzept in der Mediensoziologie. *Sociologia Internationalis : Internationale Zeitschrift Für Soziologie, Kommunikations—Und Kulturforschung, 46*(2), 161–181.

Zipes, J. (2013). *The irresistible fairy tale: The cultural and social history of a genre.* Princeton, NJ: Princeton University Press.

About the Authors

Crystal Abidin, *PhD, Senior Research Fellow & ARC DECRA Fellow in Internet Studies and Research Fellow at Centre for Culture and Technology (CCAT), Curtin University, Australia, wishcrys.com,* crystalabidin@gmail.com

Crystal is an anthropologist of vernacular internet cultures, particularly young people's relationships with internet celebrity, self-curation, and vulnerability. Her books include *Internet Celebrity: Understanding Fame Online* (2018, Emerald Publishing), *Microcelebrity Around the Globe: Approaches to Cultures of Internet Fame* (co-edited with Megan Lindsay Brown, 2018, Emerald Publishing), *Instagram: Visual Social Media Cultures* (co-authored with Tama Leaver and Tim Highfield, 2019, Polity Press), and *Mediated Interfaces: The Body on Social Media* (co-edited with Katie Warfield and Carolina Cambre, 2020, Bloomsbury Academic).

Andee Baker, *PhD Associate Professor Emerita of Sociology at the Ohio University, Lancaster Campus, USA,* andee9@gmail.com

Andee is retired from teaching sociology, currently writing for both academic audiences and general readers. Her research on 89 couples published in *Double Click* (Hampton Press, 2005) was an empirical, academic book on couples who first met online and then in person. Andee also wrote *You Get What You Need* (Miniver Press, 2014) about fans of The Rolling Stones, online and offline, and

and is finishing a memoir on her relationships. Andee served on the board of the Association for Internet Researchers and on its Ethics Committee.

xtine burrough, *MFA, Artist, Professor, School of Arts, Technology and Emerging Communication, University of Texas at Dallas, USA,* xtine@utdallas.edu

xtine burrough is a hybrid artist. Working at the intersection of media art, technology, and digital poetry, she uses remix as a strategy for engaging networked audiences in critical participation. Professor and Area Head of Design + Creative Practice in the School of Arts, Technology, and Emerging Communication at The University of Texas at Dallas, burrough organizes LabSynthE, a laboratory for synthetic, electronic poetry. The second edition of burrough's book, *Foundations of Digital Art and Design with Adobe Creative Cloud* (New Riders, Voices that Matter Series) was published in 2020.

Kevin Driscoll, *PhD, Assistant Professor of Media Studies at the Department of Media Studies, University of Virginia, USA,* kdriscoll@virginia.edu

Kevin specializes in the study of technology, popular culture, and communication. His recent research traces alternative histories of the internet and examines the politics of amateur telecommunications. In collaboration with Julien Mailland from Indiana University, he co-authored *Minitel: Welcome to the Internet* (The MIT Press, 2017) and runs the *Minitel Research Lab*, USA at https://minitel.us.

Cathy Fowley, *PhD, Independent scholar, Ireland,* cathy.fowley@silverthread.ie

Cathy holds a PhD in Internet Research. Her deep interest in life stories, from an academic perspective but also a human and personal perspective, arose from a passion for literature and particularly memoirs, and an early involvement in online communities. Her academic writing is autoethnographic, reflecting on ageing and digital spaces. She is co-founder and director of Silver Thread, a social enterprise whose aim is to engage older people in writing stories from their lives, in the spaces where they live, communities or nursing homes, and to publish their stories.

Anette Grønning, *PhD, Associate Professor of Communication at the University of Southern Denmark, Media Sciences, Department for the Study of Culture,* ahg@sdu.dk

Anette researches identity, social presence and role taking in online conversations. Since 2003, Anette Grønning has worked with online communication in different domains (public, private and commercial), in particular with email and chat interaction. She has dealt with playfulness, genre conventions, role taking and face strategies between professionals and citizens in the role of student, customer, parent, client, patient, etc. Her PhD (2006) about email interaction constitutes the first Danish research study of the digital letter.

Nadia Hakim-Fernández, *PhD, Independent Researcher and Lecturer at Open University of Catalonia,* nhakim@uoc.edu

Nadia is an interdisciplinary sociologist involved since 2006 in research focused on youth, migration, sociality and power relations, from an ethnographic viewpoint to everyday life. She currently focuses on life and work conditions of mobile freelance knowledge workers in digitally saturated contexts.

Craig Hamilton, *PhD, Research Fellow at the Birmingham Centre for Media and Cultural Research, Birmingham City University, UK,* Craig.Hamilton@bcu.ac.uk

Craig's research is built around The Harkive Project and takes an experimental methodological approach derived from the use of data collection and machine-learning algorithms in the study of popular music. Craig is also the co-Managing Editor of *Riffs: Experimental writing on popular music* and the project coordinator for the AHRC-funded Songwriting Studies Research Network.

Tijana Hirsch, *PhD, independent researcher* tijana@ucsb.edu, tijana.hirsch@gmail.com

Tijana is a transnational independent researcher at the Language and Literacy Department at Wingate Academic College in Israel, currently based in Austin, Texas, USA. Her work focuses on multilingual individuals and families through the study of family language policy and transnational living patterns as captured within different social media platforms, particularly Facebook communities. Her work is interdisciplinary in nature, combining applied linguistics, sociolinguistics, linguistic anthropology, and migration studies with online ethnographic research of internet studies. She is an expert in family language policy and (re)construction of lived experiences and knowledge formation in social media over time.

Polina Kolozaridi, *Lecturer at Higher School of Economics, Coordinator at club for internet and society enthusiasts, Russia,* poli.kolozaridi@gmail.com

Polina is a social researcher focusing on the internet, specifically around issues of how people know, feel, anticipate and imagine technologies. She is from Tomsk, Siberia and now mostly based in Moscow. In Moscow, Polina coordinates a grassroots community of researchers (academic and independent ones) called club for internet and society enthusiasts (http://clubforinternet.net/). With the other club members Polina organizes initiative research projects and acts as a knowledge activist. She holds courses about internet studies, amateur online media, and critical data studies at the Higher School of Economics.

Priya C. Kumar, *doctoral candidate at the College of Information Studies at the University of Maryland, USA,* pkumar12@umd.edu

Priya studies the intersection of families, technology use, and privacy. Her research has been referenced on NPR, *Buzzfeed*, *Slate*, the *Washington Post*, the *Financial Times*, and *Time*. Priya holds a master's degree from the University of Michigan School of Information, where she designed her own curriculum in data storytelling. She also holds bachelor's degrees from the University of Maryland in journalism and government & politics. Find Priya on Twitter @DearPriya and her work at http://priyakumar.org.

Jessa Lingel, *PhD, Assistant Professor at Annenberg School of Communication, Core Faculty in Gender, Sexuality, and Women's Studies Program, University of Pennsylvania, Philadelphia USA,* lingel@upenn.edu

Jessa received her PhD in communication and information from Rutgers University. She has an MLIS from Pratt Institute and an MA in gender studies from New York University. Her research interests include information inequalities and technological distributions of power. Using qualitative methods, Lingel studies how marginalized and countercultural groups use and reshape digital media.

Annette N. Markham, *PhD, DERC Professor of Media and Communication at RMIT, Melbourne, and Affiliate Professor of Information Studies at Aarhus University,* amarkham@gmail.com

Annette is internationally recognized for developing epistemological frameworks for rethinking ethics and qualitative methods for digitally-saturated social contexts. A long-time member of the digital research community, Annette conducts sociological and ethnographic studies of how identity, relationships, and cultural formations are constructed in and influenced by digitally saturated socio-technical contexts. More information at annettemarkham.com.

Ryan M. Milner, *PhD, Associate Professor of Communication at the College of Charleston in Charleston, SC USA,* rmmilner@cofc.edu

Ryan researches everyday expression and mediated communication, assessing the social, political, and cultural significance of online interaction. He is the author of *The World Made Meme: Public Conversations and Participatory Media* and the co-author of *The Ambivalent Internet: Mischief, Oddity, and Antagonism Online.* Ryan's writing on internet culture has also been published in outlets like *TIME*, *Slate*, *The Los Angeles Review of Books*, and *The New York Times*.

Cristina Nuñez, *artist, founder/facilitator/trainer at The Self-Portrait Experience, doctoral student at College of Arts of the University of Derby,* www.cristinanunez.com, www.self-portrait.eu, cristinanunez.self@gmail.com

Cristina started taking self-portraits in 1988 to overcome personal problems. These self-portraits became her autobiographical project *Someone to Love*, which compelled her to create in 2004 *The Self-Portrait Experience* workshops that she has been conducting around the world in prisons, mental health and other vulnerable collectives. Her works have been presented internationally, published in monographic and collective books and are part of private and public collections. In 1996 *Heaven on Earth* won the award Mosaique of Luxemburg. In 2012 *Someone to Love* won the Celeste Prize and *But Beautiful* won the Prix de la Critique 2013 at the Voies Off.

Whitney Phillips, *PhD, Assistant Professor of Communication and Rhetorical Studies at Syracuse University, USA,* whphilli@syr.edu

Whitney is the author of the books *This is Why We Can't Have Nice Things: Mapping the Relationship between Online Trolling and Mainstream Culture* (2015, MIT Press); and *The Ambivalent Internet: Mischief, Oddity, and Antagonism Online* (2017, Polity Press, co-authored with Ryan Milner). She has also published the 2018 article "The Oxygen of Amplification: Better Practices for Reporting on Far Right Extremists, Antagonists, and Manipulators" (*Data & Society*). Her third book, co-authored with Ryan Milner, titled You Are Here: A Field Guide for Navigating Polluted Information, is forthcoming with MIT Press.

Daisy Pignetti, *PhD, Professor in the Department of English and Philosophy, University of Wisconsin-Stout, USA,* pignettid@uwstout.edu

Daisy's research interests include celebrity and fan studies, rhetorical theory, and qualitative inquiry, inasmuch as each area is influenced by the Internet and social media. She has published articles in *Transformative Works and Cultures* and *Computers and Composition Online* and has presented her research to the Association of Internet Researchers, Fan Studies Network, Oxford Internet Institute, and Popular Culture Association. You can find her on Twitter @phdaisy.

Patricia Prieto-Blanco, *PhD, Senior Lecturer at the School of Media, University of Brighton, UK, activist,* P.PrietoBlanco@brighton.ac.uk

Patricia's areas of expertise are visual research methods, photography and migration. She is an advocate of interdisciplinary, participatory and practice-based research.

Sarah Raine, *PhD,* Research Fellow, School of Arts and Creative Industries, Edinburgh Napier University, S.Raine@Napier.ac.uk

Sarah's research primarily explores multigenerational music scenes, focusing on issues of gender and generation. Sarah is co-Managing Editor of *Riffs: Experimental writing on popular music*, Review Editor for *Popular Music History* and a Book Series Editor for Equinox Publishing. Alongside Dr. Catherine Strong, she co-edited *Towards Gender Equality in the Music Industry* (Bloomsbury Academic: 2019) and a special issue of IASPM@Journal on 'Gender politics in the music industry' (2018). Sarah is also one of the editors of *The Northern Soul Scene* (Equinox Publishing : 2019).

Tobias Raun, *PhD, Associate Professor at Communication Studies, Roskilde University, Denmark,* tobiasra@ruc.dk

Tobias' research is focused on social media, and the potentials and challenges of mediatization processes in relation to self-representation, on the one hand in relation to gender and on the other hand in relation to mourning. He is the author of *Out Online: Trans Self-Representation and Community Building on YouTube* (Routledge 2016), and the co-editor of *Mediated Intimacies. Connectivities, Relationalities, Proximities* (Routledge 2018). Among his most recent articles is an exploration of emotional self-management in relation to mourning on Facebook, appearing in *First Monday* (2017) and an investigation of intimacy as capital in relation to the transgender micro-celebrity vlogger Julie Van Vu, appearing in *Convergence* (2018).

Sarah Schorr, *PhD, independent artist, Denmark,* schorrphotography@gmail.com

Sarah is an American photographic artist, researcher, and educator. Sarah's work has been widely exhibited with solo shows at esteemed spaces such as Yancey Richardson Gallery and Scalo Project Space in New York City. Her photographic art has been selected for juried group exhibitions by notable curators such as Elizabeth Avedon and Paula Tognarelli. In 2020, Sarah's work was honored by the Julia Margaret Cameron Award for women photographers in the categories of nude and digital manipulation as part of an exhibition at the Fotonostrum Gallery in Barcelona. Sarah recently received a grant from the Danish Ministry of Culture to create a catalogue of her current work, "The Color of Water," to accompany a forthcoming (2021) solo show of her work at Galleri Image in Denmark. Since earning her PhD, her research examines photographic practice as a mode of contemplation. Sarah currently lives, (and swims) in Denmark.

Maria Schreiber, *PhD, Post-doctoral Researcher, Department of Sociology, University of Vienna, Austria,* maria.schreiber@univie.ac.at

Maria is currently working on the project "Visual Biographies." She received her PhD in Media and Communications from the University of Vienna where she held a scholarship of the Austrian Academy of Science as part of the interdisciplinary DOC-team 'Pictorial Practices' (http://bildpraktiken.wordpress.com) and has spent time as visiting PhD at the University of Potsdam, Germany and at RMIT University, Australia. Her current research focuses on networked visual communication, media biographies and digital cultures.

Theresa M. Senft, *PhD, Senior Lecturer, Macquarie University, Australia.*

Terri's work, which tends toward feminist, critical race and postcolonial critique, explores how social media has changed the way we produce, consume and circulate performances of ourselves, worldwide. A strong believer in the power of public, free and networked scholarship, Terri founded the founded the 3000-member international Selfies Research Network (selfieresearchers.com) in 2014. In 2016, she founded Hey Girl Global Network (heygirlglobal.com), which studies the intersection of girl culture, urban culture and media culture around the world. Terri frequently speaks with and writes for both the advertising industry and mainstream media. Her website is at www.terrisenft.net

Anna Shchetvina, *Coordinator of the club for internet and society enthusiasts, BA, Higher School of Economics, Russia,* sha1205@mail.ru

As a coordinator of the *club for internet and society enthusiasts* (http://clubforinternet.net/) Anna was co-organizer of the 2019 conference *Internet Beyond* (Moscow). She also helps organize research expeditions and public reading sessions. Her main object of study is web history: practices of its archiving, public history and vernacular practices, as well as memory and nostalgia of the first Russian web users.

Winnie Soon, *PhD, Assistant Professor, Department of Digital Design, Aarhus University, Denmark,* wsoon@cc.au.dk

Winnie (Hong Kong/Denmark) is an artist-researcher examining the cultural implications of technologies where computational processes and invisible infrastructure underwrite our experiences. Her works explore topics around computational culture, specifically concerning automated censorship, data circulation, liveness and the culture of code practice. Winnie's projects have been exhibited and presented internationally at museums, festivals, libraries, universities and conferences across Europe, Asia and America. Winnie's current research focuses on critical technical and feminist practice.. She is working on two books titled *Aesthetic Programming: A Handbook of Software Studies* (w/ Geoff Cox) and *Fix My Code* (w/ Cornelia Sollfrank). More info: http://www.siusoon.net

Jeff Thompson, *MFA, Assistant Professor, Stevens Institute of Technology, USA,* mail@jeffreythompson.org

Jeff is an artist, programmer, and educator based in the NYC area. Through code, sculpture, sound, and performance, Thompson's work physicalizes and gives materiality to otherwise invisible technological processes.

Katrin Tiidenberg, *PhD, Associate Professor of Visual Culture and Social Media at the Baltic Film, Media, Arts and Communication Institute of Tallinn University,* katrin.tiidenberg@gmail.com

Katrin researches social media, sex, visual social media practices and digital research ethics. She is the author of *Selfies, Why We Love (and Hate) Them* (Emerald 2020), *Body and Soul on the Internet—making sense of social media* (in Estonian, 2017) and *Sex and Social Media* (co-authored with Emily van der Nagel, 2020). She is on the Executive Board of the Association of Internet Researcher and the Estonian Young Academy of Sciences. For more information kkatot.tumblr.com

Carmel L. Vaisman, *PhD, Lecturer at the international BA in liberal arts, the multidisciplinary program in the Humanities and the Cohn Institute for the History and Philosophy of Science and Ideas at Tel Aviv University,* carmell@tauex.tau.ac.il

Carmel is a digital culture researcher trained as an anthropologist. Her first book, *Hebrew On-Line* (Keter books, 2011) co-authored with linguist Ilan Gonen, dealt with aspects of language change and digital discourse. She earned her PhD in communications from the Hebrew University in Jerusalem in 2010. For a complete list of publications, op-eds, popular talks and media interviews, visit her personal website at absolutecarmel.com

Son Vivienne, *PhD, independent researcher, Australia,* son@incitestories.com.au

Son have over 30 years of experience in media production and research in digital self-representation, online activism, queer identities, and rhetorical strategies for speaking and listening across difference. Their current research explores the many creative ways that we 'code-switch identities' as diversely abled, classed, raced and gendered bodies, online and off. They are a Board Director at LGBTQI+ youth advocacy NGO, *Minus18*, and their work on digital storytelling is published as *Digital Identity and Everyday Activism: Sharing Private Stories with Networked Publics* (Palgrave, 2016). Son's less verbal, more earthy projects include cultivating fecundity in their garden, and generosity in their children. More info at Son's website: www.incitestories.com.au

Katie Warfield, *PhD, faculty in the Department of Journalism and Communication at Kwantlen Polytechnic University, Surrey BC, Canada,* katie.warfield@kpu.ca

Katie is the Director of the Visual Media Workshop, a center for research and learning into digital visual culture. She is an award-winning community activist and her recent writings have appeared in *Social Media + Society, Feminist Media Studies, Language and Literacy*, and *Feminist Issues, 6th ed.* She has co-edited the books *Feminist Posthumanisms, New Materialisms and Education* (Taylor and Francis) and *Mediated Interfaces: The Body on Social Media* (Bloomsbury).

Index

A

B

C

General Editor: ***Steve Jones***

Digital Formations is the best source for critical, well-written books about digital technologies and modern life. Books in the series break new ground by emphasizing multiple methodological and theoretical approaches to deeply probe the formation and reformation of lived experience as it is refracted through digital interaction. Each volume in **Digital Formations** pushes forward our understanding of the intersections, and corresponding implications, between digital technologies and everyday life. The series examines broad issues in realms such as digital culture, electronic commerce, law, politics and governance, gender, the Internet, race, art, health and medicine, and education. The series emphasizes critical studies in the context of emergent and existing digital technologies.

Other titles include:

Felicia Wu Song
Virtual Communities: Bowling Alone, Online Together

Edited by Sharon Kleinman
The Culture of Efficiency: Technology in Everyday Life

Edward Lee Lamoureux, Steven L. Baron, & Claire Stewart
Intellectual Property Law and Interactive Media: Free for a Fee

Edited by Adrienne Russell & Nabil Echchaibi
International Blogging: Identity, Politics and Networked Publics

Edited by Don Heider
Living Virtually: Researching New Worlds

Edited by Judith Burnett, Peter Senker & Kathy Walker
The Myths of Technology: Innovation and Inequality

Edited by Knut Lundby
Digital Storytelling, Mediatized Stories: Self-representations in New Media

Theresa M. Senft
Camgirls: Celebrity and Community in the Age of Social Networks

Edited by Chris Paterson & David Domingo
Making Online News: The Ethnography of New Media Production

www.ingramcontent.com/pod-product-compliance
Lightning Source LLC
Chambersburg PA
CBHW060750150926
51501CB00004B/147
* 9 7 8 1 4 3 3 1 7 4 4 9 0 *